SAMMY TIPPIT
WITH JERRY B. JENKINS

UNASHAMED

A MEMOIR
OF
DANGEROUS
FAITH

Quick Response Codes throughout this book link to videos of interviews with or eyewitness accounts from the individuals involved in the incidents, and in many cases were filmed during the events. You can access these with any QR Code reader/scanner app on your device.

A publication of ST Books

To the glory of God,
and with appreciation to my wife, Tex,
who is and always will be the love of my life.

To our children, Dave and Renée,
and their spouses and children,
God's special blessing to us.

In memory of my father,
David Thomas Tippit,
a great basketball player and a great dad.
And my mother, Lavada, who
influenced me in my foundational years.

CONTENTS

Part Three — The Using

Part Four — The Autumn of Life

INTRODUCTION

Among the greatest thrills of my life were two trips to Eastern Europe with Sammy Tippit, twice venturing into Romania—once before the overthrow of dictator Nicolae Ceausescu and once after. How stark to see memorials to recently slain revolutionaries outside a hotel where we had stayed just a few years before—to realize that a historic revolution had occurred on the very streets we had walked.

Yet this book is not about only Romania or Eastern Europe. It is about a man who would rather speak of God than of himself. It may be the most unusual memoir you will ever read.

Have you ever wondered what God might do through a person wholly consecrated to Him? D. L. Moody was challenged by that idea in the nineteenth century, and the results of his ministry remain to this day.

Some people may see Sammy Tippit as a throwback to another era. Can anyone with ability and talent remain unaffected by fame, wealth, materialism? If not, how does he deal with the attendant pride?

God has packed into Sammy a lifetime of amazing events. He seems a lightning rod for outpourings from heaven, a dynamic preacher and bold personal witness whose hallmark is obedience.

The kinds of results Sammy has seen in his worldwide ministry have ruined many other ministers. They became enamored with success, began to see themselves—rather than God—as the key, and started the slow, sure slide to pride.

Sammy is not above sin, but God has done a deep work in his heart, breaking him, keeping him humble, keeping him in the Word and in prayer. God has shown him that humility is the trademark of the true man of God. The deepest desire of Sammy's heart is to be an obedient and effective man of God.

He lives what he preaches, straight from the Bible. No doubt other Christian workers have the same burden, the same trust, the same zeal, the same talent to move people's hearts. But few are so dead to self or so honored to be used.

You will praise God for Sammy Tippit, who wants only to glorify Christ. More important, you'll learn that you can glorify God yourself by entrusting to Him every area of your life.

Jerry B. Jenkins
Black Forest, Colorado

Part One — The Calling

CHAPTER ONE

THE DAY THE CURTAIN FELL

Baton Rouge, Louisiana
Summer, 1965

I had changed overnight, and friends and family had no idea what to make of me.

I may have looked like the same Louisiana State University-bound, happy-go-lucky athlete, student leader, and award-winning speaker who hadn't met a girl or a beer he didn't like, but it was obvious I was an entirely different person.

I had gone from Most Likely to Party All Night to a fearless follower of Jesus, eager to tell everybody what He had done for me—forgiving my sins and giving me eternal life—and that He could do the same for them.

Friends didn't even believe me at first. I had to be kidding, or this had to be a phase. But I had come to faith and almost at the same instant felt called to preach. God so overwhelmed me with a burden for the souls of everyday people that I recruited a couple of friends and started preaching everywhere. I'm talking within just days of my transformation, and I mean everywhere.

I talked my way into bars and nightclubs, asking the managers if I could have a few minutes at the microphone when the band was on break. They'd ask me, "To do what?"

I'd say, "To talk about Jesus."

I had to sound like the craziest kid they ever saw, but I hardly ever got turned down.

Well, I don't want to get ahead of myself, but from that time to this, my life has been a whirlwind. My bizarre compulsion to both preach and share Christ with people one on one has grown from the bars and streets of south Louisiana to mass meetings in stadiums all over the world.

I'll tell you how that all came about, but let me start with a pivotal night in my life nearly a quarter century later.

Romania
July, 1988

For many years Romania had been the focus of my ministry in Eastern Europe. But one fateful night soldiers pulled me off a train at the border and held me under guard overnight. The next day they put me on a train to Vienna and told me, "You'll never set foot on Romanian soil again as long as you live."

I had developed such a love for the country and my fellow believers that I was brokenhearted. Soon, friends found a way to smuggle a note to me: "Sammy, remember, the glory of God comes only through much suffering. Keep praying. Don't give up."

The message had come from one of my dearest friends in the world, a compatriot, a prayer warrior, and my translator in Romania, Titus Coltea. A young medical doctor who risked everything to serve Christ against the wishes of the Communists, Titus—along with his wife, Gabi—always buoyed me with his deep, warm, affectionate, bold faith!

Despite his encouragement, I found it hard to imagine things could change in Romania. The ruthless Securitate, the dreaded secret police, helped dictator Nicolae Ceausescu rule with an iron fist. Many believed that one of every three people in the nation was somehow linked to the Securitate. There was no such thing as peaceful protest in Romania. Whenever I had visited, friends and I were followed and threatened.

And now the Securitate had made good on its threats.

Nigeria
Late 1989

My pattern had become to emphasize two priorities wherever I was invited to preach: evangelistic meetings, of course (because that was my calling), but also the inspiring and training of national Christian pastors and leaders. I called them to prayer and personal revival, and then I would conduct a major evangelistic outreach to the city.

That's what I had been doing in Africa when I awoke one night in a remote, dilapidated hotel, dehydrated and doubled over in pain.

The phone system was down, but somehow word got to a local pastor who rushed me to a hospital. There they pumped liquids into me, despite my fear of used needles in a nation where AIDS was a growing concern.

It seemed only one person was on duty in the entire hospital, and no one on my floor. Whenever my IV ran low, I had to get up and carry it with me, calling out for someone to come and help me.

When my stomach began to bloat, I was scared and so sympathetic to my wife, Tex, who had twice been pregnant. I thought I was going to burst. I prayed earnestly, "Lord, if what they're doing to me is wrong, don't let my stomach deflate. If it's right, let the swelling reduce."

If my stomach was still swollen twelve hours later, I was going to take out the needle, dress, catch a taxi, and pay whatever it cost to get to Lagos (about a three-hour drive). From there I would fly to London and find a hospital where they could help me. I didn't want to offend the people of Nigeria, but I was so sick I would have no choice.

The swelling subsided, but I was still very sick. The local pastor visited me occasionally and kept telling me, "You'll be okay, Brother Sammy. God has given us assurance. He will take care of you."

I appreciated that, but with Tex back home in San Antonio, I wanted help in the form of people who would stay with me and look after me.

Finally finding a working phone, I brought Tex up to date and said, "Sweetheart, pray for me, and get your friends to pray for me."

She assured me she would and then asked if I had heard about the Berlin Wall. I hadn't. "It's come down," she said.

I couldn't have heard her right. "You've got to be kidding!"

"I'm not, Sammy. People are dancing in the streets."

Sick as I was, I hardly slept. So much of my life and ministry revolved around the Eastern bloc that everything in me yearned to be there. I'd had the indescribable privilege of preaching all over the world, but my international ministry had begun in Europe early years before.

I had prayed since my college years for the downfall of Communism, the greatest enemy of the Gospel in Eastern Europe. Since my first ministry trip there in the 1970s, I had prayed for an end to oppression of the brothers and sisters in Christ I had grown so close to. I had heard great elderly saints cry out to God for this day, yet I can't say I truly had the faith to believe it would happen in my lifetime. So I was as shocked and thrilled as anyone when the news came.

I knew how important the Berlin Wall news was when I realized that despite my pain and loneliness in that hospital bed, I was also overcome with joy.

The antibiotics gradually began to work, and my pain and discomfort slowly lifted. I was able to preach the last couple of days of the Nigerian crusade, and I couldn't wait to get back to the States to see about getting back into the Eastern bloc.

As soon as I arrived in San Antonio, it seemed everyone wanted to know if I thought Romania would be the next country to break free of totalitarianism.

"Not without a bloodbath," I said. "The Securitate is too strong. With transportation and communication so limited, no one could pull off a coup without violence."

Just a few weeks later my family and I visited my widowed mother in Louisiana for the Christmas holidays. The adults were chatting in the kitchen when my son, Dave, came in. "Dad, come and watch the news. There's been a massacre in Timisoara."

I rushed to the TV just as CNN reported on that Romanian city that had become so dear to me. People had been killed. Multitudes had taken to the streets. I prayed I wouldn't hear the names of any of our many brothers and sisters in Christ in Timisoara. They were brave soldiers of the cross who had for so long lived out their faith under the tyranny of Ceausescu.

Reporters had never been allowed into the country, so news was sketchy. The borders were closed, and truck drivers were the only ones allowed out. I called Sam Friend, a former associate in Washington State, and asked what he knew. He told me the Securitate had come to arrest a pastor named Laszlo Tokes, who had spearheaded a demonstration. Government forces found people surrounding his home to protect him. The Securitate fired into the crowd, killing dozens.

I became obsessed with the people of Romania and believed the United States needed to take a stand. Romanians were always low on food. They had no weapons, no money. We needed to come to their aid.

I told Tex, "I know it's Christmas, but I have to do something."

"I'm with you," she said. "But what *are* you going to do?"

Early in my ministry I might have done something noisy, like chaining myself to a cross in front of the United Nations, or going to the great Romanian population in Chicago and calling for a big rally in the civic center.

But times had changed, and techniques that had once been effective could now make me a laughingstock. I called my media contacts and encouraged them to get the word out that the Securitate would march through and massacre more people while the world press was focusing on controversy in Panama.

One thing the Communists hated was adverse publicity. So every chance I got I accepted interviews as a Romania watcher who had spent years in ministry there. I called for the American people, particularly the Christian community, to raise a loud cry against the atrocities. "We need to protest every killing. We must stand for the Romanian people."

Within days the stunning news came that the army had pulled out of Timisoara. The Communists had been booted, and a transitional government had taken control. From what he knew of the passion of the resistance and his years as a Romania expert, Josif Tson, head of the Romanian Missionary Society and former pastor of the great Second Baptist Church in Oradea, predicted that Ceausescu would be deposed within forty-eight hours.

I might have dismissed that from anyone else, but Josif was a knowledgeable Romanian expatriate.

Still, I was only cautiously optimistic. I had spent enough time in Romania to know how powerful Ceausescu was, how he had surrounded himself with security and staged elaborate parades in honor of himself.

"It will happen, Sammy," Josif said. "We need to prepare."

I was so excited about the possibility of returning to Romania that I could hardly think of anything else. After years of ministering there, it had been seventeen continuous months since I had been to that precious country.

I helped arrange for a colleague, evangelist Steve Wingfield, to preach in Timisoara the next month, and for Dr. Joe Ford, chairman of the board of our ministry, to go. "It's dangerous," I said, "and I can't tell you what you should do. But, I'm making plans. I don't know when, but at the right moment, I'm going."

Steve and Joe both agreed to go.

While Ceausescu was making a speech in Bucharest, he staged another demonstration to show how the people loved him. But some university students, who had heard over Radio Free Europe what had happened in Timisoara, began hollering from the back of the crowd, "*Jos cu Ceausescu!* [Down with Ceausescu!] *Jos cu Ceausescu!*"

The crowd picked up the chant, and perhaps for the first time since he had taken power in 1974, Ceausescu realized he didn't have the support of the people.

He was the cruelest of dictators. He spent elaborately on himself, even built himself an obscenely opulent palace (one of the largest buildings in Europe), despite the fact his people lived in squalor. They couldn't get bread or meat, and they camped out in lines for gasoline. All while Ceausescu lived as a king.

So much of the population had been compromised by the Securitate that family members would turn in each other for various offenses to gain favor with the guards. Yet, all over the country signs read, "Long live Ceausescu!" "The People for Ceausescu!" "Ceausescu Peace!" It was Orwellian.

Of course, Titus and Gabi Coltea were on my mind every minute. Steve Wingfield told me a friend of his had used a phone with an automatic re-dialer finally to reach Titus after thirty hours of continuous calling. "It was strange," Steve reported. "My friend kept asking Titus how he was doing and was he safe and how was his family, but all Titus could say was, 'The glory of God has come to my country. The glory of God has come to my country. Tell Sammy that what we have prayed for so long has come. Tell him he must come immediately.'"

The next day I talked to Titus by phone, and he told me to get a vehicle, put a red cross on it, and drive to the border. "They'll let you in if you bring medical supplies, no questions asked."

I arranged for a vehicle through a friend in Germany and planned to go. That Sunday morning my pastor, David Walker, asked me to update the congregation on the situation in Romania. After I shared our plans, David added: "Sammy will not ask for money, but I will. If you want to help, just give it directly to him."

It reminded me of how God had met our needs early in my ministry. One man asked how much my flight would cost, then wrote a check to cover it. By the time I left church that morning, I had been given more than four thousand dollars!

On Christmas Day I heard the stunning news that Josif Tson had predicted: Ceausescu had not only been deposed but also had been put to death by firing squad. It was time to go.

New Year's Day, 1990

I flew into Vienna where I met Don Shelton, pastor of a church I had pastored years before in West Germany, and a few laymen with a van and medical supplies.

We were an eight-hour drive from the Romanian border at Oradea, and I was eager to get going. Titus had told me there would be a church service at Second Baptist in Oradea that night, and though he wouldn't tell anyone I was coming, I wanted more than anything to get there in time for that.

"Great Is Thy Faithfulness" was on my heart as I was reminded that when all else fails, God is faithful. No government, no dictator could keep me out of Romania if God wanted me in.

We drove as fast as we dared across Austria and Hungary. About an hour outside the border between Hungary and Romania, we started praying. Both Don Shelton and I had been blacklisted, but who would be in charge of the border now?

Before we could move on to the Romanian border, the Hungarians insisted we enjoy a lengthy meal. We kept trying to beg off, but they wouldn't hear of it.

When we finally got to the eerily silent Romania side, snow was falling. We knew that inside the nation the revolution was in full pitch. Many may have been trying to get out of the country, but we were desperate to get in.

I was hardly new to that border crossing, where I had always faced delays, searches, and harassment. Many considered it lunacy to try to get back into Romania during the height of the revolution, especially after having been banished. And maybe it was.

My heart hammered as armed soldiers approached our car. If they remained loyal to the deposed Ceausescu, our very lives would be in danger.

"Get out!"

I knew that what happened next would change my life, for good or for bad. All these years later, I still see it in my mind as though it were yesterday.

In the past, the guards' first question had always been whether we had Bibles. The old regime believed Christianity was an illness. While there was no law against afflicted people meeting together, trying to bring a Bible in was akin to pushing drugs. I didn't try to smuggle in even my own Bible, let alone any for others. I always used one from someone inside the country.

But this time the guard said, "Are you a Christian?"

My breath came short. I always made it a practice to tell the truth and trust God with the outcome. I had seen friends turned away because they had been "in-country with Sammy Tippit," only to be routinely processed through under my own name a few minutes later.

"Yes," I said, "we are Christians."

The guard smiled, threw open his arms, and said, "Welcome to Romania!" He added, "Someone is here waiting for Christians to arrive."

Here came Titus and Gabi running to embrace us. What a joyous reunion! We knelt and praised God in the very spot where I had been told I could never return.

Titus said, "We must get you to the church."

I had become so endeared to the people of that great congregation that they even had a greeting just for me. Whenever I showed up, whoever was leading the service would say, "Tonight we have with us…," and the people would say in unison, "Sommy Teepeet."

We arrived at the end of the service, and a stir arose. Titus's brother-in-law Peter was at the microphone. Although they had been about to close, he said, "Tonight we have with us…"

How sweet to hear that congregation of more than two thousand say my name in unison in their unique accents.

Titus and I mounted the platform, and my heart burst with love and joy as I looked into the beaming faces of newly freed people. I opened the Word of God, and Titus and I could only weep as we spoke.

From the Soviet Union came rumors of demonstrations, threats of secession, and Kremlin strong-arm tactics. Clearly we were on the front lines of history. The mammoth Iron Curtain had been rent, and the world would never be the same.

Neither would our ministry.

CHAPTER TWO

NEVER ASHAMED

No one predicted I would grow up to become an evangelist.

I was a stranger to spiritual things until junior high when I heard that an all-American and all-pro football player was going to speak at a church. Football players were my idols.

I hung on his every word and was intrigued when he said, "All my awards don't amount to a cup of coffee compared to what Jesus Christ means to me." When the great star invited us to "Come and receive Christ," I hurried down the aisle.

But the counselor assigned to me seemed more interested in getting me baptized so I could join the church. I filled out a card and got wet, but I didn't come to know Christ. It wouldn't be until the summer before my senior year in high school that I even considered God again.

Meanwhile, I took speech courses every year and loved every minute of them. I enjoyed wide success and traveled to several cities to speak about world peace. That summer of 1964 I was chosen as one of thirty students from Louisiana to study at the United Nations in New York. Our group stopped at the famous Gettysburg battlefield in Pennsylvania and sang patriotic songs and spirituals. As I gazed at the eternal torch, I began to wonder if there really was an eternal God.

I gained a global perspective at the UN, won an oratorical contest for the southern states, and was named outstanding high school speaker for North America. Only later did I recognize that God was at work in me even before I knew Him, preparing me for what I do today. I'm also sure that's why much of my preparation and delivery seemed to come naturally.

I returned to Baton Rouge that fall with the world by the tail. My senior year was a good one for parties, girls, alcohol, you name it. I graduated near the top of my class, excelled in college testing exams, and finished in the top three percent in the nation in math. I was recruited by several big schools, and I accepted two scholarships to Louisiana State.

My future seemed set, at least for the next four years. I had success, popularity, a serious girlfriend, and I was rushed by LSU fraternities during the summer. But something was missing. I could speak of global peace, but I had no inner peace. I felt empty and at times even wondered if life was worth living.

One night my girlfriend's father, a deacon in a big local church, told us we couldn't go out unless we went to church first. That was a laugh. I had gotten drunk at a party the night before. But her dad stood firm. No problem—I just wouldn't pay attention.

I didn't like the preliminaries at all, but when a young evangelist named James Robison stood to speak, my plan went out the window. I couldn't ignore him. He bounded all over the platform, smiling and shouting, excited about life. I didn't have half what this guy had. Even with all my success and popularity, I sensed I had nothing without Christ.

I had walked forward years before, and it made no difference. But I was ready to give God another try. I didn't care what my friends or even my girlfriend would think. I went forward, talked with Robison, and prayed, "Jesus, if You're real, be real to me tonight. I'll give up anything, I'll do anything, but come into my heart and be my Lord."

For the first time I knew Jesus Christ was in my life. He forgave my sins, and my emptiness was gone. I knew immediately that God wanted me to use for Him whatever abilities I had.

I told James Robison I felt called to the ministry, and he said, "Sam, Jesus didn't have to leave heaven to die for you. He chose to. He suffered and bled and was ridiculed and tortured. He gave His life for you. If He's called you to preach, you must be willing to give Him everything, no matter what the cost. Even if it means going to jail or losing your friends, you must be willing to pay the price."

I had no idea, of course, that I would eventually be called to suffer those very things. I didn't know either that though I was willing to pay those prices, I would be blind to my own ego and pride. The day would come when God would have to search me and break me and mold me if I truly wanted to continue to grow and be of service to Him.

As brand new as I was in Christ, I was thrilled with my Lord. I wanted to tell everyone. There were meetings every night that week at church, and a few nights later one of my buddies was there—Fred, a real boozer. During the invitation, I told him, "I want you to know Jesus."

He laughed. "I've tried religion, Tippit. It'll wear off in a few weeks. This weekend we're goin' down to Grand Isle where there'll be all the girls you want and plenty of booze."

"No," I said, "I've changed."

"I'm not listening," he said.

I was hurt and discouraged. I had failed.

Monday morning Fred called. "I got loaded at Grand Isle last night, but all I could think about was what you said. Can you come over and pray with me?"

I was so thrilled to lead someone to Christ that I couldn't wait to do it again.

Another friend, Don, also received Christ at one of the meetings, and the three of us started getting together to pray and go to church. The pastor took us under his wing and helped us grow.

I got my first opportunity to preach at a nursing home where the young people put on a service every Sunday. The only thing I knew to preach was my own testimony. I preached it each week in a different way.

Fred and Don and I went into nightclubs and bars to share our faith. We were scared to death, especially at first. We recognized a lot of people, and our mouths seemed glued shut. We held a private prayer meeting in the bathroom, but when we came out, we still just stood there unnoticed.

Suddenly Fred shouted, "I can't hold it any longer! I've got to tell you what Jesus has done for me!" The place fell dead silent, and two bouncers ushered Fred out. So Don and I started quietly sharing Christ with anyone who would listen.

That gave the three of us the confidence to overcome our fear and just go to those places and witness one-on-one, without causing a scene that would get us thrown out. Soon we were doing that several nights a week.

While it was rare to see someone come to Christ, the exercise was a great experience for us as new Christians. We learned the value of boldly, and often not so boldly, obeying the Lord when He led us to share His Gospel.

One night Fred told me he felt led of God that I should go and witness for Christ in the nightclub across the river. That place had been the scene of stabbings and even bombings. I said, "Well, if *you* feel led, maybe *you* should go."

He asked me to pray about it, and I like to joke that I made the mistake of agreeing to. Prayer can be dangerous. Sure enough, God told me to go. Fred and Don and another friend, Charlie, went along. I carried my little red Bible and asked the bartender who I needed to talk to about permission to preach.

He pointed me to a dark cubbyhole in the back. Don, Fred, and Charlie stayed in the hall praying while I knocked hard. The door flew open to reveal six glaring eyes. The manager, flanked by two bouncers, sat counting a pile of cash.

I said, "Sir, my friends and I want to tell people about Jesus."

The manager's eyes darted between my Bible and my eyes. "All right," he said.

I gasped. "All right?"

He shrugged and resumed his counting. "You can have the stage when the band takes its next break."

I walked out grinning, but as I passed my friends in the dingy, dim hallway, they didn't even see me. They still had their heads bowed, one fervently praying, "Lord, please be with Sam."

A few minutes later, when the band members unstrapped their instruments and wandered from the little platform, I knew if I hesitated I'd lose my nerve. I hurried to the microphone.

"Listen," I began, "I don't know what y'all think about Jesus Christ..." and a hush fell over the place. "But let me tell you what He's done for me."

After I told my story, the four of us split up to share Christ with people individually. Several gave their hearts to Jesus. We were thrilled, but we didn't tell anyone because we didn't want to become egotistical about it.

That week in church the pastor said he had heard that some young people had shared their faith in the nightclub. One of the deacons had been approached by a man who'd been there and heard us and wanted to know how to receive Christ. That was as exciting as the night I had received Christ myself. I thought of Romans 1:16: "For I am not ashamed of the Gospel of Christ, for it is the power of God to salvation for everyone who believes." As I looked forward to college, I prayed, *Lord, help me* never *to be ashamed.*

Near the Louisiana State Capitol building I found a little hill where I often prayed and studied my Bible. I found it beautiful to spend time alone with Jesus, and God convicted me about many things. One was my girlfriend. I knew I had to get away from the kind of lifestyle we had enjoyed, and that meant I couldn't continue dating her.

"Sammy, I'll change," she promised. "I'll give my life to God."

I said, "If you mean that, let's not see each other for two months." I knew if she truly gave her life to God, she wouldn't want the party life any more than I did.

Being apart from her for two months was going to be tough on me too. But just two weeks later, I was convinced God wanted me to break off the relationship.

Although I knew it was the right thing, still I was lonely. Like most young men, I longed for a loving relationship. But it wasn't just breaking up that made me lonely. My own mom didn't understand what had happened to me, and she didn't hide her displeasure.

Mom grew up in a family so poor that she and her sisters had to stay out of school one year because they had little to eat and had to work menial jobs to survive. Her older sister got a job after high school and bought Mom a pair of shoes to wear to her graduation. None of the sisters could afford to go to college.

I believe Mom felt her dreams would be fulfilled in me. Because I had won academic scholarships, she was infuriated when I told her I felt God wanted me to go into the ministry. One evening she beat me over the head with a belt, yelling at me to get out and never come back.

I'd seen many South Louisiana torrential rainstorms, but I doubt there had ever been a downpour to match my tears that night. I wandered the streets, sobbing.

My aunt later talked Mom into allowing me back, but the wound she inflicted that night festered for decades.

In my loneliness I developed a hunger really to dig into Scripture and increase my Bible knowledge. I knew no one would understand, but I felt God wanted me to leave LSU after the first semester and transfer to a denominational Bible school.

Mom raged that I was giving up a scholarship at a prestigious university for "religious" training—and she was not alone.

I had no idea how I was going to finance my education now, but I was excited about studying the Bible and knew God was in my decision. That kept me going at the new school when some classmates and I were told that our witnessing on the streets embarrassed other students, who considered us Holy Joes.

I couldn't believe that happened at a Christian school. Sure, at LSU we would have been laughed off the campus, but here?

On the upside, one of the guys in our young preachers group read a passage of Scripture one night that burned in my soul. It was the Old Testament passage where God puts His call on Jeremiah:

> Then the word of the Lord came to me, saying: "Before I formed you in the womb I knew you; before you were born I sanctified you; I ordained you a prophet to the nations." Then said I: "Ah, Lord God! Behold, I cannot speak, for I am a youth." But the Lord said to me: "Do not say, 'I am a youth,' for you shall go to all to whom I send you, and whatever I command you, you shall speak. Do not be afraid of their faces, for I am with you to deliver you," says the Lord. Then the Lord put forth His hand and touched my mouth, and the Lord said to me: "Behold, I have put My words in your mouth. See, I have this day set you over the nations and over the kingdoms, to root out and to pull down, to destroy and to throw down, to build and to plant. ... I am ready to perform My word... Therefore ... speak to them all that I command you" (Jeremiah 1:4-10, 12, 17).

That Scripture worked on my heart for days, and it still does decades later. No matter where I go or what I encounter, I claim those promises. Even if I hadn't felt called of God to preach all over the world, I would take great comfort in knowing that God is ready to perform His word.

Even to those who are not preachers, Jesus' Great Commission remains in force. He has commanded us to make disciples. As scary as that can be, God promises to go before us and to prepare hearts.

Soon some student stole some of my clothes just to bother me. It worked. I talked myself out of being so radical and quit witnessing on the street. I justified that by accepting invitations to speak at youth rallies and evangelistic meetings, but I felt no power. Nothing of much value happened at my meetings. My faith grew lukewarm, and I was miserable.

My father had suffered for years with Lupus, and when he took a turn for the worse, I jumped at the opportunity to again transfer to another school. I switched to Southeastern Louisiana College (now University), just forty miles from home.

At Southeastern I fell in with a bunch of Christians who emphasized the grace of God over any other doctrine. To them this meant that believers are free to live as they choose. Frankly, in my youth and naïveté, this grace-of-God business sounded pretty good. I used it as an excuse to go back to social drinking and partying, and I even took to smoking a pipe—sort of the ultimate symbol of my freedom.

I didn't realize I'd fallen into a trap. I'm a believer in eternal security, and God's grace is inexpressibly deep and merciful. But it is not a license for sin, and deep down I knew I was kidding myself, thinking I could stay close to God in spite of my lifestyle.

I was still a Christian, of course, and I truly wanted to serve God, but I was conflicted and disappointed in myself. In the midst of all that personal turmoil caused by my spiritual lapse, I met someone who would become the most important human in my life from that time till now.

Because of student elections and campaign posters everywhere, one of the more publicized names on campus was Tex, nickname of Debe Ann Sirman, a Texas girl running for office. She also came to our Bible studies. I was the first person to explain to her what it meant to receive Jesus Christ. With my inconsistent spiritual life at the time, it was a wonder she even listened.

Thank God, some girls in her dorm were genuine examples of what I had talked about, and one night Tex gave her heart to Christ. The next day I saw in her the newness of life I had experienced when I became a believer. It shook me. I envied her and realized how far I had strayed from my first love of Jesus.

Tex was excited about her new faith and often cried over all the girlfriends with whom she wanted to share Christ. I missed that kind of passion for the lost. I had really blown it. I knew I had to ditch all the habits I had regained.

Tex was magnetic and fascinating, and I was drawn to her exuberant faith. Soon she and I started to date, and I gave up drinking, partying, and even my pipe—not for her, but because I knew they were barriers to the kind of fellowship with God I longed for.

Tex and I were in love by March of 1968 when I got word that my father was dying. I didn't even have time to tell her I was leaving for Baton Rouge. God gave me peace as I drove home, consumed with thoughts about life and death and how I had failed Dad so many times. I wished we had talked more. There was much about him I didn't know. Whereas Mom was still angry with me about my direction in life, Dad gave me my first Bible and encouraged me. He had rededicated himself to God not many months before, so I didn't worry about where he would spend eternity.

We talked a while, and he told me to be sure to stay in school and get my degree. I was holding his hand at four in the morning when I saw life leave his body. It hurt to see my family go through such heartache, but I knew my father was with Christ and that God was with me.

Back at school, Tex and I began to talk about marriage. God had forgiven me for my stagnant season and instilled in me a burden for souls—and not for just a few. I wanted to reach the world for Him.

After hearing about mission efforts in Eastern Europe, my mind returned to that region often. For some reason I felt I would one day preach the claims of Christ behind the Iron Curtain.

My desire grew to further God's kingdom throughout the world, but what could I do as a student? I sent a little money to evangelistic concerns in Communist countries, but that didn't lift my burden.

Like any groom, I could only hope I knew what I was getting into when Tex and I married on June 8, 1968. I was deeply in love, and I knew Tex to be a spiritual woman with a loving, compassionate heart for me and for God. Neither of us was aware of what would be required of us in the future, and only with hindsight can I say that God provided me the perfect mate.

Although I had more to learn than I could imagine and areas of my life needed a deep work from the Lord, He had blessed me with a woman of character who cared about lost souls and would go with me anywhere to see them come to Christ. Unaware that Tex was often more victim than partner during the early years, I plunged into ministry. She could see I had the right motives, but eventually God would use her to minister to me in painful but necessary ways.

A few months after Tex and I were married, God spoke to me in a way He never had before. No one else saw what I saw in a restaurant in Baton Rouge that warm evening. As we sat eating, I gazed out the big glass windows, and my mind carried me far beyond the borders of Louisiana.

Strangely shivering despite the weather, I stared straight ahead. Chairs scraped the floor, mothers scolded children, and Tex brushed her lips with a napkin. But in my mind it was as if the restaurant had been transported across the ocean. My soda had become some sort of a hot drink. The people around me spoke a language I didn't understand.

Somehow in my mind I was behind the Iron Curtain, surrounded by people in a godless vacuum. My heart bled for them, and I burned to tell them the forbidden news. The experience felt so real that it stayed with me for days, and I felt God was calling me to minister behind the Iron Curtain.

I read about the persecution of believers in Eastern Europe, and God constantly prompted me to pray for them. I wanted to go, but how could I? I was just twenty-one, and our home in Walker, Louisiana, was a long way from Europe. Besides, we were practically penniless.

Having not shared the vision with anyone but Tex for several months, I told a group of young people at the Walker Baptist Church about it, and they were thrilled. They even held a car wash to raise money to send us overseas. They presented us with seventy-two dollars, which I cherished as an expression of their love.

But after about a year I put the money away and dismissed the idea. When I discovered what it would cost to go, I began to wonder whether my vision had really been a vision after all.

I badly wanted to reach people for Christ, but I wasn't producing any spiritual fruit. Regardless of how I preached or witnessed, I again found myself in a spiritual desert. I had no power, and nothing was happening.

It took a fiery redhead with a heart full of love to turn me around.

CHAPTER THREE

IN THE CASKET

Leo Humphrey was a muscular, stocky man in his mid-thirties, a rough-and-tumble guy you wouldn't want to mess with. A student at New Orleans Baptist Theological Seminary, he shared his faith in the famed French Quarter. This fireball didn't pass anybody without saying, "Jesus loves you!" He was happy and joyful and seemed to live by the power of God. Most impressive was that his witness was fruitful. I was determined to find out what made him tick.

I started going down to the French Quarter in my spare time to work with Leo. One of his ploys was to tell nightclub owners he was praying they wouldn't sleep until they gave their hearts to Jesus. Then he would write their names in his little prayer book and walk out. I told him, "You can't witness that way. You'll turn those guys off."

But more than one came to Leo pleading with him to quit praying for them, saying, "I haven't slept for days."

"Receive the Lord and you'll sleep like a baby," he'd tell them. And some did. I was learning that even techniques that border on the extreme could work.

The French Quarter shocked me. I saw public immorality, people high on drugs, and knife fights. Kids talked about death the way you and I talk about the weather. That only intensified my burden for a dying world. I was a college senior doing well academically, but my heart was heavy. The sin of the French Quarter haunted me daily. I prayed that God would let me help people find Jesus.

Finally the burden became so strong that I couldn't concentrate. Every minute I sat in class seemed like time I should use to spread the word about Christ. School had become an impossible distraction from what I believed I should be doing. So I dropped out—no small decision, given my father's last request.

My whole extended family was distraught. Mom shouted, called Tex and me names, and even had people call and remind me of Dad's last wish. Friends warned that without a degree I would never preach in a large church or gain any kind of ministerial reputation. Where would I go? What would I do? I had no source of income.

Somehow I knew God had put this restlessness in my heart and that He would take care of Tex and me. My reputation wasn't as important to me as it had once been. (Although I have since preached in some of the world's largest churches and in stadiums all over the globe, I would have been satisfied simply to share Christ on the street with one person at a time.)

Tex was beautiful about it. "Sammy, wherever God calls you, I'll be with you." She has kept that spirit for decades, even though she was learning that the young man God was calling had as many blind spots and weaknesses as he had strengths.

The first thing I did was call Leo and tell him I wasn't waiting for some mysterious door to open. "I'm coming down to witness with you in the French Quarter." Tex and I loaded all our furniture into a truck we borrowed from her dad and drove to Leo's office.

While we were talking with him, someone ransacked the truck. Suddenly there we were, two kids with nothing but an empty borrowed truck, a burden, and the clothes on our backs. We didn't know where we'd sleep or when we'd eat, but we knew we were in God's will. He just wanted us to start from scratch.

Leo signed me up at an evangelism conference and got us a room at the seminary. Pastors and evangelists had come from all over the country. I didn't have a razor or even a change of clothes, but I was eager to learn more about sharing Christ.

I heard a lot of ideas—some good and some not--and suddenly I felt the urge to speak up. I fought it, not sure I wanted to draw attention to myself. Already I stood out as one of very few people there without a tie and coat. Certainly I was the only one with a couple of days' growth on his chin.

Men who wanted to address the group simply raised their hands. Finally, I couldn't contain myself. I stood and told the nearly three hundred pastors and evangelists that we have to take Jesus to the people and not expect them to come to us. We must get out on the streets and present the claims of Christ to anyone who will listen. While I had the floor, I got a little carried away and began sharing my burden for the sin and degradation of the French Quarter.

After the session several pastors sought me out and invited me to come and speak at their churches. I was floored. Here I had stepped out in faith only a few days before, and God had opened the door for me to preach in churches all over.

Those speaking engagements helped meet our financial needs, and it became exciting just to trust God when we needed money. Tex and I moved into a house in Hammond, Louisiana, for eighty dollars a month.

I was scheduled to speak at a church one night, but we didn't have enough money for the gas to get there. The rent was due, and I needed clean clothes and a haircut. We didn't know what to do except to pray. We knelt in our little living room and claimed Philippians 4:19: "My God shall supply all your need according to His riches in glory by Christ Jesus."

We rose believing God would take care of us. I went to the post office to pick up the mail, and there was a gift, a check for one hundred dollars. That paid the rent, cleaned our clothes, cut my hair, put gas in the car, and even paid for a few groceries. The speaking engagement gave us enough money to live on for a while. God has met our needs many times just like that.

My burden grew, and I began to minister in many cities. We witnessed on the street, and I preached in churches, but still I wasn't satisfied I was doing all I could. I was bold, but I was still bearing little fruit. Again it would take Leo to point me in the right direction.

He and I were invited to speak at a youth crusade in Gulf Shores, Alabama, so we had some time to talk. I confided in him that I felt a lack of power, a void in my ministry.

"Sam, do you really want the power of God in your life?"

"I sure do."

"Let's go to the shore and pray about it."

I had a feeling of great anticipation as we headed for the Gulf of Mexico that evening. But before we prayed, I knew I had to admit I'd had misgivings about Leo when we first met. He laughed. "To tell you the truth, Sam, I thought you were in this whole thing for yourself."

"Sometimes I think I *am*," I said. "But I want to get right with God."

We prayed that the Lord would empower me and multiply my ministry. Then I wandered the beach by myself. I laid in the sand and gazed at the stars, listening to the waves, awed by God's handiwork.

I poured out my heart to Him, and He brought unconfessed sin to my mind, exposing some bad attitudes. I begged His forgiveness.

I see Your magnificent power before me, but I'm not experiencing it. I want so badly to bear fruit in my ministry. I need Your power.

I could feel His cleansing, and when I began to thank Him, I couldn't praise Him enough. I worshiped and lost all track of time. I didn't have what some call a charismatic experience, but I felt the Holy Spirit doing a deep work in my life.

Hours later Leo came to me. "It's almost dawn, brother. Let's go."

I grinned. "Praise God," I said. "Praise God." Jesus had taken control of my life. I couldn't even sleep. I just kept praising Him.

Tex was thrilled for me and knew I earnestly sought to serve God. But without realizing it, I was treating her as an accessory. I was in charge. I guided her. When we disagreed, I won her over. When we argued, I showed her I was right and she was wrong. I was so overly confident, I didn't even have a clue what I was doing to her.

Before the first youth crusade meeting in a tent on the beach, the weather was so bad it was about to blow the tent over. Leo said, "Guys, we won't be able to hold the meeting if this doesn't let up. Let's ask God to stop the rain."

A few of us formed a circle inside the tent and knelt to pray. I asked God to stop the rain, but to be honest, my faith was weak. Meddling in the weather was new for me, and I was skeptical. Somebody in that group must have had more faith than I did, because God stopped the rain.

Kelly, a seventeen-year-old girl from Louisiana, had overheard us praying, and she thought we were crazy. She was a biker who prostituted herself for a guy in the American Breed cycle gang from New Orleans. Leo had witnessed to her in the French Quarter and had invited her to the meetings. She also had a friend in the choir.

Kelly had been selling her body since her father had kicked her out of the house at thirteen. She saw him kill her brother with a knife.

Kelly had come only to get away from New Orleans for a while and to score some drugs on the beach. She sat listening to me preach that night with a lot on her mind. I spoke on the second coming of Christ, which was new to her. She thought about Leo witnessing to her and also the girlfriend in the choir who had shared Christ with her. And she thought about the rain stopping.

After the meeting I saw her in the parking lot. "Kelly," I said, "Jesus loves you."

"Don't give me that, man," she spat. "If Jesus loves me, why am I strung out on dope and running with a cycle gang?"

"All I know is that Jesus wants to give you a new life."

She turned and ran toward the beach, calling over her shoulder, "Just leave me alone!"

Later Leo and I found her on the shore and sat on opposite sides of her. We talked and prayed for hours. Finally, at three o'clock in the morning, Kelly asked Jesus to forgive her sins and come into her life. She wept and softly repeated again and again, "He's real."

The next day she went to church in the only clothes she owned. That night before I spoke I asked her to tell the people what had happened to her. After she did, she walked out of the tent and approached two young men across the street. I wondered if anything was wrong, but when she came back, she told me she had gone to share Christ with them.

During that week of meetings we saw more than 130 saved, mostly through personal witnessing. God had once again blessed me with His power.

Kelly didn't have a home to go to, so for the next three months she traveled with Tex and me. I saw her personally lead more than 150 people to Christ. When she went to church with us, she would stand at the door afterward and ask people—even deacons and elders and pastors, "Are you saved?"

When she finally returned to New Orleans to finish high school, her biker man told her, "Forget about religion. You're ridin' with me tonight." She refused.

The next day she had a black eye.

"I got beat up for Jesus," she said.

God's power changes lives.

When I got back to Hammond, Louisiana, I told an old college buddy, Ramsey Gilchrist, what God had been doing in my life. He was especially intrigued by what I told him Leo had said about a man named Arthur Blessitt. Arthur ministered to dopers and hippies at His Place on the Sunset Strip in Hollywood, California. Ramsey and I decided that the best way to learn from Arthur would be to go and see him. Our wives agreed, so we pooled our money, made sandwiches, and made it to California in thirty hours.

After telling Arthur about ourselves, we asked him to tell us some of his experiences, but he just looked at me and said, "You've got to get right with God."

I told him I already had, but he said, "You need to die daily. What you say you experienced that night on the beach you can experience continually if you die daily."

He showed me Galatians 2:20: "I have been crucified with Christ; it is no longer I who live, but Christ lives in me; and the life which I now live in the flesh I live by faith in the Son of God, who loved me and gave Himself for me."

Right there in Arthur's living room I again prayed for the power of God, but this time I figuratively placed my desires in a casket. I placed my wife in that casket, along with my car and my few belongings, and yes, even my secret desire to be another Billy Graham. I placed everything I could think of in that casket, and then I climbed in, telling God I was willing to die to self. Deep in my heart I knew I had Christ's control *and* the Holy Spirit's power to go along with my burden for souls.

I thought the French Quarter was bad, but the Sunset Strip was really something. Cycle gangs wearing chains and carrying blades roared back and forth. We spent only a few days in Hollywood, but it was enough to make me want to serve Christ in a large city. For some reason I felt God drawing me to Chicago, so I started praying about it. Chicago was about as far from my culture as I could get, and the Lord had a lot to teach me first.

My first lesson came in south Louisiana when I preached in a church and revival broke out. The pastor took me aside and said, "If you don't change your methods, you're going to have to leave."

I was shocked. "What do you mean?"

"You're using psychological tricks to stir up people emotionally."

"Man, I'm just preaching about God's changing power."

"And stop saying that this church can't save a person. You and I know it's true, but you're causing people to doubt their salvation."

"I didn't intend to," I said, "but if they're doubting, maybe they should be."

"Change your style or leave."

That night I pleaded with the Lord to somehow show me that I was letting His Spirit preach through me. "If it's just me doing this, then I'll quit."

At about two in the morning I was still up pacing and praying when the phone rang. It was the church youth director.

"Sammy," he said, "revival has come."

A full-time Christian worker had come to his house in tears and told him, "God won't let me sleep until I return these shirts I stole from Sam when we were in college. I saw in the meeting tonight that he has something real. I was wrong to make fun of him."

That was all I needed to know. God was blessing my preaching and that I dare not change. I told the pastor the next day that I loved him and his church but that I would have to leave if I couldn't preach the way I felt. He told me to leave.

It would have been easy for me to become bitter and turn my back on the church as a whole, but God showed me that I must model to kids how to relate to the church. They may get saved on the street, but if they can't connect with and relate to the church, they'll blow away with the wind. Many kids don't like church because too many church services are like funerals. I longed to see revival within the church.

CHAPTER FOUR

THE MONROE SEVEN

God proved what He had taught me when Pastor L. L. Morris invited me to speak Wednesday through Sunday at Calvary Baptist Church in Monroe, Louisiana, early in 1970.

The night before the first service only four young people showed up at the prayer meeting with the pastor and me.

"We might as well forget it if the kids aren't even interested," I said.

But L. L. Morris wasn't a quitter. "Sammy," he said, "before this week is over, I believe God is going to shake Monroe for His glory, and people are going to be saved."

A group from Northeast Louisiana State University sang to a fair crowd the first night and a few made decisions for Christ. But the next night I felt the presence of God in a dramatic way. During the invitation, a Sunday school teacher came forward to pray with Pastor Morris, then came to the pulpit and all but pushed me aside.

"I'm supposed to be an example," he announced, "but I've been a poor Christian, and I want you to forgive me."

Suddenly the Holy Spirit seemed to fall on that place. The singers from the university confessed they had grown lax in personal witnessing and committed themselves to do nothing but glorify Jesus.

Many came to Christ during the next few days, and the crowds kept getting larger. By Sunday night, attendance was so great we decided to extend the meetings. The next night we moved into a larger building, and by the following week we had to move yet again.

Local college kids asked for time in class to tell what God had done in their lives. Ray Mears, a music teacher in the local high school, shared Christ with his students and told them that those who were interested in hearing more could see him after class. All but two stayed.

We set aside a room in the local Christian coffeehouse, Your Place, for around-the-clock prayer. We asked God to touch the heart of former Louisiana Governor James Noe, owner of one of the television stations in Monroe, and that he'd give us free time to tell about the revival. Noe not only gave us the free spot announcements but two fifteen-minute shows besides.

"You're having trouble holding all the people?" he said. "How would you like to have the civic center?" He wheeled around in his chair to call the mayor. "I want you to donate the civic center to these boys. They're doing something positive, so let's give it to them. If there's a charge, I'll cover it."

One night about midnight a girl named Connie McCartney came into *Your Place* stoned on speed. She'd been reared in a Christian home and had received Christ as a youngster, but now twenty she was out on bond after being arrested for selling drugs. She was facing a sure prison term.

"Sam," she said, "speed is my lover. I've tried everything, even astrology and witchcraft. I want out. Can Jesus set me free?"

It was a thrill to tell her God had promised to deliver her from anything, even speed, "if you'll give Him your life. Jesus says the truth shall make you free."

That night Connie committed her life to Christ, and she said she went home and flushed her drugs down the toilet in the name of the Father, the Son, and the Holy Ghost.

Connie and a local football star testified at the next meeting, and the crowds kept growing. I was interviewed on the TV evening news, and the anchorman said, "We understand something is shaking the Twin Cities."

"Jesus is shaking them," I said. "People are finding that He is the only hope for the world."

When I called Leo to tell him what was happening, he said, "Sam, God is doing a mighty work in America. I just got a call from Arthur Blessitt on his 'Which Way, America?' walk for Christ." (Arthur was carrying a cross from coast to coast, preaching in meetings and witnessing along the way.) Leo said that at Arthur's meeting in Albuquerque there were a thousand decisions for Christ.

My heart burned to see America turn back to God. I knelt and asked God what I could do to glorify Him. He seemed to say, "Sammy, walk. Walk, walk, walk."

Outside of Arthur, I had never heard of anyone walking for Jesus. "God, I have a wife to think about. I'll go if You want me to, but You'll have to help Tex trust You in this."

A few days later I finally discussed the idea with her. She told me God had spoken to her less than a half hour before, impressing upon her that she must be willing to follow Him, regardless where He led.

"An hour ago I would have thought this was crazy," she admitted.

To my shame, I have to confess that if I had not waited for God to work in her heart, I would have somehow badgered her into going along anyway.

When Ray Mears, the music teacher, heard our plan to walk from Monroe to Washington, D.C., he told me, "I believe God is calling Charlotte and me to go with you." But Ray was five credit hours from his college degree, and Charlotte was pregnant. Besides that, they were $1,100 in debt. Ray wanted to pay off his debts before the walk, so he put his car up for sale. A dealer told him he'd never get more than $800 for it, but Ray held out for several days and finally took it to an auction where it sold for—you guessed it— $1,100.

Ken Hall, a college freshman, also felt God wanted him to go with us. His decision was made difficult by his father, who drove up from Shreveport. "Son," he said, "if you go, you may never see me again. I don't have long to live."

Ken looked his father in the eye and said, "Daddy, I love you, but I love Jesus more, and I have to do what He has told me." (Dr. Ken Hall went on to become a pastor in Texas and Executive Vice President of Baylor University.)

Richard Medaries was a former rock drummer who turned his life and his talent over to God. I felt led to approach him about the walk. Little Richard, as he came to be known, was hesitant at first. But through prayer he felt God wanted him to go. And he brought along his drums.

Connie, the former speed addict, would have to come back to Monroe to stand trial in April, but she wanted to go anyway. She expected to be sentenced to several years in prison, and she wanted to learn how to share her faith with other inmates.

There was nothing exceptional about any of the seven of us. We all simply wanted to be used of God.

Arthur Blessitt and I prayed over the phone, and he suggested a Bible as our symbol. That rang a bell with me. We would push a wheelbarrow full of New Testaments to give to people along the way, and we would meet up with Arthur in the capital.

The deacons of a large local church told us that walking for Christ just wasn't done. They said they had never heard of people selling their belongings and dropping out to follow Jesus, except, of course, in the Bible.

Several local pastors met with us and told Ray he must not love his wife, taking a pregnant woman on a march across the country!

"I don't understand it myself," Ray told them. "All I can say is that God has called us, and we're going."

Finally, one of the pastors spoke up. "If God has called these boys, we'd better not stand in their way."

Arthur called and seemed to have had second thoughts. He urged me to be sure God was in the decision. He and those with him had been threatened that they might never make it to Washington. "Pray again, and be sure."

But before we could even do that, a young man told us, "God showed me you will be struck dead on the first step."

All we had were two cars, a little food, our Bibles, a trailer-tent, and a wheelbarrow. With about $100 between us, we planned to leave the morning of March 16, 1970. I was too excited to sleep well, but the lack of rest wouldn't take its toll until we were far down the road.

Dozens of local Christians and several members of the news media gathered to see us off. Many of the kids who had received Christ during the revival joined us in a 7A.M. prayer meeting. I'd made many new friends in Monroe, and I wondered if I'd ever see them again. It was an emotional morning.

After we were interviewed briefly by the press, Tex, Ray, Charlotte, Connie, and Little Richard drove ahead in two cars. Ken and I would walk the first leg, trusting God to open doors.

As I bent to grab the wheelbarrow, my mind raced. Was I wrong to ignore the young man's death vision? I looked at Ken. "Praise God, brother. Let's walk for Jesus."

With the first step God flooded my soul with the love and joy of Jesus, and I could only praise Him.

Publicity preceded us, so townspeople gathered and kids ran along shouting, 'Those guys with the wheelbarrow are coming!" A man working in a cornfield in Rayville was the first to come to Jesus on our walk. We witnessed to people all along the way before we finally called it a day.

We set up our tent in the country, away from the highway. Ray, Charlotte, Connie, Tex, and I slept in our clothes in the tent, while Ken and Richard climbed into their sleeping bags on the ground outside.

Then the rain came.

In the morning, mud and wet equipment dampened our spirits. So it wasn't all going to be a joyride. Already we were down to the nitty-gritty.

Walking twenty-five miles a day, we made it to Jackson, Mississippi, in a week. We stopped at a restaurant just inside the city limits and looked forward to ministering at the college. But we couldn't wait. We started sharing the claims of Jesus right there.

The next morning we held an outdoor meeting during the break after the regular campus chapel service. Afterward two local pastors asked us to hold services in their churches and took up a love offering for us. God was providing.

We left the next Monday for York, Alabama, and—to our surprise—a chance to witness to Governor George Wallace, in town for a rally. We detoured, and I told one of his aides we'd like to present the governor one of our Bibles. I had just about resigned myself to not seeing Wallace, when the rally started and an aide told me, "We're going to let you do it."

When I was invited to the platform, the Lord impressed three verses on my heart: "You will be brought before governors and kings for My sake, as a testimony to them... But when they deliver you up, do not worry about how or what you should speak. For it will be given to you in that hour what you should speak; for it is not you who speak, but the Spirit of your Father who speaks in you" (Matthew 10:18-20).

I claimed that promise and couldn't believe what came from my mouth. "People," I began, "the solution to the problems that face our nation today is not found in any politician but only in Jesus Christ! Mr. Wallace, I'd like to give you the Word of God because in it is found the solution to the crises in America."

I didn't want the crowd to think we were there for political reasons, so we left immediately, headed for Livingston. My presentation to the governor was broadcast on statewide television, and unknown to us, the president of Livingston University had state troopers looking for us up and down the highway all night, wanting to make sure we didn't pass through without stopping to speak there.

As we neared the University of Alabama at Tuscaloosa a few days later, we passed a chain gang on the other side of the highway. Holding a big Bible aloft, we yelled, "Jesus loves you, brothers! Jesus loves you!" (A year later one of the men on that gang told a friend of mine that as a result of that incident, he eventually received Christ.)

At the University of Alabama, we shared Christ with a couple of young men on the steps of the student union building. One said, "Man, you've really got something. You should tell this to the whole student body."

He got permission for us to hold an outdoor meeting Monday morning, two weeks since we had left Monroe. We had no time for publicity, so we prayed God would bless Little Richard's drums. When he cut loose, the kids started coming. I spoke to two thousand that day, and many gave their hearts to Jesus.

Police stopped us at the border of Sweetwater, Alabama, and told us they wouldn't let us walk through their town. A young boy we had been witnessing to told us he was the nephew of the mayor. "Let's go talk to my uncle," he said.

A councilman told the mayor we were saying something the country needed to hear and that we should be allowed to continue. The mayor agreed.

About a mile down the road, a squad car pulled up. "Hop in," an officer said. I tried to tell him the mayor said we could proceed, but the cops put our wheelbarrow in their trunk, drove to the other side of the city, and ordered us out of the car.

"Sir," I said, "we weren't trying to give you any hassle. We just want people to know the Lord. If you don't know Jesus—"

"Son, you'd better not show your face in this town again."

I said, "All right, but we want you to know that Jesus loves you and that He died for you. And we love you too."

In Georgia, Murray Bradfield, a local youth director, invited us to a rally at his church, but Ken and Richard and I felt led instead to go to a prayer room upstairs to seek the Lord. As the meeting started below, we knelt and cried out for revival in America. Psalm 46:10 came to mind, and I quoted it to the others: "Be still, and know that I am God; I will be exalted among the nations, I will be exalted in the earth!"

On our knees and elbows, hands covering our eyes, we suddenly broke into sobs. I felt I was in the presence of Jesus, and I have never felt so unclean, so unworthy. Each of us asked God for forgiveness for failing Him so often, and for cleansing and filling. I immediately felt filled with peace and joy and power.

A few days later we arrived at the University of Georgia in Athens, where a rally was planned to memorialize the students killed by National Guard troops at Kent State. Two thousand students gathered, and someone got me on the program. The leader said, "Just don't mention the name of Christ. We also have a rabbi on the platform."

I said, "Well, then count me out. Jesus is what we're all about."

He finally consented, but neither I nor the rabbi got a chance to speak. Radicals stormed the platform and urged the students to take over the administration building.

The next day thousands there were demonstrating for peace, but we were also passing out Jesus stickers and carrying posters that read Real Peace Is Jesus and Get Back to God.

I worked my way toward a platform where a radical was shouting obscenities and calling for the destruction of the administration building. He suddenly turned and handed me the microphone, obviously thinking I was the next radical in line.

Here we go again, Lord.

"There's been a lot of talk about peace here!" I began, and the crowd cheered. "But let me tell you, there won't be any peace until we get the Prince of Peace, Jesus Christ, into our hearts!" Silence. I expected a brick or a tomato, but suddenly the students applauded. As TV cameras moved into position, I preached Jesus and challenged the students to commit their lives to Him.

The next speaker said, "Well, what *would* Jesus do if He were here?" The riot had turned into a revival. The guy who had asked me not to mention Jesus now asked me to pray there would be no more violence on campus.

That year the University of Georgia yearbook carried a picture of Tex and Connie holding a big sign: Real Peace Is Jesus.

CHAPTER FIVE

LESSONS

As we made our way from Georgia into South Carolina, one day Ken and I heard a huge trailer truck behind us and turned to see it barreling straight for us. We hurled ourselves into the ditch, wheelbarrow, Bibles, and all, and the truck missed us by inches. I have no idea what was behind the incident.

A few days later, when Little Richard and I were walking, someone fired a gun at us out their window. I'll never know whether the bullet was a blank or just missed.

The greatest lesson God taught us was love for one another. That was tough on the road. Because we slept in our clothes, we were dirty and hot and tired and miserable. God provided money and food all along the way, but at one point we were down to just some Kool-Aid, peanut butter, and bread. At the end of a day of walking, when all you've had is a scoop of grits, you need more for supper than half a peanut butter sandwich and a couple of swallows of a drink.

As I sat wearily trying to make that little sandwich last, I noticed a half cup of Kool-Aid left in the pitcher. I thought, *I'll bet ol' Ray wants that, and I'm not going to get it.* It sounds petty, but it seemed important at the time. God had to teach me daily to die to myself.

After four months and fifteen hundred miles, we finally came within sight of our nation's capital across the Potomac River. Three black guys stopped us as we neared the city, and one pulled me off to the side. "I'm going to kill you," he said.

He reared back to hit me, and I said, "Jesus loves you." Something held him back.

"I hate you!" he said, snarling.

"Jesus loves you," I said.

"Don't tell me that!"

"Jesus loves you," I said again and again. He kept cocking his arm, but he never swung.

"Is Jesus white?"

33

"I don't know," I said. "I've never seen Him. The Bible says that those who worship Him must worship Him in spirit and in truth. I used to hate black people. I thought they were lower than whites. But when Jesus took over my life, He took away that prejudice and filled me with love. That's why I can tell you I love you."

His face softened. "You mean it?"

"I sure do."

"Honest?"

"I'm not just talking."

He stuck out his hand. "Man, you're okay."

"No, Jesus is okay. I'm rotten. Jesus changed me."

It was great to see Arthur Blessitt again. Murray Bradfield met us there, and he and another friend and I did some fun witnessing by car. At red lights we'd jump out and pass out tracts, trying to get back to the car in time for the green light. Once, I didn't make it, and the guys couldn't wait. I knew they'd eventually get back and find me, so I took off walking, passing out Jesus stickers and tracts, witnessing as I went. I came to a gate and a big, black iron fence, and there, beyond the bars, sat the White House.

Knowing thousands of people peered through that fence every day, I started pasting stickers on every fourth bar. People gathered to read, "Real Peace Is Jesus."

Two guards came running and one told me, "Scrape off all those stickers, or we'll arrest you for defacing government property!"

"Yes, sir," I said. "Forgive me. I had no idea it was against the law."

One stayed with me to make sure I'd do it, and I got a good chance to witness to him.

Then I told him I had affixed more stickers to the other end of the fence.

"I'll trust you to scrape them off," he said. "You're a good Christian."

Later a guard in the security office inside the White House told me, "I'm a Christian too. We need more young people doing what you're doing."

Not far from there, I handed a tract to two girls. They looked at it and one said, "I've been lying awake nights worrying whether I'm going to heaven. Can I know for sure?"

We knelt right there on the sidewalk in the shadows of the White House, and she and her friend prayed to receive Christ.

On July 17, 1970, we marched to the Capitol and then to the Washington Monument for a rally. About a thousand people flooded the area as Arthur Blessitt and I proclaimed to the nation's leaders that Jesus was our only hope.

Arthur felt led to fast for forty days at the corner of Constitution and Fifteenth Avenue, praying for revival in America. I spent a little time with him there, and one evening as he dozed, I prayed God would use me that very day to help spark revival in America. The pay phone rang nearby (Arthur had released the number to the local press). The caller was a guy from Boston who said he wanted more information on what we were doing. I told him and shared with him the plan of salvation. I led him in a brief prayer of acceptance.

A few minutes later the phone rang again. A girl from Pennsylvania said, "I praise God for what you guys are doing. I just heard you on the radio, and—"

"The radio? No, you didn't hear me—"

"You didn't just pray with a guy from Boston?"

"How did you know that?"

"He was a disc jockey, and you were live on national radio!"

Several more people called that night, including a truck driver who was crying. "I've been searching for God for two years," he said. I led him to Jesus over the phone.

I found out the next day that the deejay had not really received Christ but had repeated the prayer so his listeners could hear it.

God had answered my prayer in a unique way.

CHAPTER SIX

GOD'S LOVE IN ACTION

God had been impressing on me that I should set up a headquarters and start a street ministry in Chicago. So after a week with Arthur in D.C. and a visit to my home in Baton Rouge, I named our ministry God's Love in Action and headed north on September 1, 1970. That proved difficult for Mom. "That walk was ridiculous enough. And now you want to move to Chicago? Why?"

We rented the upstairs of a big house in Uptown on the city's North Side. With no steady income but knowing that God had led us there, we threw ourselves into ministry and trusted Him to provide.

We never asked anyone for a penny, and that remains our policy to this day. I believe income is a gauge of God's direction. If He wants us to do something, He'll provide for it without our begging. If He doesn't, that means He's not in it. We do include a return envelope with our newsletter, and gifts to our ministry are tax deductible, but we never ask for anything from anyone but God.

Now it was time for a lesson in patience and persistence. Chicagoans were not as receptive to us or our message as people in the south had been. They didn't seem to trust us. One girl said, "Why doesn't your Jesus get you some shoes?" Northerners didn't run around city streets barefoot.

I knew we were in God's will because He kept supplying our physical needs, but the lack of results was getting to me. If I'd ever had a problem with pride, it was cured in Chicago. While I was in that wilderness and seeing no fruit, God was teaching me—yet again—that it is only He who draws people to Himself.

Finally, after three months of barrenness, we saw Big Mike come to Jesus. Mike Logston said he came to Chicago from Oklahoma because the thieving was easier. The six-foot, four-inch, 280-pounder always carried a sawed-off shotgun.

Within twenty-four hours of Mike becoming a believer, a runaway Jewish girl named Cindy gave her heart to Christ. After that, God seemed to pour out His blessing.

We started a Monday night Bible study class, but at the first meeting, Tex and I were the only ones there. We worked with several area youth pastors and their kids, I spoke throughout Chicago, and we kept holding our Bible studies no matter how many people showed up. Within a few months we were filling our attic with seekers every week.

We brought on four other full-timers, though we didn't pay salaries as such. I helped finance the operation with speaking engagements, and a few people sent a little support.

The big daily papers in Chicago referred to us as the originators of the Jesus movement in the city. We were often referred to as the Jesus Freaks or Jesus People, but we were really just old-fashioned Christians.

Within a half-year our weekly Bible studies were averaging sixty kids each week, and in July of 1971 we saw six hundred kids in four weeks. We simply studied, sang, and prayed, but the new Christians were hungry to learn about and worship Jesus.

As I preached in a church one Sunday on how God had promised Abraham a son, I had trouble keeping my train of thought. As I tried to tell the people that they should trust God in the same way Abraham did, I sensed He was trying to tell me that I would have a son and that he would be used of God in a mighty way.

Tex was skeptical. Neither of us knew she was already pregnant. When we found out, no names for girls even entered our minds. Slowly Tex came to be convinced, but she wasn't excited about my announcing it before two thousand people at a citywide crusade in East St. Louis, Illinois.

That summer Arthur Blessitt came to Chicago, and we held a rally in the Civic Center Plaza where more than a thousand people gathered, and many turned from drugs and alcohol to give their lives to Jesus Christ.

Our Bible studies grew, and we saw more and more results on the streets. When the famous acid rock group Sly and the Family Stone played for about ten thousand kids at Northwestern University in Evanston, we went to share Christ. Kids lay naked on the beach, and drugs were passed around openly.

We passed out little red stickers that read One Way, Trust Jesus and we called them "reds," which also happened to be the word for downers in the drug culture. When one of our guys stood in the middle of the crowd and yelled, "Free reds!" you should have seen the kids flock around him.

A lot of people thought we were fanatics when we painted Jesus Loves You in our upstairs window. One girl is glad we did. She stopped in one day to tell me she had run away from her home in Washington, D.C. "I've already been raped, and now I'm addicted to drugs. I saw your sign and felt like Jesus touched me."

I asked her if she wanted to give her heart to Christ and have her sins forgiven and her life changed. She prayed with me, and then we contacted her family and arranged for her to return home. She believes God led her down our street that day. So do I.

Tex and I heard there was a huge contingent of Satan worshipers in Chicago, and we knew we would have to confront them head-on. We stopped at their coffeehouse to share Christ with one of their leaders. He said, "Tippit, I have more power in my little finger than all the Christians in Chicago."

He looked surprised when I said, "I challenge you to prove that." He didn't know what to say. Tex and I left, praying God would remove the power of Satan from the neighborhood. The next night the leader was nowhere to be found, and a month later that coffeehouse burned to the ground. (We had nothing to do with it!)

In the nightclub district, centered on Rush Street, we shared Jesus with many lonely people looking for any kind of peace or love or happiness.

One night a club owner called me and said, "I don't want to see you down here anymore."

I said, "We're not doing anything but talking to people, and we're not going inside your club. We're staying on the sidewalk."

"People don't want to hear about your religion, and you're hurting our business. Stay away."

"I'm not trying to be obnoxious, sir, but God has told us to go where the people are."

"You come down here, and I'll have you thrown in jail."

LeRoy, the doorman at My Place, a club just off Rush on Delaware Street, said, "I wouldn't mind cutting you guys up if you keep coming down here."

September 1, 1971 (a year to the day since we arrived in Chicago), I returned from a week of meetings in Florida and could tell immediately something was wrong. Tex was eight months pregnant and didn't need any more stress.

She told me that two of our high school volunteers had been arrested while witnessing and charged with disorderly conduct. I couldn't believe it, and I worried about the future of our ministry. But we had been called to share Jesus in that area, and we weren't going to be intimidated.

Two days later my associate Lloyd Cole and I went to witness on Delaware Street. The first person I handed a tract to was a plainclothes detective. "Sorry," he said, "but you aren't going to be able to do this here tonight. It's not legal."

"Sir," I said, "I believe in obeying the law. What are we doing wrong?"

"I'm telling you, you'll have to leave."

"If this is illegal, I'll leave."

He pulled me off to the side. "You're taking food out of a baby's mouth. The owner of this place supports his family by providing entertainment and selling alcohol. You think it's right to deprive a man of his job?"

"I believe that if a man seeks God's will in his life, God will provide him with a better job. If we have revival in America, a lot of nightclub owners will be out of work."

"Well, you're hurting this man and a lot of other people down here."

"That's your opinion," I said, not unkindly. "There are pushers and prostitutes on these streets, and we certainly aren't doing anything illegal the way they are. We're offering something positive, and they're ruining people's lives. We're just sharing Christ with lonely people."

"Why don't you do this downtown?"

"If it's wrong here, why wouldn't it be wrong there?"

He glared at me. "If you don't leave, we'll get something on you."

The next person I talked to knelt right there on the sidewalk with me and prayed to receive Christ. LeRoy, the My Place doorman, came out and pulled a switchblade from his pocket.

When he flipped open the blade, I jogged away. Lloyd and I kept witnessing up the street, keeping an eye out for LeRoy. When two plainclothesmen came out of My Place, I returned and asked if I could talk to them.

"We have nothing to talk to you about. You're the one who's doing everything right."

"Someone pulled a weapon on me."

"A weapon!" one said loud enough so LeRoy could hear. "What did it look like?"

I pointed to LeRoy, who hurried into the alley. One of the cops brought him to the front of the club before searching him, and when he found no knife, he accused us of trying to cause trouble.

"No, sir, we're not," I said. "Our rights are being infringed upon. We just want to speak freely for Christ."

"You've got five minutes to get off the street."

"You haven't told me what we're doing wrong."

"Loitering."

"We can't get them on that," the other whispered. "Maybe disorderly conduct." He turned to me. "Don't worry, son, we'll get you on something."

"You still haven't told me what we're doing wrong."

"You're under arrest."

We were taken to the precinct station near the corner of Chicago Avenue and LaSalle a little after 10 P.M. The plainclothesman urged the booking officer to let us keep our Bibles and tracts. I was confused. His attitude seemed to have changed. "Sir," I said, "do you know that Jesus really loves you?"

"Yeah, I know. For God so loved the world and all that."

"Do you know Jesus?"

"I wouldn't exactly call myself a Christian."

"Jesus could come into your heart."

"I know. You fellas go ahead and make your phone call."

Tex was nearly in tears when I reached her. We would have to wait in a cell until someone came from our headquarters with bail money.

Lloyd and I were put in an empty cell at one end, out of the range of vision of the other prisoners. We sat on opposite ends of a steel slab. "I can't believe it," I said. "Before I got saved, I never went to jail. All the testimonies I ever heard went the other way."

We prayed, and God filled my heart with peace. I was reminded of Philippians 4:6-7: "Be anxious for nothing, but in everything by prayer and supplication, with thanksgiving, let your requests be made known to God; and the peace of God, which surpasses all understanding, will guard your hearts and minds through Jesus Christ."

People in there needed Jesus. So we sang. Then we shouted our testimonies. Soon the other prisoners banged on the bars and hollered for us to shut up.

We testified to the power of God to change lives. The men got quiet and then noisy again and then quiet. After about fifteen minutes we noticed the noise had all but subsided. From the other end of the cell block a voice called out, "Hey, are you a preacher?"

"Yes, sir, I am."

"What're you doing in jail?"

I told him, and that seemed to give us a common bond. A man in the cell next to us said, "Man, I've been searchin' for peace for six years."

Though I couldn't see him, he was just inches away, listening as I talked about Jesus. Lloyd fished in his back pocket and reached through the bars to try to hand the man a tract. But it slipped from his fingers and floated to the floor. Lloyd stabbed at it with his comb and carefully slid it as far as he could toward the other cell. Finally, the man reached it. The whole place was quiet.

After several minutes I asked, "What's happening, brother?"

"This says a lot," he whispered. "I want to know God."

"Are you willing to pray with us right here?"

"Yes."

We prayed for him, and then he prayed. He admitted he was a sinner, and he thanked Jesus for dying for him. Then he invited Christ into his life. We told him that when he got out of jail, he should look us up so we could help him.

"I'm gonna be in a long time," he said. "I cut up a guy, and they found the knife on me." But still, Lloyd was bubbling over. He told me it was near midnight, and we were reminded of how Paul and Silas saw a man come to Jesus in prison at midnight.

"Sammy," Lloyd said, "let's lead these guys in singing with us."

"This isn't a church crowd," I whispered. "You're not going to get them to sing."

"Let me try," he said. "Y'all know 'Amazing Grace'? [It was on the pop charts at the time.] We'll sing, and you follow!"

I can hardly carry a tune, and Lloyd wasn't much better, but sure enough, the men knew the song. It was an indescribable thrill. Here were these criminals, none of them real singers, growling and mumbling along, off-key and sour, but singing "Amazing Grace." It was a sweet, discordant sound. When we finished, I preached on Acts 16 and told the men how they could have peace with God even in jail.

One of our guys showed up from headquarters with the bail money, and it was a relief to be reunited with Tex. But now we worried. Four of us had been arrested in three days. Bail money was wreaking havoc on our limited budget.

CHAPTER SEVEN

AT A CROSSROADS

Aside from my preaching, our entire ministry was on the street. Not only were we being denied our freedom of speech, but if we were convicted, all the other ministries and individuals who witnessed on the streets would be jeopardized too.

How could we be denied the right to share Christ, especially when we were careful never to force anything on anyone? As we poured our hearts out to God, I began to get the distinct feeling that I should fashion a huge wooden cross and take it to the civic center, where I would fast and pray until our trial.

That sounded pretty radical, even to me. God had promised me a son, and Tex was due to deliver that month. I tried to tell myself the civic center idea wasn't of God, but I felt God telling me, "Sammy, you must." I knew deep in my heart I had to do it. How I longed for my son to grow up in a country where he had the freedom to share Christ anywhere. In the wee hours one morning, another staff member and I found some lumber in the garage and fashioned a crude eight-foot cross.

Tex was with me all the way. The next morning she knelt with me near the cross as the staff put their hands on our shoulders and prayed for us. The burden welled up anew inside me, and tears came. A long month lay ahead.

I called newspapers that had done stories on us, and the word spread quickly. Surrounded by newspaper and broadcast media people at the civic center, I explained what I was doing.

We received tremendous support from all over. The Wheaton (Illinois) Bible Church held a twenty-four-hour prayer vigil, and we received reports of many others. Petitions flooded Chicago mayor's office. One afternoon I tried to see him, but an aide turned me away. "We know who you are. You're responsible for all these petitions."

We received calls from dozens of lawyers—including the American Civil Liberties Union—who must have figured our case would bring a ton of publicity. I became convinced God wanted us to have a Christian lawyer. We waited for the right man.

43

Meanwhile, our civic center ministry was in full swing. As I sat reading my Bible near the cross one day, a girl sat a few feet away. "Hey," I said, trying to be pleasant, "do you know Jesus?"

"No, and I don't want to talk about it."

I figure if a person doesn't want to talk or listen after I've opened the conversation, I have no right to continue. So I went back to my reading, but after a few minutes the girl turned to me and whimpered, "I need help." She had run away from home in the suburbs and said she had messed up her life. In fact, the police were looking for her.

"Jesus promised to give you abundant life," I said. I shared with her the testimonies of the other runaways. "They still have the same problems they had before they came to Christ, but He has given them the strength to face them." Eventually I asked her if she would like to know Jesus, and we prayed together.

I told our staff members and even the winos in the area what had happened and asked if they could donate toward getting the girl home. Several of the drunks, who themselves had been panhandling, gave a few cents each, and we raised enough. A few weeks later the girl's mother called to tell me that her daughter had been truly changed, and she thanked me for sharing the claims of Christ with her.

That vigil at the cross became one of the greatest spiritual experiences I'd ever had. Subsisting only on liquids, I lost twenty-five pounds and felt as if I were in the presence of Jesus most of the time. Once, however, I lost my temper. Several well-meaning Christians often joined us to help witness. One such man from a large church in northern Indiana stood around hassling blacks. With my southern accent, I had enough trouble winning the confidence of blacks without this professing believer making things worse. Finally I leaped from the bench and grabbed him by the shoulders. "You need to get right with God! You need to let Jesus take the hate and prejudice out of your heart and fill you with love!" He hurried off, obviously shaken.

When he came back a few minutes later, I apologized. "I still think you need to get right with God on this," I said, "but I shouldn't have reacted the way I did."

Murray Bradfield joined me at the cross one night when the drunks were out in full force. One huge, muscular man broke a bottle and staggered around with the jagged neck in his hand. Everyone kept their distance until he threw the bottle away. Then he grabbed Murray's hair in one hand and mine in the other and smacked our heads together several times, screaming that he wanted to kill us. We just kept shouting, "Jesus loves you, brother!" When he finally let us go, we dropped to our knees and prayed for peace.

One night about nine o'clock I heard cheering and shouting in the distance. Suddenly a group of sixty or seventy students from Moody Bible Institute, Wheaton College, Judson College, and local churches came around the corner carrying posters and shouting Christian slogans. We had a great time of prayer together. Ironically, two of us had been arrested for blocking pedestrian traffic right where more than sixty of them now walked, some spilling into the street.

The day finally came that I received word from Moody Bible Institute that my case had been discussed at a meeting of the Christian Legal Society. They gave me the names of several Christian lawyers, and I called George Newitt, who had offices near the civic center.

Most of the lawyers who had approached me were slick talkers and pseudo big shots. Newitt sounded sincerely interested in our case. I told him we were just genuine Christians who weren't out to cause trouble. "We just want our freedom to share Christ."

After meeting with Lloyd and me, Mr. Newitt took on our case at no charge, which was the only way we could afford him! God was providing for our needs, though we now had ten full-time staffers we paid according to their needs. Even with that, our combined salaries for eleven people totaled less than six hundred dollars a month. Our staffers really gave of themselves.

We planned a rally at the civic center for noon on Saturday, September 25, 1971, four days before the trial. We spread the news by word of mouth, not wanting to tell the media until that day. That morning it rained for hours with no break in sight. When the noon chimes rang in the church steeple across from the center, the rain stopped, and about a thousand people showed up.

Tex was past due by about a week, and it struck me that our son might be born the day I went to trial. I have to say that if the same situation faced me today, I'd insist on a continuance. But back then I spent a lot of time away from my very pregnant wife.

Wednesday morning I awoke at the civic center with tremendous anticipation. I hurried home to get ready for the hearing, knowing this would be the most important day of my life.

Tex was in labor when I got to the house. By the time I left, she was being taken to the hospital. I worried whether I'd be free in time to be with her. My first stop was Moody Bible Institute, where Lloyd Cole and I were interviewed on the radio. Then we went to the office of a local Christian artist who had offered his place for a pretrial prayer meeting. About 150 friends joined us there, and then a hundred more joined us a few blocks away at the little precinct courthouse.

After the usual hearings over prostitutes and drunks—people merely being processed without being helped—it was finally the *City of Chicago v. Tippit and Cole.*

Mr. Newitt started boldly, referring to the charges as spurious and asking for a summary judgment. When the judge refused to dismiss the case, Mr. Newitt insisted on a jury trial.

"Counselor," the judge said, "your clients are not entitled to a jury trial."

"Why not, Your Honor? These boys' constitutional rights have been violated."

"In this state, a misdemeanor would not require sentencing to a penitentiary and is, thus, not afforded a jury trial."

Newitt acted shocked. "Your Honor, are you telling me I can't have a jury trial on a question as fundamental and vital as this? The Constitution sets forth certain rights as inalienable. If Illinois law takes away this man's right to free speech and to exercise his religious prerogatives, then that law cannot stand."

The judge appeared taken aback and reserved judgment until he could consult with the city attorney. The attorney agreed we had the right to a jury trial, and Mr. Newitt, Lloyd, and I were immediately surrounded by the press. One reporter asked if I'd heard from my wife, and suddenly all the emotion of the past month washed over me. I wept as I announced I was on my way to the hospital.

"Sammy!" someone yelled, "you're a father! You've got an eight-pound baby boy!" Then the questions really started flying. I was drained.

I rushed to the hospital only to find that Tex was still in labor!

I spent several hours with her, praying for her as she endured the contractions. The experience drew us closer, and I appreciated her more than ever. When I took a break to get something to eat, I noticed our story on the front page of the *Chicago Tribune*. It told of my going to trial and becoming a father the same day, and it even carried the name of my son, Paul David. The only problem was, I didn't have a son yet, and for the first time in months my faith wavered.

"Lord," I prayed, "what if I'm wrong?"

Then I felt ashamed. "Lord, I believe you promised me a son, and I'm still claiming it."

Tex's labor was prolonged, and suddenly I remembered I was scheduled for a TV interview at eleven P.M. I didn't want to leave Tex, but she talked me into it. "You can tell a lot of people about Jesus tonight." Lloyd's wife Gail offered to stay with Tex.

When I left she was in deep labor. It was hard to concentrate, and at a break in the show at 11:30 I took a call from the doctor. "I wanted you to be the first to know. You have a healthy baby boy, a little over eight pounds."

A fantastic day of emotional strain ended for Tex and me, and soon we just held each other and cried. I finally got to see the son God had promised us. What a sweet, unforgettable day.

During the next two weeks Mr. Newitt prepared his pretrial brief as if for a federal case. He called the lawyer on the other side and warned, "If you go to trial, you are going to lose. The city of Chicago and the police department are going to have a black eye. People are going to get the impression that all your policemen do is knock people off the streets when they are passing out Gospel tracts. There's been a lot of publicity on this case, and there's going to be a lot more. The best thing that could possibly happen to the city would be for you to slink off into the background and let this case be dismissed."

Mr. Newitt also told him that he was contemplating filing a suit in federal court against the violation of our civil rights to free speech and the exercise of our religion. The case had clearly become a personal matter to our lawyer.

When the case was called and the judge asked if the prosecution was ready, the city attorney requested a continuance to meet with the defense. "They were stalling," Mr. Newitt whispered. "When you ask for time, you're in trouble."

Both sides met in private, and the chief enforcement attorney for the city—a tough, cocky guy—conducted a minitrial of his own and then lectured all involved. He insinuated that I wouldn't know the difference between a knife and fingernail clippers and asked why I didn't simply sock LeRoy in the nose. "You don't understand how we live around here."

He was trying to make me look like a hillbilly over his head in the big city. "Sir," I said, nearly in tears, "if you think I'm lying, then let's just go ahead to court."

Newitt motioned me close and whispered, "Now knock it off. We're going to get out of this all right. We've got them over a barrel, and they're giving up."

"Well, I'd rather go to trial and prove I'm innocent."

Newitt insisted there was no need. In the end we agreed not to file a federal suit against the officer if the city agreed to drop the charges.

I didn't realize how big a victory we had won until we were threatened again a couple of weeks later. I went to the district commander and told him we'd been threatened by a nightclub owner again.

"Don't worry, Tippit," he told me. "None of my men will arrest you boys when you're out there telling people about Christ. If more young people were doing that, I wouldn't have half the problems I have today."

George Newitt told us, "We gave the city a whipping. The personal satisfaction I received from defending the rights of Christians to share their faith without intimidation will last much longer than any payment I could have received."

CHAPTER EIGHT

THE WALL

Our Chicago Bible studies were booming, but I still felt drawn to the Iron Curtain. I prayed that God would lay a deep impression on my heart if He had some specific international ministry for me. *I'll do anything to further Your kingdom.*

One morning at three o'clock Murray Bradfield and I were on our knees in my little office when we felt impressed that the Lord wanted us to walk across Germany for Him.

God would have to help us overcome three major obstacles:

We needed twenty-five hundred dollars for transportation alone.

We knew no one in Germany.

Neither of us spoke the language.

We felt led to go late in the year, but prospects looked dim. We needed to get passports and reserve flights.

That day a man came to the house and identified himself as a schoolteacher. He said he had saved money for years, but that morning as he prayed, God had touched his heart, and he felt led to bring us a check for twenty-five hundred dollars. He had no idea what our financial need was, but God did. What a blessed time we had sharing with him how we had prayed for that amount.

Many would say it was more foolish than courageous to lead a walk across Germany with no contacts in Frankfurt or Berlin and only a few on the walk route. I didn't have much of a plan beyond following the Lord.

I crammed to learn as much German as I could, and we left on November 28, 1971. Almost immediately God made it obvious He had gone before us and would be with us. One of the great surprises of my life came in the form of a "coincidence" a fiction writer couldn't have made up. We landed in Frankfurt and were transferring to a flight to Munich when I thought heard someone call out in a German accent, "Sammy Tippit? Sammy Tippit?"

Knowing no one in Frankfurt, I whirled to see a well-dressed man in his late twenties smiling at me. "Are you Sammy Tippit?"

"Well, yes," I said, rattled.

"My name is Volkhard Spitzer."

Speechless, I shook his hand.

"I read about your trouble in Chicago," he said. "The church I pastor in Berlin has been praying for you since your arrest."

"How did you recognize me?" I managed finally.

He shrugged. "You looked American, and when she called you 'Sammy' in an American accent, I wondered if it could be you."

I told him we had been praying for a contact in Berlin because I dreamed of holding a prayer and fasting vigil there.

"Don't worry about that," he said. "I'll arrange a rally for you, and we'll have thousands there."

Volkhard told me his nonstop flight from Berlin to Munich had been rerouted through Frankfort. Some coincidence, no? It shouldn't have surprised me to find we were booked on the same flight to Munich. Before we boarded, Volkhard was somehow able to contact the media in Munich and tell them he would be arriving with some Jesus People from Chicago.

We spent the entire flight planning the Berlin rally. The media was waiting for us in Munich, and with Volkhard translating I got to share my dream for preaching Christ on the continent.

I soon discovered that Volkhard's church was nationally known for its large youth outreach. I couldn't wait to minister there.

Our first personal contact with the German people came when Murray and I went the University of Munich to witness. I was scared, praying God would give me the words and help me understand the students. The Marxist party controlled the student government, and they displayed pictures of the country's Communist leaders in the student union. That was an eye-opener for me.

Two of several I shared with prayed to receive Christ. They understood only a little English, so my quoting of Scripture in German was key. They would soon get involved in a Bible study group on campus and begin to grow spiritually.

As we were leaving the university, I handed a girl a sticker that read Real Peace Is Jesus.

"*Nicht Jesus,*" she said. "*Zondern Marx.*"

"*Marx ist tot* [Marx is dead]," I said. "*Jesus lebt noch* [Jesus still lives]." When I also quoted Scripture, I could tell from the look on her face that the Word of God pierced her heart.

Our walk across Germany took us from Augsburg to Kassel through Stuttgart, Frankfurt, and Giessen. The first night of the walk would be the first time I ever preached with an interpreter, and I was nervous and hadn't slept the night before. The meeting was held at the Augsburg Evangelical Free Church, where we were warned not to be too loud or get too excited or give an invitation. We were informed that the typical German was sophisticated, intellectual, and formal. I prayed for wisdom.

An hour before the meeting, the place was already packed, yet people kept coming. Many may have just been curious about the American Jesus People, but we believed God was moving.

I had little idea how the people were receiving my message until I came to a sentence that stumped the interpreter. When he paused, several men on the edges of their seats blurted out the translation. That made it clear they were with me and that God was helping me communicate.

I kept it subdued, but I did ask the young people to respond to the claims of Jesus Christ, and about thirty did. They weren't emotional. They talked to God the way they would talk to a friend. It was new for me to see such a sober, intellectual approach to God.

The next morning I spoke to the student body of the local high school on what Christ could do for a young person and concluded, "If you would like to turn from your sin and give your heart to Jesus, meet me right now in this corner."

More than half the students rose. "Wait," I said. "Let me explain." I went through all that it meant to be a Christian, that it was no trendy, faddish thing but meant sacrifice and discipline and dedication. Again more than half started to move. "Okay," I said, "I'll have to talk to you right where you are."

Until then we had noticed little conviction of sin in Germany. Promiscuous sex was widespread, and young people seemed to have no second thoughts about it. But now, as I explained the forgiving power of God, kids asked, "Is this wrong? Is that wrong?" It was hard to leave as kids swarmed around us with question after question about the Christian life. They seemed to be starving for the Word of God.

The trip continued through one outpouring of God's power after another: through Fellbach where, before we ate, each person stood and said to the one next to him, "I love you in Jesus Christ, and may God's blessings be upon you;" through Mannheim, where with little publicity nearly fifty kids committed their lives to Christ; through Neu Isenburg, where a plot by the Communists to take over the service was turned into a great outpouring of the Spirit; through Giessen, where God taught us that one conversion could result in a Bible study that would draw an average of sixty kids each morning.

In Neu Isenburg, as our singing group opened a large meeting, a group of Communist students from the University of Frankfurt drowned out our P.A. system shouting, "We want discussion! We want discussion!"

When Murray tried to give his testimony, the chanting grew louder. He looked directly at the Communists and said, just above a whisper, "*Jesus liebt dich* [Jesus loves you]."

They fell silent, but when he finished and the music began again, so did the chanting. "Power to the people! We want discussion!"

When the interpreter and I stepped to the microphone, the noise was deafening. A member of our singing group and two Christian soldiers quickly moved into the midst of the Communists and knelt to pray. By the time the Communists decided what to do, I had gained the attention of the rest of the crowd.

About a dozen received Christ that night, and when I returned to the auditorium from the prayer room, the crowd was still in an uproar. To an American whose country has wide-open political debate, this was a shock. The news media were there, and everyone seemed to be demanding debate. I don't generally allow debate about the Gospel in my meetings; in America that would have resulted in endless, nit-picking discussion.

But this was different. This crowd was likely to come up with very direct, answerable questions. I silently prayed that God would give me His wisdom.

"All right," I said. "We'll have debate, but if there is disorder, we quit."

I had never studied dialectical materialism or even Communism that much, but God made me sensitive to their arguments and allowed me to see past the words to the real problems. I was wearing a vest with Jesus Loves You sewn on the back, and one of the first questions was about that. "I'll bet you supported a big, capitalist company when you bought that vest!"

"No," I said, "a friend made this and gave it to me because we want to share God's love with others." Much of the crowd, even some of the Communists, applauded.

"Are there white churches in America that won't allow blacks in?"

"There may be," I said, "but not my church. A few years ago I hated blacks, but when I met Jesus, He replaced that hatred with love. If you want to bring the races together, the love of God will do it."

For several minutes they hurled questions, and I felt God gave me answers. The crowd applauded each answer, which seemed to befuddle the Communists. An American pastor later told the European Baptist Press that it was the greatest outpouring of the Spirit he had seen in his years of ministry.

God provided a rickety, old van we nicknamed Aby Baby, for Abraham, an Old Testament model of stepping out in faith. We thanked God daily for that van, frustrating as it was. The only way we could start it was to push it and pop the clutch. It was hilarious when it stalled in traffic. We'd all jump out, and off we'd go, running and pushing, with Aby Baby spitting and popping and rattling and shaking.

Tex and Davey and I took a train toward Berlin. When the train developed a problem with its heating system, we had to wrap Davey in everything we could find. The only times my faith was really tested were when I started having second thoughts about dragging my loved ones on an excursion like that—which was often. As the train moved from West Germany to East Germany, border guards checked our passports and luggage. We prayed that the rest of the staff—and Aby Baby— would make it.

Aby Baby must have looked a sight! On top of that old rattletrap sat an eight-foot cross, a lantern, and a worn spare tire. We prayed the border guards wouldn't find the suitcase full of Bibles and tracts. Some vehicles were searched for hours.

Murray told us later that everyone had been ordered out of the van for the search. The guards could hardly stand the stench from the sleeping bags we had used after walking all day, so they rushed their search. Murray said they popped open his suitcase first, and when they got a whiff of his undershirts, they scrambled out with an "Okay, go on."

It was good to reunite with Volkhard Spitzer. We set up our cross for a prayer and fasting vigil in downtown Berlin at the Wilhelm War Memorial Church where many local Christians joined us. We enjoyed many opportunities to share Christ there and at our nightly rallies.

Finally the day came when God opened the door for Murray and Debbie Bradfield and Tex and Davey and me to go behind the Iron Curtain. Lynn Nowicki, a young American Christian guy studying in West Berlin, was going to cross into Soviet-controlled East Berlin to visit some of the underground Christians I'd read so much about. By law, no home could entertain more than three people at a time, so the six of us planned to cross two by two by train through Friedrich Strasse.

But I wanted to see the Berlin Wall for the first time at Checkpoint Charlie, the iconic border crossing that had become the symbol of the Cold War. I'd been hearing about the Wall since I was a freshman in high school in 1961 when it had been erected. Its purpose was to stem defections from the Eastern bloc. Some three and a half million had fled to the West since the start of the Cold War, comprising approximately twenty percent of the East German population. Making that worse, not to mention embarrassing, was that the defectors were primarily from the educated class—teachers, doctors, engineers, and the like—which proved devastating to the East German economy.

The wall, initially 830 miles of barbed wire surrounding the city, eventually became a combination of concrete and tall chain link fencing. It was supported by wide stretches of plowed earth and land mines in expanses at some points as wide as three and a half miles.

We climbed onto a little stand at Checkpoint Charlie (there were also Checkpoints Alpha and Bravo and so on), from which I could see the minefields. Every seventy-five yards or so on the Eastern side stood huge towers manned by machine gunners. Their assignment? To kill their own countrymen if they tried to escape.

Imagine how helpless I felt, trying to take in this monstrosity that had transformed a city into a massive prison bloc. What kind of regime threatens death to citizens who merely want the freedom to come and go?

Seeing it for myself moved me as I had never been moved before. My whole being raged with such sadness, frustration, and anger that I couldn't imagine what I could do, a nobody against the forces of Communism, indeed the forces of Satan.

My heart broke for the victims of this heinous death barrier. *Oh, God, there must be some way to reach these people with the Good News!*

Speechless, I boarded the train to cross through Friedrich Strasse. I could hardly believe the contrast between East and West. West Berlin was full of life and light, but East Berlin was tomblike. The dank, dimly lit streets lay silent, and everything was gray.

My relief at making it across the border was displaced by fear and a crushing empathy and love for this mysterious country and its people.

Lynn Nowicki took us to the home of an old gentleman I'll call Pastor Busch. When Lynn introduced us as Christians from America, Herr Busch greeted us with a bear hug, tears in his eyes. He had been pastor of a Lutheran church and had refused to sign a document penned by the Communist government that referred to Jesus Christ *a* savior but not *the* Savior of the world.

The Communists removed him from his church. Devastated, Herr Busch wrote an underground letter to other Lutheran clergy, urging them not to sign. None complied. Even his children turned on him. He was the only one who had stood for his beliefs.

What a blessing to me was this precious man of God! Even then he was studying Russian so he could share Christ with Soviet soldiers, risking imprisonment again. Such holy boldness.

Pastor Busch took us to a Lutheran church where I was struck by the absence of young people. Here was a nation of lost souls who needed Christ, and the church was made up of old, tired, beaten people. I admired their tenacity and felt for them, but few were equipped to win their countrymen for God.

I was encouraged that evening when we went to an Evangelical Free church packed with young people full of life and joy—defying the state to exercise their faith enthusiastically.

On the train back from the services, Pastor Busch pointed out a group of young people in blue uniforms. "They call themselves the Free German Youth," he said with a sigh. "But they're not really free. They either join the FGY or they cannot continue their education."

As the train rattled up to the border, we could see Checkpoint Charlie. The old man's gaze seemed far away. He took us to the Temple of Tears, where visitors cross the border on the way out. It was named for the tears shed there by countless parting relatives.

It was hard to leave Pastor Busch. He hugged and kissed us, our eyes filled with tears. "Someday maybe I will be able to visit you on the other side," he said, smiling sadly.

"I sure hope so," I said, but I couldn't imagine it.

If we ever saw Pastor Busch again, would it be in the West, at his home in the East, or in prison? Through him the Lord had shown us the real need behind the Iron Curtain, and we assured him we would share his ordeal with praying Christians in America.

For days in West Germany I was haunted by all we had seen. I knew I needed to do more about my lifelong burden for Eastern Europe. Love for that place exploded in my heart and lay heavy on my mind.

On Christmas Eve 1971 Tex and I were thousands of miles from home and family. "Let's go to the wall," I said.

We silently walked through the night, and all I could do was cry. The wall had lost none of its impact on me, and I was shaken anew by the overwhelming need of the people on the other side—the believers and the lost.

The colossal eyesore became much more to me than a barrier lined with machine gunners and mines, separating a city, a people, and a nation. I saw it as a wall of sin separating men and women from God. *Oh, Lord, allow me to reach these people for Jesus Christ!*

The next day, we briefly ducked out of the rain at the War Memorial Church, and our cross was stolen. It had been out of our view for only a few seconds. We couldn't imagine someone walking off with an eight-foot cross in downtown Berlin, but it was gone. It struck me that experiencing the Berlin Wall and visiting Pastor Busch had been God's way of giving me a new cross to bear.

After visiting Volkhard Spitzer at his church, I headed back toward the War Memorial Church. It was still damp and chilly, so I stopped at a restaurant to get some hot chocolate. As I sat sipping and looking out the windows, I idly listened to the people around me speaking German. And it all came back to me. These were the people speaking a foreign language that I had seen in my mind three years before! The Spirit of God came over me and thrilled me with the fulfillment of my dream. The Lord had provided one more sign to assure me that the walk and an international ministry were part of His plan for God's Love in Action.

We left Murray and Debbie in Germany to carry on the ministry, and we planned to return in less than a year. God had instilled in my heart a love for East Germany that would not go away.

CHAPTER NINE
TUMULTUOUS ASSIGNMENTS

In Chicago we began turning over the Bible studies and street ministry to others, as I sensed God leading us away from that great city. To where, I wasn't sure.

During a week of meetings in Miami, Florida, I learned of demonstrations planned by radicals for the Democratic National Convention to be held there that fall (1972). I felt the convention would be an ideal place to witness and demonstrate for Christ.

In May God laid it on my heart to walk from Orlando to Miami a week before the convention. Tex and a few other staff members went ahead to Florida to set up our office and arrange for lodging. An Orlando pastor volunteered to set up rallies along our walk route.

God had given us a tremendous burden and now an opportunity to call America and its leaders back to God. Decades since that Democratic National Convention in Miami, it's hard to imagine what a tumultuous scene it was—just as volatile as the Chicago convention had been just four years earlier.

Ten different groups announced their plans, including the Gay Liberation Front, the Southern Christian Leadership Conference, Vietnam Veterans Against the War, and assorted Yippies and Zippies (Yippie offshoots). In Dade County the Ku Klux Klan burned seventeen crosses. Another right-wing group claimed that if Miami opened to the radicals, it would bring thousands of KKKers, hard hats, and rednecks to the city to break up their campsites.

The city council worked furiously to pass tougher laws against obscenity, vulgarity, and inciting violence.

I became oppressed by a feeling of impending personal disaster. I didn't want to be afraid, and I certainly didn't want to develop a martyr complex. Yet, the feeling made me stop and think, *What am I doing for Jesus every second? With every breath I want Christ to live through me.*

Tex and I discussed what would happen if she and Davey were left without a husband and father. I couldn't turn tail and run from danger, because I believed God wanted me at the convention and that it would be the greatest opportunity our ministry had ever had. My burden for our work grew, despite the premonition.

The eight-day walk that began July 1, 1972 was one of my shortest but most intense ever. The first night we covered only thirty-two miles because so many people—including the press—wanted to talk to us. We also were eaten alive by mosquitoes, heard snakes slithering in the grass, and saw several snake carcasses.

The next day, at about four in the morning, one of the guys brought a motorcyclist to me and asked that I share Christ with him. As soon as we were alone, the man pulled a huge pistol from his saddlebag, pointed it at me, and cocked it. I believed my premonition of disaster was coming true, and I thought of my young family. I wasn't afraid of death, but the dying part made my knees shake. I just kept talking about Jesus.

The biker made me strap on a holster and said that if anyone came by, we should look like we were just talking. When one of our guys arrived, I assured the drunk that he was a friend. He pulled the gun and fired it and my friend and I each thought the other had been shot.

But the man had missed. "That's the wrath of God upon you," he said. "Power!" He put the gun in the holster I had strapped on, pulled out another, and challenged me. I finally talked him into putting both guns away and tried to pray with him, but he was irrational. As soon as I got the chance, I sprinted away from him and sped off in the van. We called the sheriff and left it to him to hunt down the gunman. I'll never forget that brush with death.

Every few days, despite fatigue and sunburn and fear, God used someone or something to refresh me and give me renewed vigor. We walked all night July 3rd until the sun come up. More and more people showed up along the route, but all I could think of was Davey and Tex. How I missed them!

The rest of the way was filled with encouragement and surprisingly accurate press reports that carried God-honoring truth.

July 7th, twenty-four hours from reaching Miami, we heard radicals had taken over a location and dubbed it People's Park, where anyone could say or do anything he or she wanted. That was good news; no one would tell us we couldn't preach and witness and pass out tracts.

Or so we thought. When we showed up with our cross and our literature a couple of days later, the Yippies told us we couldn't stay because we were too controversial and not preaching what everybody there believed.

We reminded them that they had dubbed it the People's Park. We set up a cross at each candidate's headquarters and assigned staff members to man it. We also placed one at the convention hall itself.

But when we brought a cross from the convention center to the People's Park, we didn't get fifteen yards inside before we were besieged by radicals, the press, and bystanders. Some were drawn to the cross while others were repulsed. As Scripture says, the cross divides.

The convention began July 10th, and at midnight Leo Humphrey and I began a prayer vigil that lasted until the convention was over. With just snatches of sleep here and there during the six days, the entire time seemed like one long day. Each morning we carried the cross around the convention center, and on the last day we would walk twice to make a total of seven trips, modeling Joshua's march around the walls of Jericho.

A Will

More than once our morning walk put us between rival groups of radicals or protesters. We walked back and forth between them, praying and singing and witnessing. God cooled down the demonstrators time and time again. When we knelt to pray in the middle of a potential riot, people from both sides assumed we were staging some sort of sit-in and asked, "What's happening here?"

"Jesus is happening here," we answered.

Each night we held what we called soul sessions where we sang, cheered, witnessed, and preached. One night we were interrupted by a demonstration by the Gay Liberation Front, which included a gay pastor who preached the blood of Jesus and told me, among other things, "The blood of Jesus has cleansed us. Homosexuality is not a sin. Jesus and the disciples were gay."

I confess I don't understand why some people—even believers in Christ—are plagued with same-sex attraction. But Scripture is so clear that practicing homosexuality is a sin that it is impossible for the believer to reconcile it with Christian beliefs. We should love and never be harsh or unkind to homosexuals, but neither should we rationalize such behavior in light of Scripture's clear teaching.

What a chaotic week we had! It seemed every few minutes we shared Christ with leading politicians and special interest group leaders. We were hassled by radicals and embraced by others.

After our seventh walk around the convention center on the last day, we praised God for the opportunities He had given us, and for the growth in each of our lives. We went home and immediately began a follow-up program, mailing encouraging letters and literature for spiritual growth to those we had led to Christ. I praised God that despite all the tense situations, He had protected me from any harm.

While the rest of the staff went to the Republican National Convention in August, Tex and I turned our eyes to Europe, where we would return that fall for several months of meetings. I felt drawn back to Germany with a burden so deep that I knew God had a plan for me in Eastern Europe. He was not revealing it to me all at once, so I committed myself to following and obeying as I went along.

It was great to see Murray and Debbie Bradfield again in Europe, but when they left to visit the United States for a month, Tex and I found ourselves alone for the first time in our ministry—except for those first few days in Chicago. It was strange, disconcerting at first.

We had few contacts and still knew very little German. We spent the first several days just resting and praying, seeking the will of God. One day I sensed the Lord impressing upon my heart that I should memorize my testimony in German. I didn't understand. Aside from the few times I had witnessed one-on-one on the streets, I had always used interpreters. But the message was clear; I began to memorize, eager to see when God might use me.

During the next several days we had joyous reunions with many of the people we had met and worked with a year before, especially Pastor Busch. One night we visited the Evangelical Free church again, where only German was spoken. The pastor called on various ones to share their testimonies, a most unusual practice to Westerners like us. In the States we simply open the floor to testimonies, and anyone who feels led stands and speaks. I was thrilled to hear these German Christians, but I was most intrigued that they were chosen.

My heart pounded. God seemed to be leading me to speak up. But I was scared. There were no interpreters, and English was a distant third language here, behind German and Russian. I felt locked into my seat. Had I memorized well enough? Would the people respond?

Suddenly the pastor pointed at me. *"Du* [You]," he said. *"Du!"*

It was one of the great blessings of my life to be able to share with these people in their own tongue. Later I realized that God had given me an ear for languages. Throughout the years I have had to adapt to many cultures and languages, and despite no formal training, I pick them up quickly.

I could tell by the faces of the people at the Evangelical Free church that they felt honored, and also probably amused, by my very first effort. It was just another confirmation for me that God had plans for us in Germany.

The will of God is not usually hard to determine. Where the Scripture says, 'This is the will of God concerning you..." you don't have to be a scholar to figure it out. And as a rule, if you love the Lord with all your heart and live accordingly, you will find yourself doing His will. But I believed God had a specific mission for our ministry behind the Iron Curtain, and I longed to know what it was.

He had blessed our witnessing and my preaching. People had come to Christ. I wondered if God felt there was still more I needed to learn before He would reveal our next step.

That night, after the service at the Evangelical Free church, we returned to Pastor Busch's home. It had been an exhausting day, but something he said shocked me.

"I want you to pray about coming back here next summer to preach at the Communist Youth World Fest."

I bolted upright. "What's that?"

My heart raced as he explained that there would be 100,000 young Communists in Berlin from every country in the world.

What an opportunity! "But surely they wouldn't let me preach the Gospel there."

"Oh, but they might," the old man said. "Arresting a Christian for speaking out would cause an international scene, the last thing they would want. They claim they are for freedom of expression, so they will be tolerant for the few days of the festival."

My soul burned with the realization that this was what God was calling me to. Here was perhaps one of the great opportunities in history to minister behind the Iron Curtain—and we could possibly do it without being arrested.

The next day I went with three friends to the Communist side of Berlin, so excited I could hardly concentrate. Still I felt compelled to first share my faith with people. Even before learning more about the Communist Youth World Fest, I was reassured that these people were hungry to hear the Word of God. At the three- or four-minute stops on the train I would stand and preach my testimony, then hop off and catch a train going the other way.

Not one young person turned us off or was rude. They had grown up in a country where it was normal for everyone to share his beliefs, as long as they conformed to Communist ideology, but this was something new. They seemed more concerned with our safety than with theirs. One girl told a friend of mine, "You must not do this. If the police find out, you will be in very much trouble."

I sat next to one young man and asked, "*Kennen Sie Jesus?* [Do you know Jesus?]"

"No," he whispered in German. "I have been taught there is no Jesus."

That broke my heart. Time and again I heard the same thing from young students. "We have been taught there is no God." Every time I heard that I felt a deeper burden to share Christ with the untold masses. Even as they warned me not to speak of my faith in public, I could see in their eyes the hunger for God.

It was time to find out more about the Communist Youth World Fest and whether there would be any way to get in.

CHAPTER TEN
HOLY LAND PREPARATION

We went through Alexanderplatz on the east side of the border to a travel agency Pastor Busch had told us about. From there we were sent to another office and finally to yet another building, where a girl began asking us questions. I told her in German that we might be interested in attending the Communist Youth World Fest.

"Come with me," she said.

We followed her to the parking lot, where she told us to wait in a car. We had not met anyone in East Berlin who owned an automobile, and after sitting there for forty-five minutes, I was nervous. Finally, a man came out and got behind the wheel without a word. As he drove, we looked at each other, and I wondered if they were onto us already.

Suddenly the driver pointed and said, "That's the Soviet Embassy." He escorted us inside where we were told to sign in and hand over our passports. I wasn't eager to do that, but I figured we'd better do what they said.

We were led down a long corridor where every door bore an alarm device. Covering almost the entire wall of one of the rooms was a huge photograph of American activist Angela Davis.

We finally arrived at a beautiful reception room full of French university students who spoke fluent English and had been assigned to talk with English-speaking people interested in the Fest. They made every attempt to make us feel comfortable, but I felt miserable and scared.

No one seemed the least bit suspicious, and they thanked us for our interest. We were never asked the exact nature of our curiosity, and of course we never offered to explain it. We got a lot of information, but I never wanted to get myself into that situation again. I was relieved when they returned my passport.

As we stepped into the sunlight, I noticed the girl who had told us to wait in the car. I felt led to give her a *Four Spiritual Laws* booklet, but I hesitated.

Lord, I can't do that. She's part of the Communist Party.

Immediately I felt rebuked. If we went to the Communist Youth World Fest, everyone we encountered would be a Communist. I handed her the booklet. *"Jesus liebt dich,"* I said.

She shot me a double take, then smiled. *"Danke,"* she said.

We had been given a glimpse of the wide-reaching tentacles of the Communists. They seemed to know all and control all, and if we weren't careful, we might play right into their hands.

While on a mountain retreat with several Christian brothers and sisters, I sensed a new call of God. About ten of us were fasting and praying, seeking the will of God for our lives. At one point we all concentrated on what God would have me do next, and one of the brothers read aloud from the Bible: "Your eyes will see the King in His beauty; they will see the land that is very far off" (Isaiah 33:17); and "Look upon Zion, the city of our appointed feasts; your eyes will see Jerusalem, a quiet home" (Isaiah 33:20).

As I prayed, I sensed God speaking to my heart, telling me to visit Jerusalem. I was intrigued that He seemed to be leading me not to the whole nation, but specifically to Jerusalem. I expressed my willingness and put it out of my mind.

Until two weeks later, that is. At three in the morning I couldn't sleep. I woke Murray, and we began to pray. Our wives wondered what was going on. They knew anything could happen when we prayed in the middle of the night.

Go to Jerusalem kept echoing through my mind, and I believed God wanted me to go soon. Murray didn't feel the same leading, but we knew that if God wanted him to go, He would give a definite indication. I believe in the biblical model of ministers traveling in pairs, so I wanted him with me.

A few days later Murray received a check in the mail for one hundred dollars, designated for the Holy Land. That would pay for a one-way ticket. About two weeks later an undesignated check for the same amount arrived.

January 2, 1973, we flew to Jerusalem. We were there for twenty-eight days, and I still marvel at what He taught us during that time.

We spent the first twenty days in prayer and Bible study. God instilled in me a love for the Scriptures I had never known before and have never lost since. He opened the prophetic passages to me so that I understood not only the completeness of Christ's first coming but also His second coming.

Murray and I spent hours at the Garden Tomb, and we made friends with the Dutch warden there. Praying at that special place for hours, I became impressed by God that now, more than ever, the church needs to be rooted in His Word. I sensed a leading from the Lord that I should not concentrate solely on evangelism, as I had been doing. I felt He wanted me to exhort and educate and train believers to help with the work, to get them back into Scripture and holy living and then motivate them to share their faith.

By January 6 enough extra money had come in that our wives were able to join us. One Saturday, while on an errand for Tex, I was taught an invaluable lesson. I got lost and drove into the Orthodox section of the city, and immediately our rented car was surrounded by angry Jews. They shouted and pounded on the car as I furiously shifted gears, trying to find a way out of the neighborhood.

The nerve of someone to drive a car on the Sabbath! I learned later that I was lucky I had not been stoned to death. God delivered me, but only after I got an idea of what Jesus went through when He "worked" on the Sabbath.

The last week we were there, Murray and I walked to each of the gates that surrounded the city, praying and speaking to people about Christ. What a blessed experience, one that will likely never be duplicated in my ministry. The sweet joy of the Lord often drove us to our knees. There was no fear and no opposition; in fact, we didn't even have to seek out people to talk to. God kept sending them to us, and they had questions. We never approached one person to tell him about Christ. It was as if we were in a heavenly situation, where God did all the work and all we had to do was the fun part—tell people about Him. Can you imagine the joy and ease of having God put the listeners right in front of you, eager to hear the Gospel?

On the sixth day, we had no one to witness to. A spiritual battle was raging. It was the Sabbath, and over loud speakers the entire city heard an eerie cry in Arabic: "In the name of Allah, the merciful and compassionate, praised be Allah… ."

On Sunday morning the Lord impressed upon me that I would give my testimony at the Garden Tomb. Murray and I had planned to go there for Communion before our last walk. When we arrived, we were told that the warden, John, wanted to see us. "Would you take the service this morning," he asked, "and give your testimonies?" I shouldn't have been surprised.

It was a beautiful experience and a thrill to be able to commune with believers that day. Later, when we arrived at the Golden Gate, one of Jerusalem's closed gates, we felt victorious. Although no one was there to hear our witness, I was overwhelmed with the power of God, and seven times I shouted, *"Yeshua Hamashiach!* [Jesus the Messiah!]" All I could think of was *Jesus is coming soon. Hallelujah, praise be to God! My eyes shall behold the King!*

As I've been able to reflect on that strange, wonderful trip from the perspective of several decades, I'm struck that it was primarily a work of commissioning my life. God removed me from my usual ministry and taught me, focusing my mind and heart on His essentials. I still had opportunities to minister; in fact, that five-day period during which He sent people our way instead of requiring us to seek them out remains one of my sweetest memories. But above all, I learned history, studied the Old Testament, the big picture.

God had much, much deeper work to do in my life and character—work I had no idea was needed—but right then He was preparing me for a ministry He had not yet revealed. I lived in a constant state of anticipation, eager to see where He would lead me next.

Slowly the Lord taught me lessons about spiritual matters. I had been empowered to witness and preach, and I had learned the importance of dying to myself daily. But I had been making the mistake of putting myself in the position of authority without submitting to any authority. I felt like a traffic cop without proper authorization. I needed a church, a local body of believers to whom I would be spiritually accountable and who would pray for me.

Once while witnessing with Lynn, the friend who had introduced us to Pastor Busch, we were chased by Soviet soldiers and barely eluded them on a train. That was my closest call since visiting Europe, and it made me think twice about counting the cost.

I had been threatened, run off the road, run out of town, held at gunpoint, shot at, arrested, and even jailed during my street ministry in the States. I've always felt willing to die for my Lord. But dying is one thing. Prison is another. I have to say truthfully that I would rather die for Christ than to live for Him in prison.

My German was improving as a result of ministering in and around Frankfurt, but as the time grew near for the Communist Youth World Fest, I felt the need to go back to America and submit myself to a local body that believed in our ministry and would send us out. I had met Texas pastor Bud Gardner at an international conference and felt led to move to San Antonio, Texas, and become accountable to the Gateway Baptist Church. We would have a home base, and I believed God would grant our ministry all authority in heaven and earth if we would submit ourselves. That authority could tear down the gates of hell and was what we would need to combat Communism, atheism, and Satan behind the Iron Curtain.

I wrote to Fred Bishop, a pastor from southern Illinois who had ministered with us at the Democratic convention the year before. He was a bold witness with a good youth work going. Just before leaving for the United States, I learned that he felt led of God to help us in Europe, so we started making plans for him to go with us to the Fest.

Meanwhile, I had to make one more trip to Berlin before leaving for Texas. If I needed one more confirmation that we needed the backing of a local body, I got it on that trip.

Somehow Lynn got hung up in Poland and was unable to meet me in East Berlin. I had always depended on him because he knew some Russian and spoke fluent German. Now I was all by myself, and when I needed my poor German, it wouldn't come to me. I could hardly get simple sentences to make sense. I can't describe the loneliness.

Somehow the Lord helped me get more specifics about the Fest, and I was never so glad to get back to the West.

Fred Bishop and his wife moved to San Antonio to prepare for the ministry at the Communist Youth World Fest. He and I met every morning for prayer and Bible study; then we memorized Scripture, the *Four Spiritual Laws*, and some choruses in German. Once we had the basics down, it was time for God to give us a strategy for the Fest.

CHAPTER ELEVEN

STRATEGY

One morning Fred came by with two twenty dollar bills someone at church had given him—one for each of us. "He said the Lord led him to do it and seemed to be telling him we would need these today."

Neither of us had any immediate needs, so we prayed about it and decided to use the money to rent a hotel room for the day just to seek God. There He spoke to our hearts and led us to various Scripture passages, including Acts 13, where Saul and Barnabas were sent out and John Mark was commissioned as their helper.

I certainly didn't see myself as a modern-day apostle Paul. But I would be proclaiming the Gospel as he did, and Fred would be helping me, as Barnabas had helped Paul. I also felt there was another lesson in that passage, that three of us should plan to go. Fred Starkweather, a young man who had come to Christ through Fred Bishop's ministry, would serve as our John Mark.

I couldn't escape the impression that God wanted me to preach publicly at the Fest, though that seemed impossible. I had assumed we would minister to people secretly, individually, trying to keep ourselves, as well as those we ministered to, out of trouble. We would witness and pass out as many *Four Spiritual Laws* booklets as we could get across the border. I didn't see how I could possibly preach to one hundred thousand Communists without getting arrested or at least deported.

God led me to Isaiah 58:6-8 where He talks about loosing the bonds of wickedness to let the oppressed go free, breaking every yoke. We were to "share [our] bread with the hungry, and ... bring to [our] house the poor who are cast out... Then [our] light [would] break forth like the morning, [our] healing [would] spring forth speedily, and [our] righteousness [would] go before [us]; the glory of the Lord [would] be [our] rear guard."

That thrilled my heart. God was going to bless us in a way we couldn't even imagine. I believed He was going to pour out His Spirit and do a tremendous work if we would just obey. With the glory of the Lord as my rear guard, how could the gates of hell prevail against us, even in an unthinkable situation?

Provision

It was June 1973, and we were to leave in about six weeks for Germany. I was certain we were ready to go except for last-minute Bible study, memorization, and brushing up on the language.

It turned out God had another lesson for me. A brother from our church came over one night to pray for our family because we had all been down with colds and the flu. He prayed with such compassion that I realized he knew something about prayer that I didn't. He seemed to be willing to take our sickness upon himself, if that were possible. I asked him to teach me about intercessory prayer.

He told me that a true intercessor is a bit different from a regular prayer warrior. He not only identifies with the need he is praying for, but he is also willing to take that burden upon himself. The greatest example of intercession, of course, is Jesus, who knew no sin, yet became sin for us. It moved me deeply to think that we can know some of the suffering of Christ on the cross if we are willing to take the problems of others upon ourselves.

That was an important lesson because it revolutionized my prayer life. I had been praying for months about the lives I wanted to see changed and the souls I wanted to see saved for God's glory. But was I willing to face the persecution these people would face as a result of their decisions?

God had promised to work a spiritual miracle at the Fest. But was I willing to pay the price? Was I willing to go to prison for any or all of the people He would draw to Himself through my preaching? I battled with that question for days.

Was I in it for the glory of marching into the Fest and being able to say I had preached there? Was I on some spiritual ego trip? Or was I ready to lay my freedom on the line for Christ?

God taught me a hard lesson. He showed me that this ministry was His and not mine. If I wanted to play in this league, with this much at stake, then I had better get myself in gear and get close to Christ.

That would mean joining in the fellowship of His sufferings, according to Philippians 3:10-11: "That I may know Him and the power of His resurrection, and the fellowship of His sufferings, being conformed to His death, if, by any means, I may attain to the resurrection from the dead."

I searched my soul. In the flesh, Sammy Tippit was not ready to give up his freedom for anything or anyone. But I wanted to be obedient. I wanted to serve Christ. I loved Him and wanted to share Him. I wanted more than anything to say that I would do that at any cost, but I knew that only He would be so perfect in His love as to give Himself. I prayed He would give me that supernatural love for lost souls. That was not a part of my natural self, so it would have to come from Him.

I also knew it was no game. If I prayed for souls, expressing my willingness to go to prison for them, God might require me to do just that. He is not in the business of providing a cozy life for Sam and Tex. He's in the business of drawing people to Himself. If I wanted to be a part of that ministry, I really had to count the cost.

This was no mere spiritual exercise. This was ominous. Fred Bishop, Fred Starkweather, and I drew up wills and made arrangements, in the event we never returned.

A week before our departure we were flat broke. New to Texas, I was enough known yet to be speaking regularly. We needed at least $1,100 more to get us to the World Fest, and I didn't have it. I even considered swallowing my pride, admitting my lack of faith, and borrowing the money to obey God. Fred Bishop didn't believe God would have us borrow it. "If He has called us, He'll provide."

I was to speak at the crusade of an evangelist friend (David Stockwell) and then at a seminary class, but I didn't even have the gas money to get there. The day before, my pastor had invited Fred Bishop and me to a ministerial luncheon. We went along, not knowing how we would pay for our meal. The pastor paid, though he was unaware of our plight. On the way out I was greeted by a man from the Billy Graham team I had met a few years before. He pressed a five-dollar bill into my palm.

That gave us enough to put two dollars' worth of gas in the car and three dollars to eat on that evening. Later, in the restaurant, I thanked God for providing. When I opened my eyes, a man approached us and introduced himself as a pastor on vacation. "God touched me when you were praying. We need more young men who will stand for Jesus Christ. Allow me the privilege of paying for your meals." I was beginning to see that, as always, God will take care of His own. There we were, paupers eating as children of the King.

That night, at the end of the evangelistic meeting, people came up to chat and pray with me. On the way to the airport I discovered they had stuffed more than seventy dollars into my shirt pocket.

The next day at the seminary a girl came to me, telling me she had heard me preach the year before. "I didn't do it then," she said, "but I must do it now." She handed me a check for one hundred dollars.

David Stockwell said the Lord had laid it on his heart to give me $250. I was overwhelmed. When he and a few others joined me at a nearby restaurant, I was overflowing with the goodness of God. We joined hands around the table and softly sang, "God is so good, God is so good, God is so good, He's so good to me." I knew it, and I meant it!

On the Sunday evening before we were to leave for Germany I was invited by a member of the First Baptist Church of Castle Hills to go with him to the airport to pick up Harlan Popov, author of *Tortured for His Faith*. Popov, who had been imprisoned for years by the Communists, was to speak that night at Castle Hills, and I was thrilled that I could meet him.

But Popov's flight was delayed, and I was asked to speak until he arrived. There were more than a thousand in the service that night, all excited about hearing Popov. I spoke for just twenty minutes, sharing what God had told us to do at the Communist Youth World Fest and what He had done for us in recent days.

The congregation then knelt to pray for us. When the last amen was heard, Popov arrived. It was perfect. An offering was taken, then the regular service took place, and another offering was taken for Popov. That made it even more incredible later when people began stuffing my pockets with money.

When I got home, I had almost forgotten about the money. I first told Tex all about the service and the people who had promised to pray for us, and then I began pulling wads of money out of my pockets. I counted $350, and with what had come in the mail that week, we now had a total of $1,000, exactly $100 short of what we needed the next day. By now there was no doubt in my mind that God would provide.

We planned to get a good night's sleep and leave the next morning at eleven for our flight to Germany. At seven I was awakened by a phone call from a man who had heard me speak the night before; he asked if I could meet him at the union stockyards. "Not really," I said. "We're going to be on a tight schedule today."

But he insisted, promising it would take but five minutes, so I left early. When I arrived at the stockyards, this brother said, "All I know is that the Lord laid it on my heart to give you this." He handed me two fifty-dollar bills. Fred and Fred (as I came to call my compatriots) and my family were on our way, with the Lord providing what we needed, right down to the last penny.

CHAPTER TWELVE

ATTACKED

A few days before the Communist Youth World Fest, the Communists closed the borders and no Westerners would be allowed in. We had prepared for months and months and God had provided for us to come all this way. Now Satan seemed to be frantically attempting to discourage us.

But God gave me a Scripture passage as I poured out my heart to Him. He impressed upon me Revelation 3:8: "I know your works. See, I have set before you an open door, and no one can shut it; for you have a little strength, have kept My word, and have not denied My name."

When God opens a door, we don't have to worry about any earthly government. God said the doors would be open. We didn't know how He would open them, but we trusted that He would.

The night I took Fred and Fred to the Berlin Wall for the first time, I experienced three events that I believe were calculated to shake me up.

First, a weird, wild-eyed man tried to speak to me. I sensed the Lord telling me to stay away from him, so I told him my German was not very good and moved away.

Then a woman let loose a German Shepherd from more than a block away, and it ran straight past everyone else and leaped to attack me. I froze in fear as Fred and Fred dropped to their knees, praying the dog would leave me alone. It ran off.

Then the weirdo returned and said in German, "How would you like to go across the border with that dog?" Again I kept my distance.

Finally, I asked some guards what they knew about the border being closed during the Fest. One said, "That order had been rescinded."

On the way back, I twice noticed the weird man on our train. We finally lost him. Then I tried to share my faith with a young woman, glad to have my mind back on our purpose and off the experiences at the wall. She seemed interested, but then clearly came on to me while giving me her address. I tore up her information, relieved to get away. The whole evening had been a nightmare.

Two days before the Fest we made a dry run, giving Fred and Fred the experience of crossing the border, checking out the area, and getting a feel for what we might encounter. Tex would be our daily prayer warrior. If anything happened to us, she would inform Christians in the States and within hours the news media would know.

Fest delegates had already begun to flood the city, and it took us more than two hours to get across the border. Waiting proved exhausting, laden down as were with tracts and some twenty thousand Russian language Jesus stickers stuffed in our shirts, pants, shoes, and jackets. The long lines became a blessing in disguise, because the border guards seemed eager to keep things moving. We were quickly processed and given twenty-four-hour visas.

I took Fred and Fred to Alexanderplatz, which was to be the center of evening activities once the Fest opened. The place was bustling as organizers set up the huge sound system that would boom Communist teaching to the hundreds of thousands of delegates. Estimates were that half a million people would visit the Fest daily and that 100,000 would fill Alexanderplatz every night. We stuck the Russian Jesus Loves You stickers on anything and everything.

An air of expectancy permeated the area, but no one could have been more excited than we were. We had something no one else had, and we planned to share it. This was not political warfare. The solution to the problems of these people was no anti-Communist crusade. The solution was an outpouring of the Holy Spirit. The Bible says we wrestle not against flesh and blood but against principalities and powers. This would be spiritual warfare. Our weapons would be prayer and witnessing and preaching, in the boldness of the Spirit.

What an air of expectancy washed over the city of Berlin the day before the Communist Youth World Fest! Hundreds of thousands of elite Communist young people poured into the city from all over the world, and the news was filled with what was to come.

The day before the official opening the sun was shining, the air was cool, the borders were jammed, and the city was ready. Somehow I knew when we crossed the border that day that this tomorrow would be one of the most monumental days of my life.

Every fourth or fifth person was pulled from the line and searched. As the line inched forward, we prayed we would not be chosen. The border guard passed over us as he chose those to be searched.

I knew the city would be crowded, of course, but I was not prepared for what I saw as we passed through. I stood gaping at thousands upon thousands upon thousands of young people jammed into the main train station. Hardly anyone could move. I'm not exaggerating when I say there was a uniformed policeman every ten feet. I hadn't seen so many men in uniform anywhere, including Israel during a war!

I was struck with an overwhelming sense of defeat. The Fest had not even officially opened yet, so the crowds would get bigger! Who was I to think I could possibly preach in this environment? I was in over my head. All I could do was try to remind myself that with God nothing is impossible.

I thought I had counted the cost, but now I gave up trying to prepare for every obstacle. I was walking through a brick wall, trusting God to move in some mighty way to glorify Himself.

We rode trains from station to station all day, passing out tracts and stickers and speaking loudly to each other about Jesus right in the middle of a packed car. When the Communist young people got quiet enough to hear what we were shouting about, I'd take over and start preaching.

We boarded one train with three Russian soldiers, and I hesitated. Would it be wise to start preaching right in front of people who could arrest us?

We were going to witness and preach in front of the military at the Fest anyway, so there was no sense waiting.

The only Russian I knew was *Jesus loves you.* I said that to one of the soldiers and handed him a tract in Russian called *How to Find Peace with God.*

One soldier answered, "Jesus loves you," and another patted me on the shoulder. All three looked at the tract, as one read it. When they got off the train, they waved and smiled.

As evening fell, we headed back toward Alexanderplatz, distributing more and more literature as we went. Not far away lay Marx-Engle's Platz, where a huge statue of Karl Marx stood. Its concrete base seemed a good place to affix our Jesus Loves You stickers. We arranged them in the shape of a cross, and as we walked away, we could see the luminescent stickers glowing in the dark.. Even from two hundred yards away that cross of stickers glowed red under the statue of Marx.

Another cross that came to mean much to us at the Fest strangely reflected from the huge television tower in Alexanderplatz. The East Germans were proud of this huge tower, which could be seen for miles from both sides of the border, but they tried to change the way the sunlight bounced off it. St. Walter's Cross, as it came to be known, just kept shining. It became the banner under which we met during the Fest. Even in the midst of persecution we could see the reflected cross and remember what Jesus suffered for us.

We returned to West Berlin that night, and I couldn't imagine any way we would be able to preach publicly the next day at the Fest. Fortunately, we would not be attempting this in the flesh. All we had was the promise of God.

CHAPTER THIRTEEN

THREE BEHIND THE CURTAIN

The Communist Youth World Fest officially opened on a Sunday evening. As far as the eye could see the area teemed young people, policemen, and soldiers. Even from the third floors of surrounding buildings we couldn't see the ends of the throng.

Lord, there are just three of us. How? How?

Suddenly I was less overwhelmed with the task as I was with the burden God had laid on my heart. This wasn't just a massive crowd; it was tens of thousands of young people who needed Christ.

Bands of young people from different cultures all over the world congregated in small pockets, singing, dancing, doing skits, playing instruments. Except for all the security, it was like a giant rock concert. There would *never* be a more ideal time to try to preach in this situation, so there was no sense waiting.

I was stunned to see a young person wearing a sticker that read One Way: Jesus.

I asked him in German, "Are you a Christian?"

"Oh, no," he said, "I found this."

As I shared what his sticker meant, a friend joined him. "We've been taught there is no God, but this is interesting. Tell us more."

I was surprised when our conversation drew a crowd. Our ministry at the Communist Youth World Fest had officially begun.

A hobby at such international gatherings was to get people from various countries to autograph your Fest kerchief. I couldn't hide my American accent, so kids gathered, asking for an autograph from someone from the States.

I pulled Fred and Fred close and told Fred Bishop, "Write in German, 'God loves you and has a wonderful plan for your life' before you sign." I told Fred Starkweather to write, "Man's sin has separated him from this plan," before he signed. Then I wrote that Jesus was the only bridge over the gap left by sin and told how to receive Him.

Curiosity drew more and more kids, and we sat there furiously writing the *Four Spiritual Laws* on more than two hundred scarves. I became bolder and bolder as we answered questions, and I was reminded that God had called me to preach and promised that His glory would be my rear guard. The time had come.

I pulled Fred Bishop close again. "Stand here and don't say a word, no matter what I do."

"What do you mean?" he whispered. "What're you gonna do?"

"Don't worry," I said, and I began shouting at him in German, preaching the love of God and the forgiveness of sin through the death of Jesus Christ. Fred stared as I continued, covering the *Four Spiritual Laws*, giving my own testimony, and then starting all over.

Nearly a hundred kids crowded around to see what was going on, and when I sensed I had their attention, I pulled away from Fred and preached to them. They seemed spiritually hungry. Even when we took a break after about an hour to get a bite to eat, young people sat with us in the restaurant, eager to know more. And they didn't seem just to want to  debate. It was as if they were hearing, for the first time in their lives, something appealing about a personal God they had been told didn't even exist.

I knew we were drawing such crowds because the kids assumed at first we were American radicals. After the Russians and the North Vietnamese military, American Communists were among the most revered at the Fest.

On our way back across the border late that night all we could do on the train was sing and praise God. We had worried and wondered and prayed over how God would open the doors for us, and He had shown us that He was in charge.

We stayed up until about two in the morning, sharing with Tex all that had happened. I was so keyed up I could hardly sleep.

Tex was thrilled, of course, and excited about the possibilities. But why couldn't I see how she might feel getting only secondhand reports when she had always been such an integral part of the ministry?

The clock couldn't move fast enough for me. All I wanted was to get back to Alexanderplatz.

Fred and Fred and I felt like revolutionaries in the midst of the Communist camp. We spent much of the next day in prayer to prepare for the evening. I spent some time with Tex and Davey, but it was hard to concentrate on anything but the Fest. Here I was in the middle of the most thrilling ministry of my life, on a super spiritual high, yet I was incapable of giving proper attention to my family. Any day could be my last on the free side of the border.

I was not being the husband and father I should have been. Later I would get some small idea of how neglectful I had been, but it would be some years before I learned the deep lessons I needed to learn in this area. The problem was that I didn't even know I had anything to learn.

Fred Starkweather felt led of God not to carry any literature or stickers across the border that evening. So Fred Bishop and I loaded ourselves up, and the three of us began the long process of being checked through the border. When we finally reached the guards, they pointed at one of us to be searched: Fred Starkweather. My heart leapt! Truly God was with us and would bless us again that night!

Although the crowd in Alexanderplatz was every bit as large as it had been the night before, things were quieter and there didn't seem to be any natural openings for witnessing. "Guys, listen," I said, "we need to get off somewhere and pray."

Fred Bishop said, "Let's kneel right here."

Ten feet away stood six Communist soldiers. "We could go to prison," I said.

"I thought we'd already settled that," he said.

"If you really feel led," I said, "let's do it."

We knelt in the middle of Alexanderplatz, with thousands of Communist young people milling about. Fred Starkweather prayed first, and people around us fell silent. Then Fred Bishop prayed. I was trembling, eyes shut tight. Feet shuffled closer, and I could feel the eyes of dozens on me.

When it was my turn to pray, my voice was shaky, but I was afraid to quit. This had to be the longest public prayer in my ministry. It took all the boldness I could muster to say those last four words: "In Jesus' name, amen."

I knew a crowd had gathered, but I hardly noticed it as I rose. The Spirit of God seemed to come upon me in such a way that I felt lifted from my knees. Before I was even fully upright, I began to preach and continued for four hours. That was a miracle in itself, because I didn't know four hours' worth of German!

Few times in my ministry had I felt the presence of God as I did that night. He quickened every word of German I had ever learned. I didn't know where Fred and Fred got to, but as the crowd grew, I shared my testimony, the love of Christ, the need for confession of and repentance from sin, the *Four Spiritual Laws*, and as much about the blood and power of the resurrected Christ as I could.

Suddenly the Communist soldiers broke through the crowd. I thought of Tex and Davey, imagined being banished to Siberia, and cherished my freedom. As the soldiers reached me, I hesitated, waiting for those fateful words, "You're under arrest." I forgot God had promised that His glory would be my rear guard.

The soldiers began firing questions at me.

"Who is Jesus?"

"How do you know He's real?"

"How did He come into your life?"

The crowd picked up on the questions, everyone seeming to talk at once. A young man shouted, "I don't believe in God! But this man has something to say, and we must listen! Spread out and sit down so everyone can hear!"

I fielded questions, full of the joy of the Lord. There was no place in the world I would rather have been. These were non-Christians, ignorant of the things of God. A love for them welled up within me, and I felt immense assurance that now, as never before, I was in the center of God's perfect will for my life.

This was more than merely something I did that God decided to bless. No, this was a divinely planned event to which I had been called, an opportunity that would not likely come again.

I don't put much stock in emotions, but I felt such compassion for these kids that I burst with joy and love for them. I loved them so much that I knew it had to be of God, because humanly I didn't have the capacity for loving on such a scale. God was loving lost souls through me. Though they were dedicated followers of a philosophy opposed to Christianity, He loved them.

Their hearts seemed hungry. Their minds had been filled with the lies of Satan from the time they were born, and I wanted to give them all of Jesus that was in me. After four hours I could hardly talk anymore. My words wouldn't come fast enough to convey my thoughts.

One boy asked me a question, and I missed part of it. As I strained to hear him better, I noticed a young girl with a beautiful smile. I wondered if she could be one of the underground believers I had heard so much about. She caught my eye and translated into English the boy's question.

When I was finally exhausted and the crowd began to break up, some stayed to ask pointed questions:

"How do I receive Jesus?"

"How do I pray?"

"I want to believe; what does it mean to believe?"

The girl approached and whispered, "My name is Use *(pronounced Usah)*. I cannot talk to you now. If I am seen, I will be in very much trouble. People are watching who could mean trouble for you. Can I meet you tomorrow?"

"At the fountain at 6:30," I said.

I went looking for Fred and Fred. As I walked the perimeter of Alexanderplatz, fatigue overtook me. Thousands ran and sang and danced, looking for causes, for purpose, and I understood what the Gospel writer meant when he said that Jesus saw the multitude and felt compassion for them.

All I could do was weep. For an hour I walked in a daze, unable to contain the depth of my feeling for these young people. *How can we reach them, Lord? There are just three of us and* 400,000 *of them.* God reminded me that Gideon's army was not big either and that He would do with us what He had done with Gideon if we continued to trust Him.

Threading my way through the crowd, I came upon Fred Bishop preaching! A little farther away, Fred Starkweather was preaching too. The crowd had gotten so large when I was preaching that Fred and Fred had gone to the edges and gotten Communists to interpret for them!

Fred Bishop was arguing with a black man, and when Fred saw me, he asked me to take over. "I'm bushed," he said.

"Where is your Jesus?" the man said. "I can't see him."

I turned to a boy and girl holding hands. "Do you believe in love?" I asked.

They giggled and nodded.

"Then where is love?" I said. "Show it to me. I can't see it."

The man said, "You Christians hate blacks."

I said, "Eight years ago I would have hated you just because you are black. Now I can say honestly that I love you in Jesus Christ."

He looked taken aback.

"Do *you* love people?" I pressed.

"Yes!"

"Do you love Communists?" I said.

"Of course. I'm a socialist myself."

"Do you love capitalists?"

"Well, uh—no."

"That's the point," I said. "Communists love Communists and capitalists love capitalists, but only a believer in Jesus Christ can love every person. Only a person who knows God can even begin to understand love."

The first night of the Fest was the happiest of my life, but the second topped even that. After telling Tex all about it and praying for every face I could remember, I finally fell into an exhausted sleep. The next day we were to meet Use, the underground believer.

CHAPTER FOURTEEN

OPPOSITION

The next evening at the fountain, young people from all over the plaza recognized us and asked if we were going to talk about Jesus again. How thrilling to know that they wanted to hear more!

An article in a Communist women's magazine warned delegates about Jesus People types and even advised them about how to debate us, but all that had done was stir up more interest.

It was rarely the young who resisted us but rather their older leaders. If this Communist Youth World Fest was supposed to be a showcase for the Communists' freedom of speech, the young people seemed to want it to be just that.

One young person pointed out other kids lounging on the grass, talking and playing. "When they return home, they will not be allowed such leisure time. The only reason they are allowed now is because the news media from all over the world are watching."

Finally, Use showed up with her brother and a girlfriend. What a joy to hear how they had come to Jesus, where they worshiped, and how glad they were that we were there. Even our conversation brought Communist kids from all over. "They're talking about Jesus again," one said. "They're going to start preaching soon."

When I began to preach, more young people swarmed. Fred and Fred moved to the edge of the crowd and began preaching, breaking off clusters of Communists to keep the groups small. Soon, however, each of us had crowds too big to handle. Use and her friend and brother each took on groups of their own!

Use told me she had been warned a year earlier that she should never again talk about Christ in public. Knowing how scared she had been to talk with me briefly the day before, I knew this was a major step for her now.

Suddenly the Communist leadership had to take us seriously. We had grown to six witnesses, each with a group listening to this new idea: a God who is and who loves. A Communist from Israel shouted me down and said he had worked for Christians in Chicago who were rip-off artists. "They took money from the poor and gave it to the capitalists!"

When he accused the Chinese for Christ of taking money and not using it for ministry, I said, "Listen, I lived in Chicago, and I know that organization is honest!"

"You calling me a liar?" he said, grabbing my shirt.

"Yes, I am!" I shouted, infuriated, but in that instant God spoke to my heart. "I'm sorry I yelled at you," I said.

"You calling me a liar?" he demanded again.

"All I want to say is that Jesus loves you."

"Are you still going to say Jesus loves me when I smash you in the face and fill your mouth with blood?"

I was scared, but I said, "If you hit me, I pray that every drop of my blood will remind you of the blood of Jesus that was shed for you."

"I ought to kill you!" he said, rearing back to slug me. The crowd backed away.

"Jesus loves you."

"You *want* me to hit you?"

"Go ahead," I said. "I'm willing to put my life on the line for Jesus Christ."

He stomped off, leaving me trembling. Two Free German Youth approached. "We've never seen so much love," one said. "How can we get that kind of love?"

"Jesus Christ can give it to you if you give yourselves to Him. If you want Jesus in your life, you can pray and ask Him."

To my surprise, they both said they would like to do that, but not in front of everybody. I told them how they could receive Christ at home and tell me about it the next day.

A couple of university students asked if they could talk with me alone. "We want what you have been talking about."

We moved away from the crowds and sat on some steps near the Alexanderplatz. I told them that Jesus loved them and wanted them for His own.

"We want to know Jesus," one said, "but it costs so much here. When we were fourteen, we had to choose either to join the church or join the Communist party and become Free German Youth. If you join the church, you cannot complete your education or get a good job. We, along with almost all our friends, joined the FGY. Now we feel terrible about it."

"God knows and understands," I said. "He can give you a new life in spite of your circumstances, but you must be willing."

"You don't know what it will cost," they told me. "A friend of ours, a good student, stated publicly that she had become a believer, and she was kicked out of the university."

"Jesus Christ gave His all for you. Are you willing to give your all for Him?"

"Yes," they said, tears in their eyes. "We are willing." We prayed right there, and I realized they had more at risk than anyone I had ever prayed with before.

I was very proud of Use and her brother and their friend. The worst that could likely happen to us Americans would be banishment from the Fest and maybe the country. They faced imprisonment.

Use invited us to go with them to church the next evening. (Fest organizers permitted one church service each night, provided it was orderly and held in a church.)

When we got back across the border, we learned that Lynn Nowicki and his brother and a friend would join us for the rest of the Fest. I welcomed the increased manpower, especially Lynn's ability to speak both German and Russian.

Never should it have been clearer to me that I had the perfect wife. She'd followed this preacher-boy all over the world, sometimes not knowing if I would return. Often we had not known where our next meal would come from.

Now, while we were out on the front lines, seeing God work, Tex washed our clothes and had meals waiting for us late each night. Though she always got the news secondhand, she was as important to the cause as any of us. While hers was a humble and selfless ministry with few obvious rewards, it was an indispensable one she persisted in diligently fulfilling.

It was hard for Tex to have me gone every evening and most of every night. She tried to tell me in many gentle ways that I was neglecting her and Davey, and she admits that when I didn't pick up on it, she grew irritable. I was self-righteous enough to consider her mood an attack of Satan to which she had fallen prey.

With the right motive, but little sensitivity, I looked her in the eye and told her I loved her. "But, please. You're going to have to bear with me a while longer. This is the greatest opportunity we will probably ever have."

She admits she worried mostly for my safety. Every night she sat waiting in unbearable tension, only to have us finally burst in with stories of how wonderful everything had been. Instead of acknowledging her worry and appreciating her prayers, I expected her simply to be an audience.

Tex and I stayed up late to have a difficult discussion about our roles, and the next evening, as my compatriots and I walked to the central train station in West Berlin, I finally succumbed to the fatigue. I had been going on nervous energy and excitement, and I was suddenly struck with a wave of depression.

Torn between my desire to spend an evening with Tex and Davey and what I felt God had called me to do, the last thing I wanted was another night of Communist leaders screaming in my face. I stumbled as my strength drained away. "Guys," I said, "I can't make it."

I could see they were stunned, and I shouldn't have been surprised. I was their leader. This whole effort had originated with God's direction to me through Pastor Busch. Now here I was, the first one to break.

I believe that was when Fred and Fred fully realized their roles. I needed them. Without them I could never have withstood the pressure.

They took me to a corner where they prayed for me. That helped, but I carried on only out of obedience, not in the fullness of joy and enthusiasm I had felt the first three days.

Six of us crossed the border that night, and only Lynn and Fred Bishop were searched—the two who had felt led not to carry anything across! We rushed to meet Use and her friends at their church, only to endure a dead, boring service. The kids seemed excited and ready to live for Christ, but the church had little to offer.

As soon as the kids got outside, about a hundred of them started singing and several played guitars. Lynn joined in, and we all sang choruses. A church official emerged to tell the kids such activity was not allowed outside.

"Okay!" one of the kids shouted, "we'll leave. Let's march to Alexanderplatz for Jesus!"

I could hardly believe it. A Jesus march in the middle of the Communist Youth World Fest?

About halfway to Alexanderplatz a church leader and a government official overtook us and informed us that what we were doing was an act of provocation and a criminal offense. "You must confine your activity to the church or risk being charged with a crime."

A young man shouted, "We have already decided! On to Alexanderplatz!"

Another said, "The Free German Youth say there's freedom at the Fest! Let's prove it!"

When we got to Alexanderplatz, however, Communist party members monitored us and appeared to be writing down names, and suddenly the kids fell silent. One suggested singing in Hebrew or Latin so no one could understand, which—of course—made no sense. It kept the authorities away, but it also eliminated the witness. The crowd that had gathered to see what the Jesus People were up to fizzled.

About fifteen of the Christian young people came to me. "Sammy, we want to go all the way for Jesus. Will you lead us?"

The six of us and fifteen of them made a good-sized little band, playing and singing praise to God. The Communist kids thought it was some kind of a game, so several joined in. As we circled the plaza, we kept picking up more and more marchers, only a few of whom we knew were Christians. By the time we circled the place, we were about a hundred strong, and no one knew what to make of it. Their favorite argument had been "Why should we trust Jesus? There are hundreds of thousands of us and just a few of you!"

But we had grown from three to six, then to more than twenty, and now it appeared we were a hundredfold. When I began to preach, an adult antagonist shouted, "You've all been propagandized! This is a lie of the American capitalists!"

Before I could respond, one of the young people said, "I'm from East Germany, and I want to tell you that Jesus Christ is in my heart and is real to me."

Every time we were shouted down, someone else stepped forward to testify of the work of God in his life. That should have at least convinced them we had not been victims of propaganda but that God had truly changed us.

Later I ran into the two young men who had promised the night before that they would go home and receive Christ. "Did you?" I asked.

They beamed. "Yes!"

"And?"

"Jesus is in our hearts."

By now word had spread so far and wide about us that delegates sought us out, asking how they could know Christ. We knew that if we had become that well known, the authorities would soon find us too. Sure enough, a Fest official came to Fred Bishop and me and said, "Stop this or you will be arrested."

I had no fear for myself by this time, but what about the new believers and the underground Christians? I didn't want to be responsible for seeing them go to prison.

CHAPTER FIFTEEN

THE CHOICE

I gathered everyone and said, "Listen, we have to quit or we'll all wind up in prison."

A girl stared at me sadly. "Sammy," she said, "Jesus gave His all for us, and we are willing to give our all for Him. You can go back to West Berlin. We can't, and we don't want to."

All I could do was pray, *God, forgive me.*

We laid low for a while and met at a secluded park near the church, where I began discipling the new believers. These kids drank in the teaching, and the burden God had given me for the people behind the Iron Curtain expanded into such love for them that I can't describe it. Their boldness, their openness, their hunger for the Word endeared them to me. Here were twentieth-century young people living in the dark ages of oppression, yet they had decided to live for Jesus through the simple preaching of the Gospel.

This was no decision made lightly or in the emotion of an evangelistic service. They had counted the cost, and this would be no joyride. They had made the most dangerous decision anyone could make. I longed for them to know all there was of Jesus.

Satan had attacked, making me think I was too weak to cross the border that day. Then I'd been scared by the threat of arrest. But nothing could prevail against the cross of Christ. This was a day I would remember always, humbled that God had chosen to make me part of it.

New believers who had come out of the Free German Youth told us party leaders had been teaching counter-tactics every morning to combat us. What they didn't realize was that God gave us the strategy, and He never gave us the same idea twice. We rarely knew what we were going to do, so they certainly couldn't either.

Day Five, Thursday evening, I considered concentrating more on discipleship to keep everybody out of trouble, but almost immediately I was convicted that that was a cop-out. God was not in that cowardly plan.

We knew from the FGY that the party troublemakers were just waiting for us. We had scored a major victory the night before, so they were eager to counteract us. Our first appointment, however, was at the home of an underground believer.

At the first meeting I saw what Communism had done for its people. I had lived in Chicago, so I knew what slums were. This neighborhood was worse than anything I had seen. And this was supposed to be an average neighborhood, equality at work. The families were equal all right; they all lived in squalor.

We felt immediate rapport with these believers and enjoyed beautiful fellowship. Then they took us to a little clearing in a nearby woods where we met underground Christians from Hungary, Poland, both sides of Germany, and Czechoslovakia. Someone from each country shared about the persecution of his land, but each rejoiced in the goodness of God in bringing him to this place of international fellowship.

Our East German hosts could have been imprisoned because of our very presence, as in both East Germany and Czechoslovakia, it was illegal even to meet with anyone from the West.

How we cherished that time. This must have been the way the first-century Christians met during the height of their persecution. What beautiful fellowship we enjoyed as brothers and sisters in Christ!

After someone from each country shared, we sang and testified, and then I preached. For a couple of hours our little church in the woods was the most precious place I had ever been in.

By the time we got to Alexanderplatz, the new believers were eagerly waiting for us and the Communists had to wonder where we had been. When we formed a circle and began to sing, the Communists surrounded us. We were the talk of the Fest by now, and when I began to preach, the three hundred or so Communist young people surrounding us tried to drown me out by singing their own songs.

The Lord gave me the idea to have our kids sing "We Shall Overcome," originally a Christian song but now used internationally as a theme for the oppressed. In fact, it had become the young Communists' theme song.

When we broke into that number, they looked delighted, probably thinking they had caught us off guard. Since we were singing "their" song, they joined right in. Until, that is, they ran out of verses about peace and unity and we were still coming up with new ones. Now we had caught *them* off guard.

We switched to "We Shall be Like Him" and then "Jesus Christ Loves You," and the Communists didn't seem to know what to do. When they dispersed, that made room for other delegates who wanted to hear what we were all about. We had the freedom to preach uninterrupted for the rest of the night.

More and more kids came to Christ. When we broke into a chorus like "God Is So Good," it was thrilling to hear even brand new converts make up new lyrics in their own language, like "He's coming soon, He's coming soon, He's coming soon, He's so good to me."

Soon there were at least a hundred of us, with more coming to Christ by the hour and putting their freedom on the line. I taught them a Jesus cheer: "Give me a J,*"* etc. In America such cheers had become meaningless fads, but hearing those underground Christians shout for their Lord in public for the first time sounded like heavenly music. Each time they spelled out His name, I'd ask, "What's His name?"

They'd shout, "Jesus!"

"Who is God's Son?"

"Jesus!"

"Who does the world need?"

"Jesus!"

"Who loves everybody at the Communist Youth World Fest?"

"Jesus!"

"Who is our Lord?"

"Jesus! Jesus! Jesus!"

By Friday we were exhausted and had to lean on the Lord every step. We planned to meet some believers at a little church for some training before heading to Alexanderplatz, but when we arrived the room was packed.

Among the young people was an elderly lady who approached me after the session. She gave me a small notebook and a plaque, which said in German, "We are truly brothers in Christ."

In the notebook she had written, "Blessed are you when men revile you and persecute you for My name's sake." It was a token of love I still cherish.

I offered the young believers the opportunity to spend the whole evening in discipleship training, but they said, "This is the chance of a lifetime. We may never get another chance to be missionaries. Kids from all over the world are at Alexanderplatz."

We headed back to the Fest, one hundred strong. One young man told me he would rather be a Christian in a Communist country than in a free one "because we are like trees. Oppression pushes on our branches and makes our trunks and roots strong."

When we got to the plaza, the Communists were waiting. More than five hundred surrounded us, booming, "Peace! Friendship! Solidarity against the imperialists!" They screamed as if at a soccer game, and there was no way we could sing, cheer, testify, or preach.

We could think of no counterattack, yet we did not want to run. We joined hands and knelt. The Communists didn't know whom they were up against. They thought they were opposing men—some backwoods evangelists from America who had stolen some of their number.

But they were coming against God Himself. As we prayed, we wondered what would stop the chanting, what could drown out such hateful, boisterous noise. Suddenly, lightning flashed, thunder rolled, and torrents of rain washed over Alexanderplatz. The chanters ran to escape showers we believed were meant just for them.

Still hand in hand, we moved quickly under a shelter that had room for a couple of thousand people. It rapidly filled with delegates, and suddenly we had a captive audience. As the rain continued, the Communists had nothing to do but listen to us. We didn't want them to be bored, so we proclaimed the Gospel the rest of the evening.

I preached five different times that night as we all testified to the love of Jesus Christ. We doubled our number, seeing the total of believers jump to about two hundred. I can't overemphasize the magnitude of these young people responding by praying to receive Christ right there in public. They were saying, "I'm taking a stand that may cost me my freedom, my family, even my life, but I believe that Jesus Christ is Lord."

If these young people, in the prime of their lives, could risk everything for God, I could certainly continue to trust Him and to obey.

We had moved under the authority of the resurrected Christ. Satan might have been able to come against us individually, but he could not come against the body of Jesus Christ. The Bible says the gates of hell shall not prevail against His church.

The Fest was to end Sunday at noon, so Saturday evening at the plaza would be crucial. Had I known what was coming, I might not have gone.

We first spent some time at the home of an underground believer who could have been prosecuted just for entertaining foreigners. But by this time the believers were bold enough to sing choruses loudly, even with the windows open.

As we headed out to go to Alexanderplatz, the police met us at the door and demanded to see our passports. While most were East Germans registered for the Fest, a Czechoslovakian and I could have been responsible for the imprisonment of our host.

I fully expected the two of us to be arrested, and prayed the Lord would intervene. The officer ignored my passport and studied my twenty-four-hour visa. "All right," he said, finally, and I breathed a sigh of relief and a silent prayer of thanks. The same happened with the Czech.

At Alexanderplatz I met a young man who had read about our ministry and spread the word through occupied Europe that we had come to the Communist Youth World Fest to share Christ. He told me we were an encouragement to underground believers.

The Free German Youth, determined to stop us, had been frustrated in every attempt during the week, but they came prepared this final night. More than a thousand surrounded our two hundred, and when they began their incessant chanting, we knelt again. As if on cue, God sent the rain again.

This time the FGY were ready for us. As we moved under the cover, they stayed right with us. When we started to preach, they started in again with "Peace! Friendship! Solidarity!" Unable to be heard, I felt the Lord leading me.

"Let's march for Jesus!" I shouted, and two hundred of us rose as one and moved out into the rain. The FGY fell right in behind us and kept chanting all the way around the plaza as we sang and praised God. To the tens of thousands of other delegates it must have looked as if twelve hundred Christians were marching for Jesus.

People ran everywhere shouting, "The Jesus People are coming!"

We kept changing direction, shouting cheers as we went. All over Alexanderplatz Communists came running, and soon we were surrounded by about two thousand. Finally, in one corner of the plaza, the Communists locked arms and kept us from moving.

As they screamed jeers at us, thousands more delegates came running and we found ourselves in a sea of shouting Communists.

An elderly German man, out of place among all those young people, held up a hand. A few fell silent as he said, "We are all for peace, friendship, and solidarity," and the place grew still. "But that comes only through Jesus Christ!"

He was immediately drowned out by the snarling, fist-waving crowd. One of our guys caught my eye and pressed his palms together under his chin. He and I knelt, and two hundred Christians followed our lead.

I felt vulnerable, exposed. I might never again get the chance to preach to that many lost people. *Lord,* I prayed, *I can't do it on my own.*

I stood and raised my hand, and the crowd must have thought I was going to plead for my life, because they quieted. I cut loose with a rapid-fire declaration about how Jesus had changed my life. The Lord quickened me, and I said more words in a few minutes than I thought possible.

The two thousand FGY burst forward, nearly trampling our little band as they shook their fists in my face and shouted threats. I believed I had preached my last sermon. Authorities tried to break up the crowd, but they could do nothing.

A Free German Youth convert shouted, "I'm a Christian. Let me talk!" But they would have none of it. The Communists grew louder, their eyes wild. I was responsible for these young Christians, and I feared a riot.

I shouted to the Christians to "Start a human train!" and led the way. Each grabbed the one in front of him, and we began to move through the massive crowd. I fought through the locked arms of the Communists and kept walking, leading that huge line of believers from the center of hostility.

At the back of the huge crowd were curious delegates who knew only that the FGY had the Jesus People cornered. They couldn't see us escaping. In about five minutes I moved all the way to the edge of the crowd and circled around the back. To people at the edge I said, "Have you heard?"

They said, "No! What's going on?"

March

I said, "Jesus loves you."

"Oh, no!" some said. "They're everywhere!"

Our impossible mission had been accomplished. Jesus Christ had become the major issue on the last night of the Communist Youth World Fest.

During our last two days in Berlin we spent several hours fellowshipping with the believers and discipling them. Many rode the train back to the border with us, and my heart broke as I thought of leaving them. I wanted them to remain one in the Spirit so they would be able to stand in the evil day and hold fast the testimony of Christ. Even today my heart breaks as I think of that last ride with them.

As we passed Alexanderplatz the sun reflected like a cross from the huge TV tower. "There's our church," I said. "And there are the people who need Jesus."

When we got back to the Temple of Tears, the last night of the festival filled my mind. Use said, "Sommy," (the way all the German young people pronounced it), "please come back. We need you."

Kids from other countries gathered, and we embraced and wept. "Sommy, please come back."

"*Danke*, Sommy."

Tears ran down our faces.

"*Danke*, Sommy."

"*Danke*, Jesus," I said, smiling through tears, my voice thick. "*Danke, danke,* Jesus."

All the way to West Berlin and then all the way to the States, all I could think of were those precious brothers and sisters we had left behind. I did not know what their futures held, but I praised God for their boldness.

I couldn't wait to return to our new friends in Christ.

CHAPTER SIXTEEN

NARROW ESCAPE

For the next few years, Tex and Davey and I lived in Europe, my passion for the lost and for the oppressed believers in full bloom. I ventured behind the Iron Curtain as frequently as I could. I was learning to travel internationally, to negotiate with travel agencies and bureaucracies, to be unintimidated by gruff responses and seemingly shut doors.

Prior to that, some saw me as a little flaky. Our ministry was small-time. We didn't claim to be a well-oiled machine. I even sometimes referred to myself as a ding-a-ling, because we often appeared to just take advantage of whatever the Lord put in our paths. I can be a driven person, knowing exactly what I want to do and how I want to do it, but on the other hand, I can be like an absentminded professor.

I'm obsessive about local customs and protocol. I care about being on time, deferring to our hosts, and dressing, speaking, and carrying myself in ways that will not offend. At the same time, I've been known to get to the airport with a passel of luggage and travel companions, only to find I've left my passport or wallet.

I'll spare you the ordeals brought on by my being young and naive and getting into situations I avoid today. But some wonderful blessings came from simply doing what I felt the Lord was driving me to do. There's a place in the kingdom for being a fool for Christ, for stepping out in faith against all odds.

Fred Bishop and I visited Bratislava, Czechoslovakia, and looked up a young born again priest we'd met at the Communist Youth World Fest. What an eye-opener for me, being as I was a kid reared as a Baptist! While he and I may not have agreed on certain doctrines and emphases, and while I still believe that some in the Catholic Church have missed the most crucial doctrine of all—salvation by grace through faith alone—I will never again wonder whether there are true believers among the Catholics.

This beloved brother had translated the *Four Spiritual Laws* into Slovakian and had personally typed several copies for us to use as we witnessed there. We could have argued about the pope, the Virgin Mary, and praying to the saints, but in a society where Christianity is hated, only the basics mattered. I don't mean that these things were not important, but when the rest of the world is at enmity with God, we who believe in Christ were able to find common ground and work together to get out the most important message of all: the saving work of His death and resurrection. We emphasized what we did agree on, and that was the death, burial, and resurrection of Jesus Christ and His work on the cross as the only basis for personal forgiveness of sin and salvation.

The young priest showed us a tiny hiding place where nuns studied and prayed, out of the view of Communist authorities. I was privileged to spend some time there alone, realizing it was a holy place. Here I was, not just a westerner, but also an American who enjoyed freedom, plenty, ease, and comfort. We practice our faith with such freedom that we take it for granted. Here people had to hide from their own government. It broke my heart, and I was deeply honored to be allowed to fellowship with and minister to suffering, oppressed saints.

Fred Bishop and I did not speak either Czech or Slovakian, the languages of the country, so when we went to a nearby university to pass out the tracts the priest had prepared for us, we hoped the educated people there understood either English or our rapidly improving German.

As was always the case behind the Iron Curtain, people were hungry to read anything new. Pass out any literature on the street, and people will flock to it, so starved are they for news and information and philosophy.

After passing out a few tracts, Fred suggested we kneel in a great hallway at the university, commit our time to God, then sing "Alleluia," which seems to mean the same in every language.

We quietly asked God to move in the great university, and then, still with our heads bowed and eyes closed, we softly sang, "Alleluia, alleluia, alleluia, alleluia. Alleluia, alleluia, alleluia, alleluia."

We knew that beautifully haunting little chorus would mean little except to underground believers. Yet we sensed and heard people gathering around us. I was afraid to look up, but eventually we had to. A couple of hundred students had gathered, just staring. We rose and began to speak to them, I in German and Fred in English. As if on cue, those who understood English moved toward Fred, and those who understood German came toward me.

Two recent graduates, young women who had just received their teaching certificates, read over the *Four Spiritual Laws* and one said, "This is wonderful. We've never seen anything like this. Would you tell us more? It would have to be in secret, but we will make sure other students come."

I arranged to come back the next day to meet with them and anyone they brought along. Just then a university official angrily told us to leave the campus.

That night Fred couldn't sleep. "Something's wrong," he said. "We're in trouble, and we need to get out of here."

This was my traveling partner, my mission companion, yet I didn't realize that God might use him to speak to me. I told him, "We made a commitment to those girls, and we have to honor it."

When we arrived the next morning, only one of the girls was there. She spoke quickly, her voice strained. "You must get out of here. The authorities have been questioning everyone. They don't know whether you're German or American or what, but they're going from hotel to hotel looking for you. They've arrested people they know were here yesterday, and it's just a matter of time before they find you."

We ran back to our hotel, packed, and raced for the last train to the West. Just like in the movies, we ran down the track with our luggage and hopped on. We worried our names might show up on some list at the border, but we got into Austria without incident. When we changed our money back from Czech currency, we realized we'd been ripped off and had  only enough to get from Vienna to Salzburg and spend one night in a youth hostel. We had no idea how to get back to our families in Germany.

It was snowing when we got to the hostel in Salzburg, and the last of our money went for that night's lodging. When I awoke in the morning, I pulled the blanket up over my head and prayed, *Oh, God, we're stranded, it's cold, and we're hungry. Help us.*

Meanwhile, Fred had his prayer and quiet time outside and came back in, smiling. "Praise God, Sam!" he said.

Miserably I pulled the blanket from my head. "For what?"

"This is the day the Lord has made!"

I wasn't in the mood. I turned over and sighed.

"C'mon, Sam," Fred said. "Get out of bed and get with God."

I groaned as I rolled out of bed and started to dress, but what should I find on the floor but a wadded-up bill, one hundred German marks! It must have fallen out of a pocket the night before, and I hadn't even known I had it. That would get us home! Suddenly I felt ashamed and at the same time at peace. God was in control.

If nothing else, I learned never to despair when things looked bleak. That was a lesson I needed for our continued forays behind the Iron Curtain.

Fred Bishop and Fred Starkweather and I planned a trip into East Germany to meet at a castle outside Dresden with underground believers —many of whom had been converted at the Fest. The three of us preached and taught about forty young people who had risked their lives by sneaking to the meeting.

Afterward, a young girl told me, "I'm a Christian and want to serve Jesus. But I have sin in my life, and I don't know what to do about it."

I showed her 1 John 1:9: "If we confess our sins, He is faithful and just to forgive us our sins and to cleanse us from all unrighteousness." Because she was a new believer, that was a revelation to her, and she wept as she confessed and thanked God for forgiving her and empowering her to continue to serve Him.

At the end of her prayer, as the rest of the room was hushed and listening, she added a poignant phrase God used to grip us all. She asked God to make her willing to follow Him, and in her own language she added, "No matter what it costs."

The rest of the young people immediately went to their knees, many weeping, all praying to commit themselves to Christ. I prayed with each of them, and one after another they vowed to live for Jesus, "no matter what it costs."

We can say that same phrase in the West, but such a life may cost us no more than a little embarrassment or poverty. We may get laughed at or even ridiculed, but we don't lose educational opportunities, jobs, or our freedom. Our families don't get arrested on bogus charges.

When these kids vowed to follow Jesus no matter what it cost, they meant it. They put their very lives on the line.

I was there to minister to them, but I had been taught a lesson in real obedience. I wanted to be willing to do what James Robison counseled me the day I came to Christ—to be willing to pay whatever price necessary. But I had the option of escaping to the West if things got too hot.

Was I really ready to give up everything to do what God wanted? Or would the faith of these new believers in the underground church in East Germany put mine to shame?

The Cost

CHAPTER SEVENTEEN

HOUSE ARREST

In Leipzig one day we met with young people so enthusiastic that they boldly marched into the streets, singing and inviting others to join in. They filled a cathedral with about fifteen hundred kids where I shared my testimony and challenged them to commit their lives to Christ.

When we went to Dresden, where it was illegal to preach, I was told the people would find a way for me to bring a "greeting," and it could become a sermon as long as I wanted. At a meeting of about two thousand young people, the host asked who had come the farthest. Eventually he narrowed it to, "How many from outside Europe?" My hand was the only one still raised.

"And where are you from, sir?"

"San Antonio, Texas, in America!"

"Aah, as the one who came the farthest, you must bring us a greeting!"

I went to the platform and greeted them on behalf of their brothers and sisters in Christ in America. "They know of you. They care about you. They love you. And they pray for you."

And then I spoke for forty minutes on the cross of Christ.

During my long "greeting," I spoke of a conversation between Jesus and the apostle Peter. Rather than having Peter respond, *"Nein"* for "No," I used *"Nay,"* common to that local district. The people immediately broke into applause. I smiled and said, "Didn't you know Peter came from Sachsen?" and they roared.

In our travels to East Germany we found that about 90 percent of the young people who had prayed to receive Christ at the Communist Youth World Fest followed through with their commitment and became active in the underground church. How thrilling to feel like their spiritual father and to see them growing in faith.

All this time I viewed the Soviet Union as the ultimate center of atheism. It was still a "a riddle wrapped in a mystery inside an enigma," as Winston Churchill once said. We had no contacts there, but Fred Starkweather and I were eager to go anyway. To me, there could be no greater thrill, no greater privilege than to proclaim Christ in the Soviet Union. Even if that meant witnessing to only one person, it would be worth every risk.

By now, Davey was a preschooler, and Fred Starkweather and I lived with our families in two camper vans in Berlin. We worked with the young people in a church under a pastor named Herr Schoch. The entire church, especially the young people, was excited about our plans to venture into the Soviet Union.

I believed God had great things in store. Fred stuffed thousands of Russian-language tracts into the lining of some ski clothes, and we thought we were ready for anything.

The day before we were to leave, I lost my passport. It could have been stolen. Berlin was a city of spies, and an American passport was worth a lot of money. People at the American embassy told me I'd need a written statement from the German police saying I'd lost mine. But the police told me, "It's not our business."

"It's not your business?" I said, "Well, I'll tell you what: I'm going to sit right here and not leave until you give me a statement that says I reported losing my passport."

The officer said, "You can sit here until you starve to death."

I sat there for an hour until he finally got tired of me and rolled a form into his typewriter. "Here's your statement. Now get out of here."

I raced back to the American embassy, where I was given a ninety-day passport. But the Soviet embassy was closed. I couldn't let the whole trip fall apart on this one turn of events. I banged on the gates until someone came.

"I need a visa to go to Leningrad," I said, quickly spilling the whole story of my lost my passport and getting the statement from the police.

"Come in, come in," the man said.

I was stunned. When they issued me a new visa on the spot, I knew God was at work.

Our plan was to fly into Leningrad and witness there, then get to Moscow by Easter 1974. The desire of my heart was to preach the Gospel in Red Square near the Kremlin on Easter morning, in the shadow of Lenin's tomb. I longed to proclaim that Christ is risen.

Knowing it would be foolish to declare we were going there to win people to Christ, we went as tourists. So when we arrived in

Leningrad, we were met by Intourist, the Soviet travel agency and national sight-seeing host organization. We took a tour with them, checked into our hotel, then prayed, *Now what, God?*

We slit open a tiny compartment in the ski jackets and pulled out a few tracts. Then we asked someone to direct us to the university. The school covered several blocks, but that we were pointed to the linguistics department was clearly of God. Nearly everyone there would understand English.

We just looked the place over at first. It looked like any other European university, perhaps more somber. We found a small cafe where students milled about, and as we sat having a bite, we noticed a young man sitting by himself.

I had memorized a few words of greeting, as well as my testimony, in Russian. We approached, and I greeted him and asked if we could talk with him. Fortunately, he understood English. "Could I share with you the truth of the Bible, about how God loves you and wants a relationship with you?"

The young man's eyes grew wide, and he held up a hand. "I need to tell you something," he said, his accent thick. "All my life I have been taught there is no God. My parents taught me there is no God. My teachers have taught me there is no God. My government has taught me there is no God.

"But two weeks ago I was staring into the sky and looking at the stars, and I began thinking: *This could not be an accident. Could it be there is a God?* I prayed for the first time, and I said, 'God, if You exist, would You reveal Yourself to me?'" He looked solemnly at Fred and me. "I believe He has just answered my prayer by sending you here to me."

My heart nearly burst. What a privilege! What a great God we serve! Everything we had gone through was worth this conversation alone. I gave him a tract, and he asked if we had any more. "If I brought my friends, would you give them some?"

"Sure! Go get them."

A few minutes later he returned with nearly two hundred people! The hallway filled with students clamoring for a pamphlet. We began to preach to two different groups, and more people gathered. Four girls approached and called out, *"Habla Español?"*

The only Spanish I knew was the *Four Spiritual Laws*, so I went through them quickly. All the while I still passed out tracts as the crowd surged. Suddenly six men in dark suits hauled Fred and me into a room and interrogated us for hours, two men at a time.

I assumed they were KGB, but whoever they were, they were scary. At one point a university official asked for one of our tracts and put it into his pocket. We prayed he would read it later.

Our interrogators kept demanding to know where we got our pamphlets and how many we had. We directed them to our suitcases.

"More?"

Fred asked for scissors and cut open our ski jackets, producing hundreds more. The men's eyes bulged, and their faces flushed. They were convinced that we were part of some international conspiracy against the Soviet state.

After about eight hours they shot pictures of us and our tracts and told us to write out our confession.

"Our confession to what?" I said.

"To your crime."

"Crime? I thought the Soviet constitution guaranteed the freedom to practice religion. What is our crime?"

"The people have the freedom to believe in God, but they are considered sick. If they spread their sickness among the masses, that is a crime against the state. To bring this sickness in from the outside, as you and your organization have done, is even worse. You must write your confession."

So I wrote my confession:

"It began when a man told me about Jesus, that He is God come in human flesh, that He lived a sinless life, and that He died for the sins of the world. Three days later He arose. I gave my heart to Him. Whoever is reading this confession now can know Him too." I added a prayer of repentance and faith in Christ.

Later they came back with what they said were our confessions translated into Russian. I studied the document and knew enough to know that they were not what we had written.

"Sign it."

"No," I said. "We won't sign unless we can speak with someone from the American consulate."

"No. You must sign."

"No."

"Ah, so you *are* spies."

"No."

"Charge them as spies unless they sign."

"I think we need to sign it," Fred said.

And so we did. It was wrong, and I wouldn't do it today, because we were admitting to something that wasn't true.

We were then taken back to our hotel room and told not to leave. Someone was stationed at the end of the hall, so we were under house arrest. We heard nothing for several hours, so Fred ventured out and got on the elevator, hoping to find us something to eat.

The elevator stopped between floors, and the phone rang. "You will be taken back to your floor," a voice said. "Stay in the room."

For two days we heard nothing and ate nothing. If they were trying to work on our minds, they were succeeding. But it also made me mad. I had learned in the German police office that authorities seem to admire persistence and eventually get tired of resisting, so I called downstairs every so often and demanded to be put through to the American consulate.

Finally, they put us through. I spilled out our story, and a man said, "Listen, whatever happens, don't leave with anybody. This is serious and extremely dangerous. I'm coming straight over there. It will take me about a half hour, but I will be there."

I hadn't been truly frightened until then. But now I wondered whether they had really put me through to the Americans. I decided we would test the man when he arrived by asking him who had won the most recent Super Bowl. Only a real American would know that.

Finally, a knock came on the door.

"Who is it?"

"American consulate."

"Before we open the door, tell us who won the Super Bowl in January."

There was a pause. Fred and I looked at each other. "I have no idea," the man said. "Who did?"

I shrugged. We were Americans, and we didn't know either. (It was the Miami Dolphins.) So much for our safety test!

"Look," the man said, "I have identification. Let me show you."

We cracked the door and saw his ID. He marched us downstairs and started in on everyone involved. "You have no right to force these boys to sign anything about being at the university. I'll be filing an official protest, but right now I'm getting them something to eat."

Our money and plane tickets had been confiscated, but after some negotiating with the authorities, he said, "You're going to be deported to Helsinki, and then you'll be on your own."

After he left, an official bawled us out for trying to spread a disease among the Soviet people. Then we were taken back to our room, where we waited—for what, we didn't know.

Finally, at about ten that night, two tall plainclothesmen came for us. We didn't know what was going on, and by then I wondered even about the man who claimed to be from the American consulate. For all I knew He could have been involved in a plot to get rid of us. We were driven to a train station and put aboard a train, but no one would tell us where we were going.

The farther we got from Leningrad, the harder it snowed. The train stopped briefly at a depot in a little village, where a guard with a machine gun paced the platform.

As vividly as if it were yesterday I remember fearing we'd been banished to Siberia. I began to weep, wondering if I would ever see Tex and Davey again, remorseful that I had gotten Fred Starkweather into a situation from which there might be no escape. I asked myself if this had all been a result of my own stupidity. *Was God in this at all, or had I just been foolish?*

I told God, *Even if we do end up in Siberia, that one young man coming to Christ was worth it all. Thank You for letting us be part of the answer to his prayer.*

Well past midnight, thick flakes fell in the faint light of the train. I had no idea where we were going, but it sure didn't look like Helsinki.

Part Two — The Breaking

CHAPTER EIGHTEEN

A RESTLESS SPIRIT

As that drafty train clacked into the desolate Soviet night, I searched my soul. It took a couple of brash young people, blindly stumbling through a university, to find the one young man God had sent them there to minister to. One person coming to Christ back then was as great a miracle as the thousands who come forward at outdoor crusades in the same nation today.

Maybe we *were* foolish. I say we were naive but obedient. But we learned the depth of the spiritual hunger of the people. Those students hadn't mobbed us because we were foreigners, spoke English, or espoused some radical new philosophy.

No, they knew immediately what we were about because in that setting when we got the floor, we preached Christ. Sure, they may have been curious about two ding-a-lings kneeling to pray and sing, but what made them stay and ask questions and clamor for tracts? Our speaking of God, of Jesus, of forgiveness, of life.

I breathed a huge sigh of relief when that train did finally pull into Helsinki, Finland. Fred and I thanked God for everything that had happened—even the scariest times—but especially for the privilege of talking about Christ where few ever had.

Finding our way back to our families in Berlin without money, tickets, or passports became typical of what I would endure for years. Traveling internationally is an ordeal, and you can either cave in or be creative and trust God.

Without a penny, we placed a collect call from the American embassy to God's Love in Action board member Morris Todd, asking him to get hold of Herr Schoch in Berlin and have Tex wire us airline tickets to Berlin via Oslo and Hamburg. Finally we were reunited with our families.

After a couple of years of traveling and speaking in Europe and making occasional forays behind the Iron Curtain, Tex and I spent eight months in Switzerland, where Renee was born in 1976. Davey was then about four and a half.

The next year, while on a brief speaking tour in the States, I met Dr. Sam Friend, a pastor in the Seattle area. God began to burden his heart for ministering in Eastern Europe, and he later became a key factor in my ministry plans.

Perhaps because our second child had come along and I was nearly thirty, I sensed something within me. A certain maturity made me more reflective, introspective, and restless. I began to realize that my character development had stopped somewhere along the line. I was still active, still burdened, still enthusiastic, but something was wrong. And that something was me.

Needs in my personal life, family life, and an uneasiness in my spiritual life made me wonder for the first time whether it was time for a shift in my ministry emphasis.

As an evangelist I had traveled and preached the same types of sermons numerous times. That made it even more crucial for me to be continually growing spiritually—which requires great care and maturity. If I were a pastor, I would be forced to study the Word, to feast on it and live it.

Whatever my blind spots were—and they would be revealed to me throughout the next few years—I desperately, sincerely wanted to serve God. I began to read voraciously, and several books had tremendous impact on me. Two things struck me when I read *The Life and Diary of David Brainerd* by Jonathan Edwards. First, Brainerd was a man of deep prayer. Second, he was a man of deep humility.

I prayed a lot, but I knew nothing of the kind of prayer life Brainerd had. And I fell far short of the type of humility that characterized his life. I wanted to glory only in the Cross, but I tended to glory more in the success God had granted our ministry. I knew deep in my heart that grace would be planted only in the soil of humility, and that humility was found only in Jesus and what He did on the cross:

> Let this mind be in you which was also in Christ Jesus, who, being in the form of God, did not consider it robbery to be equal with God, but made Himself of no reputation, taking the form of a bondservant, and coming in the likeness of men. And being found in appearance as a man, He humbled Himself and became obedient to the point of death, even the death of the cross (Philippians 2:5-8).

I decided to read biographies of the great saints—like Wesley and Whitefield—and also to study the life of Moses. I discovered qualities of character of which I knew little. Moses was eighty years old before his ministry began. For forty years he was proud and strong. During the next forty he was in the wilderness, devastated and broken. God used him most mightily during his final forty years.

I was troubled in my spirit, knowing God needed to do a deep work in my heart, maybe even breaking and reshaping me so He could most fully use me. Only by grace could I become a man of godly character, a worthy goal God Himself desired for me.

As I delved deep into the Word I found myself actually praying, *Lord, give me a wilderness. Put me where nobody knows me and You can do in me whatever You want to do.*

I told Tex what I was thinking and that I sincerely wanted God to teach us simply how to be like Him. Whereas I knew I needed something deep and lasting from the Lord, I was so blind to my own specifics faults that I had no idea this was the answer to her prayers and that I needed it *much* more than she did.

Some might fear a deeper work of God in their hearts, but in truth I longed for it. Ignorant of my weakest areas, I didn't know where He would start. I just knew I had to get more serious about prayer and the Word.

Where might God put us? Where might I land? In the States? In Europe? In a pastorate?

I was preaching in the Atlanta area when I ran into an old friend, a preacher named Manley Beasley. He turned white as a sheet when he saw me and was nearly speechless, but he quickly said, "Sammy, I just returned from Europe where I spoke with a missionary familiar with you. He told me, 'God has his hand on Sammy for Europe. Sammy needs to be in Europe.'"

"Really?"

"That's not all. Another pastor said the same thing. Then, in Stuttgart, I saw a bunch of young people in a McDonald's, and I could just see you telling them about Jesus."

"Wow."

"But listen, I told these people who mentioned you 'No way I'm going to try to tell a man what God's will is for his life.' But they were persistent, so I said, 'I'll tell you what, if God brings Sammy across my path, I'll tell him what you told me.' Sammy, I just told you, and now I have to catch my plane."

Somehow I found my gate, boarded my plane, and wept. Call that encounter a coincidence, but to me it was a divine appointment. I believe God was telling me to get out of traveling evangelism, at least for a season, and take a pastorate in Europe, away from where I was known.

Within a month, I received the first two calls to churches I'd ever had in my ministry. One was in Stuttgart, and the other was the Hahn Baptist Church in Hahn, West Germany. I had preached there once.

One of the definitions of the word *hahn* is *rooster*, so I was asked to consider becoming pastor of the Rooster Baptist Church in Rooster, Germany! It mostly served a nearby American military base but was otherwise on the backside of nowhere. It sounded like just what I was looking for, so I accepted a three-year call beginning in 1978.

Many friends told me I was making a mistake and that I should stay in evangelism. But I felt certain this was what God wanted.

After the first month I was no longer sure. I had gone from an exciting world of traveling and evangelism—and enjoying all that goes with that—to the middle of typical church hassles.

Though that discouraged me, the Lord reminded me to keep the focus on Christ and call the people to holy living. I believed the key was spiritual leadership in each home—ironically one of the blind spots in my own character—so I started discipling men. The Lord gave me both a deep love and a deep hunger for His Word at the same time. I believed He wanted me to "preach the Word," so I started in Genesis.

We set a goal for every member of our church to develop a quiet time, and we began to build the church on prayer. That started a thrust in my whole ministry that has stayed with me to this day: the prayer factor, trying to build a prayer team around our efforts. Prayer became foundational to that church in discipleship, teaching, preaching, and outreach. Based on that, a church can mature by leaps and bounds, and Hahn Baptist did just that.

I also began to develop deep friendships with a group of guys committed to one another. We had fun together, won people to the Lord together, grew together.

I put a challenge before the men: I agreed to study and pray with anyone willing to meet at 6 A.M. That's how I knew they meant business. That small group grew in number and in maturity, and as these men influenced their homes and families, the church became healthier and began to grow too.

I became prayer partners with two guys in particular, Don Shelton and Ken Leeburg. When Don first came to the church, he merely took up the offering. I asked him to teach Sunday school, and after he had taught twice, he told me, "Sam, I'm just not a public speaker."

Growth

But in the discipleship group, he grew in the Lord and became a teacher, a deacon, then chairman of the deacons. Eventually, he became pastor of the Hahn Baptist Church!

Ken Leeburg was an attorney who became my best friend. We became jogging and prayer partners, our families grew close, and our friendship became very special to me.

When my mom came for a brief visit, it marked the first time she'd shown interest in what God had given us to do. What a blessing to see her seem to warm to God's call on our lives.

Soon we had to take out the pews and hold multiple services. Eventually we moved out of the church and into a local high school for Sunday evening services. People came to Christ, and attendance soared. Some of us went to the European Baptist Convention in Interlaken, Switzerland, where I was voted program chairman.

I loved lining up exciting speakers from the United States, and I knew the English-speaking churches in the European Baptist Convention would be thrilled to hear them and be motivated to live out their faith.

The night I was elected program chairman, Tex nudged me and nodded toward Davey, now a third grader, who had dozed off between us during the meeting. His eye twitched uncontrollably, which worried Tex and me. I put my hand on him and prayed for him, but his eye kept twitching. It eventually stopped, so we didn't think any more about it. I looked forward to getting back to Hahn and finishing my study of the passage where Abraham is asked to sacrifice his son to God.

The night we returned home I was roused out of bed by a noise coming from Davey's room. I found his eyes had rolled back and he was in the grip of a grand mal seizure. I yelled for Tex, who came running, and we prayed over him, pleading with God to give him relief, but he continued to convulse. Scared to death, we rushed him to the hospital.

CHAPTER NINETEEN

DEEP WATERS

The doctor on duty, in God's providence, was Chuck Patterson, a member of my discipleship group. He and I sat up all night with Davey, whose right side was paralyzed.

Only if you've been there can you imagine the pain of watching your own young flesh and blood suffer like that. I wept nearly the whole time.

The next day, with Davey's condition still a mystery, I was to preach on Abraham offering his own son as a sacrifice. It was one of the hardest things I have ever done, and I cried through the whole message. I knew God was doing something in me, but I had no idea what it was.

As civilians we could use the military hospital only on a one-time emergency basis. And as salaried Americans we had no access to German socialized medicine either. We had to take Davey to a hospital in Wiesbaden. There a neurologist asked him to walk, and it broke my heart to see my normally rambunctious little guy move in a horribly spastic way.

The neurologist said, "I'm afraid he will never again have full use of his limbs. This will get only worse."

The doctor could not pinpoint a reason for Davey's condition, but I suspected an incident when he was younger. Davey had a tiny plastic toy lodged in his throat and couldn't breathe for several minutes until we rushed him to the hospital. He seemed to come out of it all right, but this strange seizure occurring years later made me wonder.

The Wiesbaden neurologist put Davey on medication that had to be carefully monitored. Often we feared the cure was worse than the symptoms. He would wake up in the middle of the night screaming with headaches. On Christmas Eve he ran a fever of 105 degrees.

For a year and a half we went through hell on earth with him. We had to hold him down every time they drew blood. Tex and I would have given anything to trade places with him, as any loving parent would.

Meanwhile, I tried to concentrate on my Bible study and discipleship, and as the church grew I was invited to speak in various places around Europe. I struggled to balance all the demands.

We maintained our family devotions every evening, and one night Davey asked if he could talk to Tex and me.

He began to cry and said, "I want Jesus in my heart." We prayed with him, and that remains one of my sweetest memories as a father.

At about that time in 1979, Sam Friend came from Bothell, Washington, to hold a church growth conference at Hahn Baptist. He checked things out in Eastern Europe and, after talking with Josif Tson, asked if I would go in with a five-member singing group to try to reach Romania's youth. I had always wanted to minister there, so we agreed I would go into the country for the first time in June of 1980. Of course, I didn't know what a significant relationship I would begin with that country and its church.

In February of 1980 my friend Manley Beasley held an international congress on revival in Interlaken, Switzerland, where I also spoke. Britain's Roy Hession, author of the classic *Calvary Road,* was one of the keynote speakers, and he enthralled me.

At one point, when I shared all the wonderful ways God was blessing our church, I added, "But I have to be honest with you, I don't understand why God seems silent concerning our son." I asked the people to pray for us. Later, when we were checking out of the hotel to return to Hahn, Roy Hession approached me. I was honored, but chatting was not what he had in mind.

He said, "Young man, God is not only calling you to give your son back to Him, but He's also calling you to give back your self-righteousness."

I was speechless. I couldn't imagine what this great man, whose preaching I loved, had sensed in me. As soon as he turned away, my face fell. I was hurt, but more than that, I was offended. Had he gotten to the root of something God wanted to do in me? I was devastated.

I went to Don Shelton, Ken Leeburg, and John Labash, another friend and key man in our church. I said, "If what he's saying is true, I don't know if I can even preach." They encouraged me to take it at face value but not to let it discourage me. That wasn't easy. God was nudging me to be as receptive as possible to His Spirit.

In June, the five young singers from Bothell and I squeezed into a rented van with their sound equipment and headed toward Romania. At the Romanian border at 10 the next morning, I got my first lesson in Romanian bureaucracy. They demanded a two-thousand-dollar deposit to ensure we would bring all the sound equipment out with us when we left.

They confiscated three Romanian Bibles and our personal Bibles, which caused one of the girls to start pleading with me to get hers back.

"The man has a machine gun," I said.

But the guards put the Bibles into a small shipping container, so when they weren't looking, I dug out three of the Bibles and slipped them back into suitcases that had already been searched. When we got into the country, we discovered that the guards had given all our Bibles back anyway, probably because of the girl's crying!

As soon as we crossed the border, we headed for Josif Tson's house. We had been instructed to park down the street so the secret police wouldn't know whom we were visiting. Romanian citizens were required to report in writing their entire conversations with foreigners or risk prison.

Josif's wife, Elizabeth, gave us our itinerary and advised us how to deal with authorities.

Josif's church, the Second Baptist Church of Oradea, one of the largest Protestant churches in Europe, was nearly full an hour before the service. As we set up our sound equipment, people sat in pews—men on one side, women on the other—praying and weeping.

I preached how God builds character in us by allowing hardship. I shared our terrible experiences with Davey's illness. Years later I learned that Elizabeth Tson thought it was the best sermon she had ever heard on the subject and that it had deeply ministered to her.

After the service I met a sharp, dynamic young man named Paul Negrut, whom Josif was discipling. At the restaurant in our hotel he pointed out two secret police at the other end of the table. "If they're secret," I asked him, "how do you know who they are?"

"Because they call me in every day and interrogate me for two hours before I go to work."

I could hardly believe how much Christians endured in Romania. In later years, Paul would put a transistor radio in his window and play it loud when we spoke, to negate any bugging devices of the Securitate.

On our travels across the country to various meetings, we picked up an interpreter and a relative, so now there were eight of us in the van. Despite the discomfort, I found Romania a beautiful fifty-year throwback to a culture with rudimentary farm implements, horse-drawn hay wagons, and livestock by the side of the road.

We arrived at one church half an hour before the service and began unloading the equipment. People stood watching, then pitched in to help. After the group sang, I preached through our interpreter, and then—as is their custom—the church fed us. We discovered they had never gotten word we were coming. They had scheduled another man to preach, and here we had taken over their whole service!

'That's awful!" I said. "We're so sorry!"

But they insisted, "No, no, no! No problem!"

I learned on the trip that if you don't present hotel clerks with small gifts (like coffee), you may not get rooms. We also learned that we couldn't leave the van parked just anywhere. I had to talk one policeman into returning our driver's passport.

At several stops I had to sleep on the floor. Once I had to sleep in the van to protect it and nearly froze to death. After one meeting people gathered to ask questions until someone whispered "secret police" and everybody disappeared.

One church backed out at the last minute on a Monday night, so we scheduled an alternate church. I asked our host, "How are they going to get people out on a Monday night?"

He assured me I needn't worry.

I shouldn't have. When we arrived, the church was so full they removed the doors so people could see from the outside.

The next night Radu Gheorghita, a recent high school graduate, traveled all the way from Deva to Bucharest to join us, and I found him a most enthusiastic and warm believer, eager and hungry for the Lord.

I took to him right away, and when one of the young men in the singing group said there was no room for him in the van, I said, "Then you take the train and make room for him." That was one of the best decisions I ever made. Radu became a dear brother in the Lord and remains so to this day.

At one of our meetings the huge crowd kept asking for more music and preaching. I had never experienced anything like it. It had to be what heaven will be like.

Soon we enjoyed our first meeting in Timisoara, where I fell in love with the local Christians, just as I did with all the Romanian believers. We had tearful good-byes all around before heading to the border, and I knew I would be back.

I don't engage in situational ethics, such as lying to border guards. Because we had left three Bibles with believers inside the country, the number we brought out didn't match the number we'd brought in. When the guard asked us about the discrepancy, I said nothing. He probably assumed I didn't understand.

I had preached in a country during the flowering of its revival. The crowds, the hunger and thirst for God, and the intensity among the young people was unlike anything I had ever seen before. I couldn't wait to get visas for Tex and me so we could go right back.

The church in Hahn shared my excitement, so we started making plans. My friend Ken Leeburg and I prayed together and dreamed of winning the world for Christ. I used to kid him and say that I had planned to be an attorney before I got saved. He shot back that he had intended to be a minister before he got right with the Lord.

Ken challenged me physically, spiritually, and intellectually. He even demanded to be shown evidence from Scripture if he disagreed with a point, and I loved it! We disagreed on one basic doctrine, but instead of trying to ram my view down his throat, I challenged him to memorize Scripture as we jogged. Then I chose several verses that drove home my point. Before long, with no input from me other than Scripture, he began to espouse the same doctrine.

One of the things I learned best from Ken was persistence. He pushed me to where I was regularly running six and seven miles a day. We dreamed of running in races and marathons. Running me up a huge hill we called "Difficulty," he would shout, "C'mon, Sam! You can do it! Up the hill! Over the hill! Through the hill! Conquer the hill!"

Ken and I ran in a half marathon and dreamed of running in the Athens Marathon, following the path of the original marathon. I met a man at the Hahn Air Force Base who had once won that marathon, and I peppered him with questions. His answer to almost every one was, "Run hills, man. Run hills."

I was so inspired by that counsel that even though I had already finished my workout, and it was the dead of winter with deep snow all around, I hurried home and changed and took off jogging on the little country roads, heading uphill toward the church.

On the road I spun around just in time to see a car sliding right into me. It knocked me thirty feet into a field of snow. As I lay with my head sticking out, I saw a terrified young boy at the wheel of the car. He took off.

I was afraid to move for fear that every bone was broken, but I tried to wave for help, and I wondered why people just looked at me and didn't notice there were no footprints between the road and the crazy guy lying in the snow.

Finally a couple drove by, and the wife recognized me. She was a member of our church, though her husband—a policeman—was not. She called out, "Brother Sammy, what are you doing out there?"

I asked that she notify Tex and call an ambulance.

Half an hour later at the base hospital, I found the couple and Tex and the young man who hit me. He looked worse than I did. I was cut up and bruised but had no broken bones. He was frightened and remorseful, and I wound up assuring him I knew it was an accident and not to worry about me.

The husband of the woman from our church was so impressed that I had not chewed out the boy for his carelessness that he started coming to church, committed his life to the Lord, and became one of the key men in our discipleship group. God had allowed me to suffer to bring someone else to Himself. As I look back on it, I can say it was worth the pain.

God brought me low for my own benefit too. Tex and I were exhausted from being up with Davey in the night, trying to comfort him as he screamed with headaches caused by the medication. It tore my heart out every time he had to have blood drawn, and I wished I could promise him it would be the last time.

God humbled me through Davey's illness, something that took me to the edge emotionally and over which I had no control. Despite my fatigue and worry, I tried to stay in the Word and maintain my preaching schedule. While God continued to bless my ministry, and the church continued to grow, I grew more vulnerable, maybe even more sensitive. Though my nerves were raw, God somehow made me more reflective, more introspective.

I had long been impressed by Tex's dedication to Jesus. She read her Bible and prayed every day, and she studied my sermons right along with the congregation. She said she wanted to be fully right spiritually before we went to Romania, where God was at work, searching people's hearts.

One evening as we sat to dinner with Davey and Renee, Tex was unusually quiet. By nature, she's always been the steady one, hardly showing her feelings unless very upset. But now I could tell something was troubling her.

After I prayed and we began to eat, she began to tear up. "In my quiet time today," she said, "I was studying the holiness of God. Sammy, I need to talk to you."

She had my attention.

CHAPTER TWENTY

THE BREAKING

Looking back, it's clear God had been preparing me for this ominous moment, but I didn't see it coming. After dinner Tex and I sat in the living room, where she told me she had some things to say and didn't want me to say anything until she finished.

The very fact that she felt she had to say something that could have offended me was troubling. Here I was, the pastor of a growing church, sought after to speak in many places, becoming known in Europe and behind the Iron Curtain as a man of the Word and a man of prayer. I didn't go so far as to think my wife should feel privileged to live under the same roof with a man of God who should be able to counsel her through any difficulty, but if I had probed the depths of my heart, I might have discovered that was, indeed, my attitude.

But Tex didn't want my wisdom or counsel. She didn't want me as her pastor just now. She had something to tell me.

"Sammy," she began, voice thick with emotion, "there are things in my heart not pleasing to God. Studying the holiness of God I'm broken, and I need to confess it to you."

I was puzzled. I knew this woman, this love of my life. Surely she couldn't have committed some major sin without my knowing.

"Okay," I said, gently as I could. "What is it?"

She looked down, and the tears came again. "I have had misplaced priorities. I've drifted from the unity we used to know. I've not been the wife God wants me to be. And I've had bitterness in my heart toward you since early in our marriage."

Toward me? What could *I* have done to cause *anyone* to harbor bitterness toward me? I fought to remain silent.

"I was deeply offended by things you said, by your attitude when we disagreed, by the way you treated me. I've harbored bitterness toward you for that, and I want you to forgive me."

Of course, I would forgive her, but what had I done? I didn't remember having said or done anything to hurt her. I loved her, believed her to be a great spiritual wife and mother, and thought we had a good marriage. In fact, compared to most, I believed ours was great.

I stared, begging with my eyes for specifics. It crushed me to see the tears streaming down her face. "When we argue, whenever we disagree, you always win. I never win. Have you ever noticed that?"

But most of the time I *was* right, I thought. In truth I saw myself smarter, quicker, more knowledgeable in the ways of the world. Skilled in debate, I could win any argument whether I was right or wrong. Worse, I was convinced I was always right.

Except on those rare occasions when I had been so obviously wrong and had bullied her to where she cried, and I had to apologize, I had simply pressed on till, as she said, I won.

Slowly, because of her courage in finally speaking up, it was getting through my sick, self-righteous head how all that made her feel. Tex was a quiet, reflective person. Until now she had believed it pointless even to express herself. So I had gone on believing I was right.

Had it not been for my reading about humility, my preaching from Genesis, and what we were going through with Davey, no doubt I would have leapt to some defense, turned the spotlight on her, and made her feel worse for bottling this up over the years. Why hadn't she told me? How could I do anything about a problem I was unaware of?

But God was working on me through her, and somehow I knew enough to keep my mouth shut. Tex had tried to take some of the blame by focusing on the bitterness she had harbored against me.

But now I was exposed, and I didn't like the harsh glare of truth. What she said finally gave me a glimpse of myself, and I wanted to turn away from it.

I thought my marriage was great because my wife was so easy to live with. I was this macho, driving, successful guy with a wife who knew he was always right. I had been living in a fantasy world, leading a fairy-tale life.

Humiliated, I held Tex's hands and told her that I had heard her, really heard her, maybe for the first time. "Sweetheart," I said, "I want to make this right. I love you and want to treat you the way I should, the way God would have me treat you."

I sensed there was more, that she had merely awakened me to the problem. Deep in my heart I wanted to please God and be the kind of husband and father He wanted me to be. All of a sudden, I realized what a miserable failure I had been.

I asked the deacons for a few days off, we found someone to take the kids, and we spent three days in a Luxembourg hotel room, determined to get everything on the table. Now the day of reckoning had come.

In Luxembourg I learned there were many things Tex could never talk to me about because I won all the arguments. In the beginning, I had included her in the witnessing in the French Quarter, the walks to Washington and Miami, and the street work in Chicago. But I began to cut her out as soon as Davey came along.

I had bought into the myth that you shouldn't put your family at risk for the sake of the ministry. I had told myself it would be poor stewardship to subject her to the same dangers I faced. But then I would come back with exciting stories of the blessing of God, insensitive to the fact that she was once right there on the front lines with me. If she responded by accusing me of not spending enough time with her and Davey, I lashed out with an unanswerable argument and shut her down.

Painful as it was to hear, I realized that my rationalization for protecting my family actually exposed my lack of faith in God. I was being macho, protecting my loved ones rather than relying on God.

When I finally realized how deeply I had hurt Tex with my sinful attitudes, I cried for hours. The Lord showed me that cutting Tex out of my ministry had shut off a major part of our life together.

My motive had not been love; it had been rooted in fear for her and the kids. I had kept her from serving God and being used of Him. Our communication had broken down, and I didn't even know it. We had drifted apart, and who knows what might have happened to our marriage if I had continued on that destructive path.

I was truly broken now in that area, and Tex could sense it. I asked her to hold nothing back, to give me both barrels so I could prove my love for her. She says she never doubted my love, but she had sure become aware that I didn't know how to express it. She forgave me, and I believe she knew I had simply been blind to my faults.

From that point on, however, I had no excuses. I immediately rearranged my priorities to get my life in order. It had to be God first, family second, and ministry third.

Putting God first meant I had to get to the root of my problem as a husband. I needed a deep work in my heart related to motives. I could not identify with the humility of David Brainerd, who said he was humbled to speak to pastors, worrying that they had to hear such a poor speaker. When I was asked to speak to pastors, I reveled in the opportunity, and I didn't understand why.

I also knew that after two and a half years in Hahn, I had to take my family back to the United States to find proper medical treatment for Davey. We simply couldn't go on this way.

It was hard to leave our friends and the church, which had grown from about 150 to more than 500. Friends said, "Within six months you'll see a church in America grow to 5,000," and I actually believed that.

I hated to postpone that second trip to Romania, but I knew God would allow me back there one day. I left my best friend, Ken Leeburg, with the dream that I would take a church in the U.S. and from there we would venture out to win the world for Jesus. We just knew we would be involved in the effort together.

Back in the States we were able to get Davey's medication regulated and his condition began to improve. What a relief! It was a slow process, but full recovery came within a couple of years.

Meanwhile, God worked in our marriage. I had been brought low, and while I still needed to change habitual responses, Tex and I really began to communicate for the first time in years. This was no phony, first-aid solution. I wanted and needed her input and correction. As she gradually gained the confidence to speak frankly to me, I got to where I longed for her advice. Because of her love for me and the Lord, she did not abuse her right to bring me up short when necessary. I was a better man for it and a better servant of God. It also helped soften my heart for one more deep work of the Spirit, necessary for God to prepare me for further service.

I accepted the pastorate of a small church near Portland, Oregon, Mt. Hood Baptist in Gresham, which was similar to Hahn Baptist. It was filled with people who seemed to be growing through discipleship, which struck a chord in me. Interestingly, the church had been founded by the first man who had ever witnessed to me, when I was in seventh grade in Baton Rouge.

We moved to Oregon in January of 1981, and it wasn't long before I was miserable. It wasn't the church or the people. They were good. Had they been a bunch of rebels not committed to evangelism or godliness, I could have understood why the church didn't grow. But nothing I tried worked. What had turned to gold at Hahn turned to dust in Portland.

I still had a heart for winning the world, and I'm sure the people did too. But the chemistry or something wasn't right. I tried the same discipleship techniques, but little succeeded except the building program.

Not long after we arrived, the assistant pastor's baby daughter died. Our daughter, Renee, then five, was deeply moved by that and got a sense of her own mortality. Soon she came to us, as Davey had done, and asked Jesus into her heart.

Of course, I was thrilled about that, but I couldn't hide that I was unhappy in my work. I called Ken Leeburg, and he tried to encourage me. Sam Friend was in nearby Washington State, and he too encouraged me to slug it out. I finally realized God was still taking care of unfinished business in my life.

My personal worth and identity had to come from who I was in Christ, not from the results of my ministry. I had to redefine success. In asking myself if I had missed God's will by going to Oregon, I was forced back to the mirror of the Word to reexamine my motives. I knew because of the improvement in Davey that it had been the right move to return to the States. But what did it mean that I saw no success, no fruit, no church growth?

I struggled with these issues day after day, seeking God through His Word and in prayer, and He finally revealed to me my problem. It was me. My ego. Roy Hession had been right, and Tex had touched on it too. God had to teach me that true success, His kind of success, came in obedience, not in results. My self-worth could not hinge on the size of the ministry, not even in how many people came to Christ. I had enjoyed being known and respected and in demand.

Frankly, I had enjoyed pastoring a church that was exploding with growth. Who wouldn't? I believed we were doing the same things in Oregon as we had in Germany, so what was the problem?

The question was, "Have I obeyed God?" I came to see that He was interested in neither my ministry nor the results. Those were His responsibility, not mine. My job was to be conformed to the image of His Son, and He would bring the increase. All I could do was obey.

I knew God had allowed circumstances to reveal these truths to me. I was becoming the husband God wanted me to be, but the price had been humiliating. Davey's illness had also exacted a huge emotional toll. But when God showed me I was self-centered, even while wanting to please Him, that was a lesson I desperately needed.

Deep down I was glad I was learning it, but I was also felt whipped. I had asked God to humble me and teach me, to do a deep work in my life and character, but I'd had no idea how much He had to do— or how painful and comprehensive it would be.

God had revealed myself to me, allowing me to see a picture I didn't find so pretty. One requirement for true humility is the ability to see yourself for what you are. I didn't like what I saw, and for the first time in my ministry, I felt like giving up. I actually began looking into secular work, believing I was doing nothing of any spiritual worth and that I would see more people come to Christ if I was out in the world.

After about a year and a half, when I got as low as I thought I could go, it was time to move on. I had learned that success is in obedience rather than in fruit, but had I stayed there, it would have been unhealthy.

When friends told me that University Baptist Church in San Antonio needed a pastor, I thought that might be the answer. When I accepted the call in mid-1982, we looked forward to returning to Texas. I would learn that this was just another small step on a long journey.

CHAPTER TWENTY-ONE

HIDING FROM GOD

The best thing that happened at University Baptist was that several people from Hahn transferred to San Antonio. John Labash, Ken Leeburg, and Jerry Anderson were among them, and Jerry became my assistant pastor.

I wasn't happy that when the church started to grow, the people began planning to build. It was good we were growing, and building was the only option, but the idea of raising money for a building really got me down.

The death of the assistant pastor's baby daughter in Oregon had planted a seed of urgency in me, and people noticed it in my preaching.

Here I was, fast approaching my mid-thirties, and I hadn't found my niche. I felt like a square peg trying to fit into a round hole.

Ken Leeburg continued to encourage me. He believed God had His hand on my life and that I was destined to serve Him in a mighty way. I knew by now that mere obedience was what God wanted, but I wasn't even sure I was giving Him even that anymore. I knew there would be joy if I was in His will.

Late in 1982 Josif Tson came to speak at our church. At lunch one day he looked at me soberly. "Sammy, what has happened to you? Where is the young man who shook cities across Romania for the glory of God? Where is the young man who was afraid of nothing?"

I hung my head. "I don't know."

I was like Jonah, hiding from God. I wanted to go to Romania, to all the countries behind the Iron Curtain. But I still had not released from my grasp my own family. How could I take them? How could I risk Davey's health or take a young daughter so far away? What kind of husband subjects his wife to such an ordeal?

But still, my motivation was not really love and protection. It was fear. I didn't trust God to protect my family. I wanted to handle that myself.

Josif's words stung. I felt torn between the call of God and fear for my family.

I asked Tex to pray earnestly that I would get a word from God when I went to the Texas Baptist State Evangelism Conference in January of 1983. Fifteen thousand pastors, staff, and lay leaders would be there for spiritual refreshment and training. I told Tex, "I need God to do a work in my life."

When I arrived, still pierced by what Josif had said to me the month before, one of the first people I ran into was Manley Beasley. Warm and affectionate as usual—and unaware of my struggle--he said, "Sammy, God has uniquely gifted you. There's a call of God on your life. I don't know what it is, but I believe He still has something for you in Europe."

Arthur Blessitt spoke about people he had known on the front lines who were now on the shelf somewhere. Then I ran into an old friend who thought he was funny. He said, "Why, Sammy Tippit! Talk about a has-been who's been on the front lines and is now on the shelf!"

I was so agitated I was about to burst, but not because of the wisecrack. I felt on the verge of a serious decision. Should I resign my pastorate and get back out where I belonged? I'd like to believe the churches I've pastored have benefited from something I've given them from the Lord, but I fear they had to endure the deep water I was treading in my own life at the time.

I made my way up to the empty balcony of the huge civic center auditorium to be alone with God. My heart was heavy, and I felt a lump in my throat. I needed something, anything, some word from God. And who should walk in and sit down with his back to me but Arthur Blessitt. I hadn't spoken to him in years.

"Arthur," I said quietly.

He turned. "Sammy!" He quickly came to sit with me. "How are you doing, brother?"

"Not so well," I admitted, and I quickly brought him up to date.

"Sammy," he said, looking me dead in the eye, "I can count on the fingers of one hand the guys who have been courageous enough to go where you and I have gone. Lots of men are called to the pastorate, but not many can do what you've done. That's where you belong. I hear what you're saying about your son, but you know you have to give him to God."

We knelt and Arthur asked the Lord to make clear to me His direction and give me the courage to make the right decision, no matter how hard.

I sat thinking and praying until the great hall filled and Dr. Stephen Olford spoke on God asking Isaiah, "Who shall I send?" and Isaiah replying, "Here am I. Send me!"

During the invitation, I went forward and knelt, praying, *Here am I. Send me!*

There was no need to stay for the rest of the conference. At the airport I glanced into a restaurant, and there was another face from the past: Leo Humphrey of the New Orleans French Quarter.

I hurried in to greet him. Never one to hesitate to get to the point, he said, "I just brought Arthur to the airport, Sam, and he told me what you're going through. You know you've got to give your son to God, and you know I know what I'm talking about."

I sure did. Leo's own son, Kelly, was dying of cancer in his early twenties. "Leo," I said, "how do you deal with that? How can you travel with Kelly in the hospital?"

He told me that one day he was pacing the hospital corridor when his son called him in and asked why he wasn't following the Lord's leading to preach in Honduras. "I told him I was afraid. He asked me what I was afraid of—that he was going to die? I said of course.

"You know what he told me? He said, 'Dad, you've got to give me back to God and trust Him to take care of me.' Sam, it was the hardest thing I've ever had to do, but I gave Kelly back to God."

An hour before my flight, I found a secluded corner and just sat crying. On the plane I was still crying, and I'm sure people wondered about me.

As soon as I got home, I called my family together and told them everything. "I've got to give you all back to God," I said. "We need to go to Eastern Europe together." We knelt and committed each other to God.

A few weeks later I flew to New Orleans for Kelly Humphrey's funeral, a beautiful service where several people were saved. I came back with an even deeper sense of urgency.

I reestablished the board of God's Love in Action, putting layman Frank Corte on it with Morris Todd, John Labash, and Ken Leeburg. We began dreaming about getting back into Eastern Europe and especially Romania.

That summer (1983) I got a call from Sam Friend in Bothell, Washington, when I was about as ready as I could be to move on. He said, "I know what you're going through because I'm going through the same thing." He suggested I become co-pastor of his church and trade off covering for each other, one preaching while the other traveled in Europe.

It sounded good, but I worried about being the second man. "I've never been in that position, and I don't know how I'd function."

"That's going to have to be your call," Sam said. "But in my opinion, if you can't be an associate pastor, you have no business being senior pastor either."

That was the last nail in the coffin of my ego. I told Sam it would have to be only temporary. "My restlessness will make me want to get back into traveling and speaking full time."

I joined the church in November of 1983 and stayed two and a half years. It was good for me to sometimes disagree and keep my mouth shut. I handled Sunday evenings, counseling, and young marrieds, and I administered the church when Sam traveled.

My first major trip was set for the summer of 1984. We planned to go to East Germany, Poland, and then the beloved Romania. We would start at Hahn Baptist Church in West Germany, where Tex and Renee would stay until it was time for all of us to go to Romania. A major step for me was taking Dave for the first time.

Now almost fourteen, he would go with me into East Germany and Poland with a young student, Brent Saathoff; my former assistant pastor at Mt. Hood, Cork Erickson; and Don Shelton, then pastor of Hahn Baptist.

When we crossed the border from West Berlin to the East, I enjoyed reuniting with Pastor Schoch. But for me the Berlin stop was important for another reason. God seemed to burn into my mind two words: *availability* and *adaptability*. I sensed He was telling me to make that a hallmark of our ministry, especially in foreign cultures. I believe God has helped us avoid unnecessary conflict because of it.

We picked up Tex and Renee and headed back into Romania, where I hadn't been in three full years. I had served four churches and had been through deep waters. I believed God had broken me so I could be used for just such a ministry as this. I trusted Him with my family, but that trust would be sorely tested.

CHAPTER TWENTY-TWO

DANGER

Romanian border guards were stereotypical movie types—formal, pompous, strutting, and grim. Often we were detained for five to ten hours before being allowed through.

Sam Friend arranged with Dr. Nick Gheorghita and Paul Negrut to meet us just outside Oradea. We quickly transferred foodstuffs and gifts from our cars to theirs, wary of the Securitate. They scheduled us to preach in various churches and to meet secretly to disciple believers in the woods. That was the most dangerous of all because nationals were not to interact with foreigners without reporting it.

The first three nights I preached at the Second Baptist Church of Oradea, Renee began playing with a little girl from the family of Nelu Dronca, a lay leader from the First Baptist Church of Timisoara. He asked if I would preach in his church, and that started a relationship that knitted our hearts together over the years. Who knows if I would even have met this family had it not been for Renee.

Monday morning we headed toward a little village in the mountains where Dr. Nick had a shack in the woods. We were to meet several new college-age believers. It was illegal for them to get Christian training, especially from a foreigner, so this would be the most dangerous part of our trip.

At a prearranged time, we met Radu in the village, but we could not speak to him or appear to be with him. We passed him going the other way, and he said quietly, "Follow me to the edge of the village." We followed him into the foothills to the shack.

The college kids came by train and made their way in pairs through the trails to the cabin. If we were caught, we would be deported, and the students would likely lose their opportunity for education. We all could just as easily have gone to prison.

What a wonderful time we had with those kids!

Normally we ate at churches or in the homes of believers who saved their meager rations for months and fed us like royalty. They hardly ever ate with us but hovered over us, eager to meet our every need. In the U.S. we would have appeared to be taking advantage, but in Romania anything short of stuffing ourselves offended them.

In the mountains we ate what the people did, mostly onions and potatoes for every meal. It broke our hearts to see their meager rations and poor diet.

We did, however, feast on the Word of God, and they couldn't get enough. With Radu interpreting, then teaching others to do the same, we talked hour upon hour about how to witness, how to pray, how to argue for the faith. The fellowship was sweet.

One day one of the girls had a high fever, and we suggested that she go to a doctor and not climb the mountain for the secret meeting.

She absolutely refused. "I may never have this chance again. I wouldn't miss it."

The day before we were to leave, we were tossing a Frisbee with the kids when someone spotted men coming from the village.

Radu whispered urgently, "Say nothing in English. Don't let them hear your accents. I'll handle it."

When the men arrived, I was inside. Radu told the authorities he was with a group of friends and families, most of them young university students. They didn't demand to see passports or visas and didn't lecture anyone.

I had never really had such a close call. Seeing these kids freeze in fear reminded me that education, freedom, and lives were at stake.

That night we visited Pastor Peter Dugalescu in a small town called Haţeg. He would eventually move to a church in Timisoara and became a major player in the Romanian revolution, but when we met him he was a struggling pastor. About 150 people jammed into a church so small that the balcony looked as if it could fall at any time. Peter had petitioned for years for permission to add on to the church, but local authorities considered him a troublemaker. We found him jovial, full of humor and the joy of the Lord.

The next morning, we wedged ourselves into our little mountain shack with no electricity or running water and enjoyed with the students one of the most beautiful Communion services I have ever had. The Securitate walking in on that would have had all the evidence it would need to put us away.

We felt like the early church, meeting in secret, and we wept as we sang "You Are My Hiding Place" — softly so as to not attract attention.

Dave began feeling sick in the car on the way to Timisoara. By the time we covered the three-hour drive, he was in the throes of diarrhea and high fever. Nelu Dronca directed us to a Christian doctor, who told us what to feed him and to watch for dehydration.

At about two in the morning his temperature rose to 105, so we rushed him to the hospital—such as it was. I was heartsick. Only Tex was allowed in the room with him, and I chastised myself for ignoring my original fears. What kind of a father was I to subject to the dangers of a new culture a young boy who had suffered seizures for years?

Everything I had struggled with and thought I had come to terms with was coming to pass right before my eyes. My son lay in a pathetic facility where years later parents would see their children die from gunshot wounds at the hands of the Securitate. I couldn't know in 1984 that God was allowing me a foretaste of their grief and suffering. All I knew was that I felt I was to blame.

I got back to the hotel at about three in the morning and stayed awake all night, weeping and pleading with God to give my son some relief. I had given him to God, but I didn't want Dave to suffer like this.

At six A.M. I returned to the hospital to find he was not much better. I headed to the First Baptist Church to preach, and discovered that the pastor was so afraid of what the authorities would think about our being there that he didn't even show up.

The Lord laid on my heart a message from Philippians on joy in the midst of suffering. It was something I had studied and preached on in Bothell, but I sure didn't feel like talking about it just then.

Before the service I noticed that most of the people were crying. They would pray, and they would cry, pray and cry. "Radu," I said, "what is this?"

"Sammy, to these people, your coming is a miracle. They need revival. They have not seen anyone come to the Lord for years. They have never wept like this. They are deeply moved that you would bring your family and enter into their suffering with them. They are praying for your son and weeping for him."

That touched me. God was making me confront my every fear. Had I not been willing to bring Dave, their hearts would not have been softened by what had come upon him. They were ready for that message that morning, and God moved in a mighty way, knitting with ours the hearts of the people of that church.

I listened to my own sermon and stood on the promises of God! That service became a turning point for that church. Inviting a foreigner to speak and later holding a full-blown evangelistic crusade, the First Baptist Church would become a major force in Timisoara and play a key role in the revolution years later.

None of this would have happened had it not been for Renee and Dave coming with me. She had struck up the friendship with the daughter of the lay leader, and Dave's crisis had melted the hearts of the people. More than just another American preacher, I had been led of God to risk bringing my family, had suffered for it, and thus truly had identified with them.

After the service we went to the home of an opera singer for lunch. Dave had been released and was waiting for us, and he grew better from then on.

Before I left, we went back through Oradea, and I spent some time with Radu. Though only in his early twenties, I considered him a mature brother in the Lord." As someone who's been with me the whole time," I said, "give me a critique. What should I do to be more effective?"

In his direct Romanian way—which I expected and wanted—he said, "I have seen you teach, disciple, and preach, and though I believe you do them all well, you are gifted and anointed in preaching. Bring someone else in to do the other things. You preach."

I found that wise counsel and followed it. I emphasized the gift God has given me, and our ministry has been more effective for it.

Having again bonded with the believers in Romania, I couldn't wait to get back. A few months after our return to the States, I got a call October 5, 1984 from John Labash in San Antonio. He said, "I've got news about Ken Leeburg."

Ken was my best friend and had just a couple of weeks left in the military. He and his wife, Lyn, and their daughters were moving to a horse ranch he'd bought, and he was going to have time to travel with me. We had begun laying plans for him to go with me on our next international trip.

"What's up?" I asked John.

"Sam, you'd better sit down. I don't know how to say this. Ken's dead. He was killed in a wreck."

I could barely comprehend it. My friend, my encourager, the man who really knew my heart, was gone. And how?

John explained that Ken had been on his way back from his last assignment for the air force to start his private law practice and live on his new horse ranch. Ironically, he had been killed when he struck a horse with his car.

Our families had been close, our kids close in age. Tex and I flew all night to be with Lyn the next day.

She couldn't bring herself to identify the body alone and asked if I would go with her. I did, which was therapeutic for me, but I wish I could have been of more comfort to her. What could I say in my own grief? I know we're not to grieve as do those with no hope, and I know God is sovereign. But no platitudes apply when a man is cut down in the prime of life, a man who loved the Lord and served Him. Ken was the healthiest and strongest person I knew, a man with a vision for the world and for his family.

Lyn asked me to preach the funeral, and though I was honored and agreed to, I wasn't sure how I could get through it. But if his daughters could sing "Our God Reigns," I could manage a brief message.

We held the service in a tiny military chapel, packed with his colleagues. I told of Ken's urging me up and over and through the hill called Difficulty. One of the pallbearers told me he had never seen such faith and love in his life.

From the baby girl in Portland to Leo Humphrey's son, and now my best friend, I couldn't ignore the harsh truth: people are here one day and gone the next. It is the way of life. I had long ago accepted the task of trying to reach my generation with the claims of Christ. But now the urgency overwhelmed me.

The Bible says that today is the day, now is the accepted time. I may not have tomorrow to tell a lost person about Christ. I had come to grips with eternity for the first time.

Three months later Sam Friend and two associates were detained for several hours as they left Romania. Authorities found names and addresses of Romanian believers among their things, along with a note from a Romanian citizen to someone in the West.

Although they had done nothing illegal, they had fraternized with nationals and been active in churches. They were blacklisted, not allowed to return to the country.

The thought of never again seeing his beloved Romanian friends broke Sam's heart. I ached for him and also worried about my own trip planned for the summer of 1985.

Would I be allowed in?

Part Three — The Using

CHAPTER TWENTY-THREE

TITUS

We put together a singing group from our church, First Baptist in Bothell, Washington, and took them overseas in June. Besides my family and the singing group, I took Mike Mahan—who had been my associate pastor at Hahn, and Gary Maroney, a Portland, Oregon, pastor and longtime friend.

Gary is a big guy who border guards assumed was the group leader. That took a lot of pressure off me. We rented two vans, started in Hahn again, visited East Germany and Poland, and then went to Romania.

Our Poland visit put us so close to the Soviet Union that before the service we drove near the border, and I walked out into the night, praying, *Oh, God, someday, somehow let me reach those people for Christ.*

The Poles were especially sweet and seemed to take to us, but none of us knew Polish, and only their interpreter knew English, so it was almost impossible to communicate with them after the meeting.

We embraced and shook hands, murmuring words of peace and love in our own tongues and tried to communicate with our eyes and our smiles. Suddenly one of them began to sing an old hymn of the faith. We joined in English. What sweet fellowship, finally understanding what each other were saying through the lyrics to that song.

In East Germany I preached in a great old cathedral to two huge crowds of young people who met regularly to worship. I learned that two pastors had prayed for a year before the Communist Youth World Fest that someone would come and preach there.

These devout kids knocked on the pews when they heard something they liked. I was welcomed by loud knocking, and they interrupted my message often the same way.

I had given my son Dave back to God, but for some time I had been fretting over his spiritual temperature, wondering if he was really on fire for Jesus. Some of the kids in Karl Marx Stadt recognized him from the previous year. He got involved praying with them and being exposed to their enthusiasm for the Lord. I could see the love of Jesus growing in him, a real turning point in his spiritual life.

When it was finally time to drive across Hungary to Romania, the two vans headed to separate borders in the hope at least one would make it through. Those with me would try to get through a southern border, while the music group and a few others would cross at Oradea and head directly to the Second Baptist Church. We'd join them as soon as got through.

We got to our border midmorning, and when the guards found Bibles and Christian literature, they confiscated our twenty or so cassette tapes and began listening to them, looking for any hidden messages.

They found a birthday card I had translated into Romanian for Paul Negrut's daughter. That made them demand to know who we were going to see.

We sat for hours as the guards tore apart our van, and I learned a lesson, vowing I would never again attempt a border crossing without checking all the suitcases first myself.

It's a good thing the van was rented and insured, because everything that could be unscrewed or unsnapped was removed. The guards detached the quarter panels, tore out the gearshift, and unfastened the ceiling and floor panels. When they finished their search, they couldn't reassemble it.

Meanwhile, several of our people were strip-searched. I paced the small guard booth, hearing the familiar Christian songs coming from the tape player the guards were listening to.

One of the young men looked glum. I'd had to tell him to get rid of a prank tape he had made, which included a funny skit about being detained at the border.

"I'm sure glad you got rid of that tape," I said.

He looked away.

"What!" I said.

"Sam, I'm sorry. I forgot."

I couldn't believe it. I said, "Do you have any idea what's going on here? We're in so deep now with the birthday card and the other stuff they've found, there's no chance we're going to get in."

"I'm so sorry."

From the limited Romanian I could understand, it was obvious the authorities thought Gary Maroney was in charge. He was strip-searched and interrogated, and the team grew more solemn as the day passed. We finally quit looking at our watches and hoping we could make the service at Second Baptist. I was wracking my brain to come up with where we could go when they turned us away.

Then I got an idea. When I was sure no guards could hear, I told the others, "Let's pretend crossing the border doesn't mean a thing to us. Just have fun and look casual. In fact, let's scrub down the van. It's filthy.

We found a bucket and a faucet and got to it. The guards looked at us as if we were crazy. When we were finished, they put the vehicle up on a rack and removed the oil pan and everything else underneath that they could.

I believed they already had enough on us to justify turning us away.

Inside we invented games like football played with our fingers and a wad of paper. We whooped and hollered and laughed, and even the guards seemed amused.

We'd been at the border about eight hours before they finally determined that I was in charge. They asked me to come out to the van as they tried to reassemble it.

By this time they knew who we were and what we were about. I figured it couldn't get any worse, so I asked them in broken Romanian if they liked the music tape they'd listened to.

They said yes, and I told them it was about Jesus, how He was God's Son who had died for their sins and would come to live in their hearts if they asked Him to. They seemed very interested and full of questions.

As the hours dragged on, I knew the service at Second Baptist had long since ended. Finally, I was summoned to the guardhouse where a guard slid our passports across the desk and told me they were going to keep all our materials but that we would be allowed to enter the country.

I resolved never again to bring anything remotely suspicious to the border. Our mission was evangelism and revival, not smuggling. I'm not against anyone who does that, and I praise God for those who obey Him by doing it. But that was not our calling, and we had risked our ministry.

(When we got back to Bothell a few weeks later, one of Tex's praying friends told me, "While you were over there, God burdened me to pray for a border guard." Needless to say, she rejoiced at my report.)

When we finally reached Oradea, Nick and Paul said they'd worried all day wondering what had happened to us. But when we realized nothing had been heard from the other van—which was to cross the border right there in Oradea two days before, it was our turn to worry.

But all we could do was wait. There was no way to check on the others without drawing suspicion from the Securitate.

That Sunday morning after I spoke on revival at Second Baptist, a striking young man approached and spoke intensely. He quietly introduced himself as Titus Coltea, a medical doctor who had been vacationing with his wife, Gabriela, and their baby daughter at the Black Sea.

"We were having a good time," he said in precise but heavily accented English. "But the Lord gave me a deep impression that I was to return to Oradea to meet someone who would be very important in my life. That is why we are here. Sammy, my heart burns to see revival in Romania. I have been praying for it for fifteen years. Please, can I travel with you and learn more about revival? I can interpret for you."

One thing I needed was a bright, articulate translator who was both mobile and available. "I'd love that," I said, not knowing that Titus would soon become one of my dearest brothers in the world. "Let's see what Nick says."

Dr. Nick was enthusiastic and encouraged us. Titus immediately called pastors in the hinterlands, setting up meetings where outside speakers had never been heard. He told me of all the places he thought would be ripe for revival because they were off the beaten path. He was speaking my language. I had been called to the hard places, not just to big cities and successful churches where revival had already taken place.

From the moment we hit the road, I recognized in Titus a heart for God. He dedicated himself to the task, willing to sacrifice all for the sake of the Gospel. He asked question after question and made many good suggestions. He told me that Romanians have a commitment orientation. "If you preach about something today, when you come back a year later, they will still be doing what you said."

We decided I should challenge these small congregations to be people of prayer for the sake of reviving their country for God. Then we'd come back a year later and preach evangelistic crusades built on that prayer.

Titus became like a twin. He shouted when I shouted, whispered when I whispered, and gestured the way I did. If I misspoke, he would cover for me without making it obvious. After each meeting he critiqued my message and made suggestions, direct and blunt in the Romanian way. Throughout the years we have not always agreed on everything. Like  me, he is human and can be a Type A personality, but I have never questioned his heart, his motives, or his commitment.

Sometimes during the invitation, Titus would simply take over and plead with his countrymen on their own terms, beckoning them to receive Christ. That was fine with me, because it always seemed right for the occasion. Titus risked everything to become a minister of the Gospel, and he was an evangelist in his own right. How I grew to love him!

After preaching in several small towns, we gravitated to Cluj, a university town. Who should we meet up with there but the music group! They told me they had been turned away at the border because of their sound equipment. The guards believed they planned to sell it in country. "You told us never to give up, Sammy," they said, "so we drove back out, stored our equipment, rented another van, and tried another border."

After Cluj we had a four-day meeting lined up with our dear friends at First Baptist in Timisoara. My family and I had looked forward to that for a year after the people had rallied around us and bonded with us over Dave's illness. He was healthy this trip.

I was thrilled to have Titus with me, especially because on the first night the fearful pastor was again absent. Dave gave his testimony, and the people wept. It was great to fellowship with the Dronca family again.

The pastor attended the second night, but the next day he invited us to a picnic lunch deep in the woods where no one would see us.

"What you're doing is dangerous," he said. "There will be problems from this."

I didn't try to correct him, though I politely disagreed. I told him I had once been paralyzed with fear for my family but that when I trusted God to take care of them, He blessed our ministry even more.

One day in Timisoara I was secretly introduced to a man named Buni Cocar. As a pastor, he defied authorities by expanding his church. Now he was on the run and hadn't seen his family for some time. "I have been living in hiding, Sammy. Could you help me?"

I promised I would do what I could, aware that many Americans make such promises and promptly forget them. I decided to follow through. I didn't know how successful I would be, but I would try.

In Romania crowds tend to get bigger every night, and the next night about fifteen hundred crowded the church, the balcony, the courtyard, even the street. But for some reason nothing seemed to click for me. I felt no freedom as I spoke, and though Titus clearly noticed, he couldn't help either.

Here was a big, enthusiastic, sympathetic crowd, and we had a message for them, but I didn't really know exactly what it was. I spoke a line and prayed while Titus translated. Then he would pray while listening to the next line, but we weren't flowing.

Finally, I stopped. "Folks," I said, "for some reason I don't feel God wants me to finish this message. I feel led to just share with you the Word of God."

I began to recite verses and passages God brought to mind, without commentary. It was then that I learned how much of a man of the Word Titus really was. I could tell he had to be in the Bible regularly, because as soon as I would start a verse, he would translate it.

Suddenly we were humming like a well-oiled machine. I would step forward and shout out a verse, and he would translate it and be ready for the next. It seemed he even knew exactly where I was going and what would come next.

Titus and I simply quoted the Word as the Lord led, back and forth, back and forth, rapid-fire and with conviction. The Spirit fell heavy on that place, and people began to weep as they basked in God's truth. Emotion rose in my throat as I continued, mirrored by Titus.

The message consisted entirely of Scripture, leading to passages on the need for salvation and how to receive Christ. Hundreds came forward to accept Him.

Scriptures

Nothing is so powerful as the unadorned Word of God. He promises that His Word will not return to Him void. No preaching, no matter how anointed, can match the sheer impact of Scripture.

I had never in my life been in a service like that, and I'll never forget it. We need to allow the Bible to speak for itself more often.

When it was over, the pastor pulled me into his office and stood there in tears. "Tonight was for me," he said over and over. "My life will never be the same. The fear is gone."

We left to head back to the West, but the people lined the street and shouted to the glory of God, praying and weeping and singing. It took about half an hour just to get our van down the block.

Outside Arad we dropped off Titus, who had to change clothes in the dark and take a train back to Oradea. He and I were bound by that divine experience, and it remains one of our sweetest memories. That was the beginning of God thrusting us throughout the nation of Romania in a mighty way.

CHAPTER TWENTY-FOUR

CLOAK AND DAGGER

Not long after we returned to the States, I got a call from an old high school classmate, Woody Jenkins, a member of the Louisiana House of Representatives. A Christian active in evangelical concerns, after reading some of my books, he reestablished contact with me. Now, he introduced me by phone to David Funderbirk, recently resigned U.S. ambassador to Romania.

Funderbirk had resigned after a vain attempt to end the United States' favored-nation trade status with Romania. He had told the President, Congress, and the State Department that Ceausescu regime atrocities must not be ignored. Eventually his efforts would succeed, but at the time we spoke, he was still lobbying.

I told him of Buni Cocar and asked for any help he might be able to give. He encouraged me to contact the U.S. embassy in Bucharest. "It's important that they know you and that they know when you are in the country. What you are doing is dangerous."

I told him that I tried to avoid the political arena and that I traveled to Romania as an ambassador of Jesus Christ, not of the United States. Mr. Funderbirk insisted it was still a good idea to stay in close touch with U.S. representatives over there. "You'll in no way compromise your own mission. And if I you're not protected and are arrested for any reason, you would likely be charged as a spy and could simply disappear, never to be heard from again."

That got my attention. I assured him I wanted to make it clear I was there on a mission for Christ. Our ministry would not exchange money on the black market. If we got into trouble, it would be for preaching the Gospel, not for breaking the law.

In January of 1986 I coordinated my return to Romania with both evangelist Barry Wood and pastor Jon Randles of Graham, Texas. Barry and Jon had been with Sam Friend the year before.

The three of us took different traveling companions and staggered our arrival dates so as to be careful not to draw attention to each other and all get deported at the same time.

Randles planned to land in Bucharest January 1. I would come in on the 2nd, and Wood would come a few days later. I didn't realize Randles had not made it in. His blacklisting was in the system, as authorities had warned. Fred Gough, a former professional football player, traveled with Randles, but they didn't go through the line together, and he was allowed in. But it was his first time in the country, so he knew no one, didn't know the language, and could only try to contact people he had heard about from Randles.

Frank Corte, of our board, and Don Shelton, by then pastor of Hahn Baptist, went in with me January 2 without incident.

Pastor Vasile Talos led us to his church where I was to preach. Meanwhile, Fred Gough had found the church. The people knew an American was coming to preach, so they asked him about his message.

"I'm not the speaker," he said. "I don't have a message."

"Praise the Lord, He will give you one!"

Fred panicked, afraid and alone in a strange country, unable to make himself understood. He feared for his freedom, knowing he was probably being watched by the Securitate.

Just then the door flew open, and in I walked wearing a long, black coat that looked to Fred like Securitate. He breathed a huge sigh of relief when he realized I was an American and was *really* relieved to find I was the speaker!

Fred and I hit it off right away. I admired him for coming in on his own when many others would have given up and left immediately. I advised him to take off his rings and not put his hands in his pockets while speaking, and he gave his testimony that night. Westerners appear to be showing off their wealth with even simple jewelry, and to the Romanians, hands in the pockets is a sign of dishonesty.

Fred

The next morning Fred went to the U.S. embassy to check on Jon Randles, who had been deported to Budapest. Fred said he had told the embassy personnel about me and that they wanted to meet me. Had it not been for my phone conversation with former Ambassador Funderbirk, I would not have been happy about that. I planned to be extremely careful.

I was escorted to Funderbirk's former office, and the U.S. operatives began asking questions. "Let me ask you something before we go any further," I interrupted. "Is it safe to talk here?" I didn't want them asking me about key people in the country unless they could assure me we weren't being bugged.

"This is as safe as any place in Romania," they said, eyebrows raised. That was all I needed to hear. That meant it wasn't safe at all.

"Well," I said quietly, "the conversation basically ends here." I wasn't about to compromise my friends.

"Come with us," one said, rising.

We moved to another area, where they punched a button and a fake wall slid open to a state-of-the-art soundproof room. What in the world I had gotten myself into? We sat at a table, and they said, "It's safe to talk here."

They told me all that had happened with Randles, and they also repeated what Funderbirk had said: that I could disappear and never be heard from again.

They told me the Romanians were as sophisticated as the Soviets in their bugging devices and warned me not to trust any public place, hotel room, or restaurant. "The woods are the safest."

They told me the microphone in a hotel room could be in the ashtray, the TV, the phone, or even behind a picture. "They might even sit outside in a car with a directional microphone pointed at the window."

We learned to talk about our friends only by their initials whenever we were indoors.

Embassy officials asked us to keep them informed of our itinerary, and they offered to help if we suffered any oppression or persecution. I wondered if I had done the right thing by even talking with them, and I worried about Barry Wood who was scheduled to arrive that day.

I drove to the airport and watched as Barry approached passport control. I caught his eye but we were careful not to try to communicate. While others were admitted and headed to baggage claim, Barry was pulled off to the side. When he looked away from my gaze, I knew it was bad news.

I preached that night and visited the U.S. embassy again in the morning to report what I had seen at the airport. They traced Barry to Budapest.

Knowing Tex would be worried, I called her from Fred's room at the Hotel Intercontinental, and we spoke in code. I told her I had arrived safely and that the weather in Bucharest was beautiful. "We're enjoying the scenery and meeting a lot of new friends." That meant that I had been to the churches and gotten reacquainted with our friends.

I about had a heart attack when I got a seventy-dollar bill for that two-minute call!

That night after I preached in Bucharest, Nelu Dronca arrived. He had taken off work to make the eight-hour trip from Timisoara just to talk to me for a few minutes. He said, "I knew if I came all this way, you would not be able to say no to me. You must come to see us and preach to us in Timisoara on this trip."

"You're right, brother," I said. "I couldn't tell you no. I'll work it out somehow, and I will be there."

We embraced, and he hurried out to catch the train back so he could be home by morning.

Back in Oradea Dr. Nick admonished me for having spent too much time in small churches in the dangerous areas the last time I was in Romania. "You risk too much by going to where the churches are small and the work difficult."

I told him, "Look, you have to understand I'm not a rich American. I'm just one little guy. People who support me know I'm not going to sit around in the big cities and wait for events at the large churches. I come to minister, and too many cities here have never had an evangelist come and preach the Gospel. I would violate the trust of the people behind me if I didn't do that."

"But your ministry is so valuable. Do you want to risk that?"

"My ministry is nothing. Obedience is everything. I'm risk-oriented. For me, it's about faith. My whole life has been going where very few people go."

At a small church in Galati the year before, one of the men asked why I was the first preacher from the West to visit his town. "Why haven't you ever been here before?"

I accepted the rebuke, not knowing what to say. Oradea is a great city with a wonderful church close to my heart. But there were needier places, places just as important, where persecuted people struggled. Many of the most well-known preachers in the world had spoken in Oradea. Who would go to the hard places?

Not many interpreters were available in the small, out-of-the-way places, which was why it was so important that Titus go with me. Nick implied that I should minister to Oradea and let them take the message to the rest of the country. But when I asked the people elsewhere whether ministers from Oradea came there, they said, "No."

I apologized for having been insensitive to Nick, and by the end of our discussion I believe he understood that I could not be restricted from preaching to the small churches in difficult areas.

After we cleared the air, I felt much more freedom to preach the rest of the campaign in Oradea. On Thursday night the daughter of a local Securitate commander risked everything to receive Christ.

Afterward one of the church leaders asked me if the Lord had worked that night. I told him the place had been full, many were saved—including the daughter of the Securitate official, and many more rededicated their lives. "Weren't you there?" I said.

"Oh, no. I was with a hundred other men in a prayer room. In another room a hundred women were praying."

I firmly believe that was the reason the Lord had, indeed, worked.

Prayer

I enjoyed many hours of discussion and debate with Titus and Radu. I loved discussing strategy with them. Radu was intrigued by the concept of humility being a basis for revival, according to 2 Chronicles 7:14. "I find humility elusive," he said. "Once you know you have it, you have lost it." To him, true humility was really seeing God for who He was and seeing yourself in comparison.

I loved preaching and being with Romanian believers, but, boy, those trips were draining. Don Shelton, Frank Corte, and I preached twenty-seven times in twelve days, sometimes four services in one day. The Romanians didn't allow us to get to bed at a reasonable hour because feeding guests is part of their spiritual gift of hospitality, and the biggest meal of the day comes late at night after the services.

I was spending myself, but what better, more fulfilling way to be used up than for Jesus?

CHAPTER TWENTY-FIVE

MAKING THE BREAK

When I got back to the States, I told Tex, "No doubt it's time to leave the church. I've got to go full time."

Despite all God had taught me about trusting Him, I admit my biggest hurdle was money. I had lived by faith before, but now I was used to eight years as a pastor, where the salary may not have been lucrative but it was steady. My kids were growing up and had more needs. Would my income be enough?

Throughout the years, people who had supported me before I took my first church had slipped from our list. We kept in touch with about five hundred through an occasional newsletter, but we didn't want, need, or seek financial support. For international trips, I used the love offerings from my occasional outside speaking engagements in the United States.

Then one day, in response to news that we were planning another overseas trip, an old acquaintance sent us a note and a pledge of fifty dollars a month. Tex said that with that check the Lord breathed faith into her heart for our future. I said, "Honey, you understand fifty dollars is not going to do it."

"Sammy," she said, "God is going to touch other people's hearts just like this."

She was right.

Sam Friend was great about our decision. That church has been behind us all the way. We moved back to San Antonio on June 20, 1986, and left for Europe ten days later. Collynn Wood, evangelist Barry's daughter, became an important member of the traveling team, as did several others. Joe Davis, a newcomer from Jon Randles' church in Graham, Texas, became a frequent companion overseas.

A highlight of the trip was returning to Bratislava, Czechoslovakia, where I had visited following the Communist Youth World Fest years before. Now I was given the name of a godly old man from the Brethren Church, a man who had been imprisoned for five years for trying to share his faith publicly.

What a blessed time of fellowship we enjoyed with this godly man of prayer! I didn't understand Czech or Slovakian, so he spoke to me

151

in German. He pointed to a huge soccer stadium and said, "I am praying that one day we will preach the Gospel in that stadium."

I smiled and nodded, but I had so little faith that I thought, *Not likely in your lifetime. Or mine.* It was an honorable dream, but it wasn't going to happen without a miracle.

The old man continued, "Many come to my country to make a big fire for God. I don't want to make a big fire. I want to be consumed by God's fire. And when I am ashes, then I will see His glory."

I just nodded and bowed my head, so moved I could not speak.

Titus and Radu organized a Romanian singing group to travel with us so we wouldn't have to bring more people from the States. To qualify, the singers were required to memorize all of James, 1 Peter, and 1 John. When they performed, they sang a song, quoted a chapter, and so forth. It was a thrill to be involved with kids so committed to the Lord.

In the town of Constanza one morning, Dave and I played some local young people in basketball, a good witnessing opportunity. After the game we headed to the beach where we were to meet Tex and ten-year-old Renee at noon. A huge crowd had gathered out on the boulevard, but I couldn't see what was going on. A young Romanian came running. "Sammy! It's Renee!"

Dave and I took off running and found Tex in the middle of the crowd, huddled over Renee, comforting her and praying for her. She had been hit by a car and had a huge bump on her head and was bleeding. Tex would not let anyone else put Renee in an ambulance because we had heard that Christians mysteriously died in Romanian hospitals.

I lifted Renee into the ambulance and climbed in with her, telling Tex to meet me at the hospital. Renee kept sobbing, "Daddy, I don't want to die." As if to be sure she wasn't losing her mind or even her memory, she said, "My name is Renee Tippit, and I'm ten years old and I have Jesus in my heart. Daddy, I don't want to die. I want to grow up and be a singer and come back to Romania and sing about Jesus."

It was all I could do to fight back my own panic and tears to tell her she would be all right. After X rays and an examination, I was told that Renee would have to stay a few days, which made me nervous. I knew Tex would insist on staying with her, but where was she? Renee and I sang, prayed, and quoted Scripture together until Tex and the others arrived.

Tex was upset because a local policeman had impounded our car—though it had nothing to do with the accident—had confiscated Tex's passport, and was threatening to imprison her for six months for being a neglectful parent!

When Renee seemed stable, we asked Collynn Wood to stay with her while Tex and I went to the police station. Through our interpreter, I told the policeman that if he didn't return our car and Tex's passport and stop threatening ridiculous punishment for what was clearly an accident, I would complain to the U.S. embassy and have his job.

Our interpreter refused to translate that, so Tex took over and shared her faith while pleading for her passport. The situation became calmer, but still he held her passport. And the threat of prison still hung over her head.

In the shower before the meeting, I dropped the soap, and while picking it up I banged my head on the soap dish sticking out of the wall. I slid to the floor crying. I had lost all hope. "God, I came here for You," I said. "Why are You letting this happen? What's going on?"

After I dropped Tex off at the hospital, I went to the church where Titus and Radu waited for me in the pastor's study. When they reached out to comfort and pray for me, I broke down. "Guys," I said, "I can't preach. I'm in too much turmoil. There's no way." Radu and Titus said they were going to find a place to pray for me, and they left.

Alone with the Lord, knowing my dear brothers were praying that He would raise me up, I got some understanding of the fatherhood of God. My heart hurt so much for Renee that I would have traded places with her in a second. But God had given His own Son, *knowing* He would die.

I had needed to give Dave back to the Lord the previous year. I thought I had given Tex and Renee back to Him, too, but now I faced the real test. What if Tex went to prison and Renee did not survive? I knew I had to get to where I was really willing to entrust them to Him alone. This was beyond my control.

"God, they're Yours," I said, sobbing. "You're our only hope."

God's supernatural peace washed over me, and I sensed He wanted me to speak that evening on how to stand under pressure. Anything on that subject would have to come from Him, and I would have to be totally honest and vulnerable.

That evening I told the people everything, from seeing my ten-year-old daughter lying in the street to banging my head on the soap dish. They wept and prayed for Renee. Many came to Christ, and many more recommitted themselves to Him.

Near the end of the service I was handed a note, which I joyfully read to the people. It was from Tex and read, "Sammy, Renee is okay. She's out of the hospital, and we're back at the hotel."

On my way out of the service a woman professor met me, her daughters in tow. "At noon my family and I were having lunch," she said, "and we were deeply burdened to pray for your family because something was wrong."

Back at the hotel, I learned that Tex's passport had been returned and the car released. Glory to God!

It seemed that on every trip I had to learn hard lessons about myself and the faithfulness of God. In November, when we went back, we visited Titus and Gabi at their humble apartment. It was tiny even by Romanian standards but minuscule compared to the homes of medical doctors in the West.

We were careful not to speak English outside. If anyone reported Westerners visiting the Colteas, Titus and Gabi would be in trouble. When Gabi opened the door, she looked as if she had seen a ghost and threw her arms around my neck. How great to see her and Titus!

We spoke to a crowd of three thousand at Second Baptist in Oradea, though the power was out and the place was lit only by candles. In Bucharest, we held a secret training session for area pastors in the basement of a church. Every time someone walked by we fell silent and the pastors looked at each other in fear. Yet every day they took copious notes and enjoyed warm fellowship in the Lord. These poor men wore their only suit of clothes day after day, grateful for training in the Word, which they hadn't had in years.

I met again with officials at the American embassy, and one of them walked me back to the Hotel Intercontinental. "Keep your eyes straight ahead," he said, "and don't change your expression while I talk. I am a Christian, too, and I have a safe, guaranteed way of getting books into the country." He handed me a paper with the instructions.

I asked how many we could ship in, because the pastors need commentaries and Bible study aids.

"All you want."

We took advantage of that, shipping in box after box of books.

In Galati, we ran into a bizarre situation. Two deacons stood at the entrance to the church telling any they knew to be Christians that they were to stand and listen outside. The church was full of unbelievers and seekers. Josef Stephanuti, the pastor, arrived a little late one evening and couldn't get in himself! He had to stand outside in the bitter cold with the rest.

Pastor Stephanuti was one of the sweetest men I have ever met, soft-spoken and godly with a beautiful, warm smile. He and his family lived in an apartment in a neighboring town, crammed into three tiny rooms with an outside kitchen and no indoor plumbing. His church's application to build him new living quarters languished for years.

After we ministered at his church, he was informed he would never receive permission to enlarge his living area. "Brother Stephanuti," I said, "I'm so sorry. Had I known, I would not have come."

"Oh, Sammy, no, no," he said. "If just one person had come to Jesus Christ, it would have been worth it. And look at all who came! I can live like this the rest of my life."

Stephanuti

Titus had to be careful in every city, unable to stay at any hotels and he could not appear to be with us, other than in the churches. One day he realized he was being followed. He couldn't have the ruthless Securitate find out what he was translating, who he was with, or where he was staying. We would all be in trouble.

He prayed and prayed about what to do and felt the Lord saying to him, "Turn around, and face your fear." So Titus turned around and looked directly at his follower. Obviously disconcerted, the man looked away. When he looked back, Titus was still staring him full in the face. The man turned and walked away, so Titus followed him all over town until the man finally eluded him. Titus was not followed again.

The Cross

Galati overlooks the Danube, across from the Soviet Union, so after we ministered each night, the team and Titus and I bundled up and walked down by the river. I looked across the border and wept and prayed the Lord would one day send me to the Soviet Union to proclaim His Gospel.

Titus too had a burden for that vast nation, because it had long been the center for atheism and socialism. All the Eastern European Communist countries fell under its domain, and he longed to see God do a mighty work there. But his main burden was for his own country.

One night as we walked, he fell prostrate on the frozen ground, his face in the dirt, and prayed, "Oh, God, if it takes the blood of the martyrs to bring my people to Jesus, let me be the first to offer my blood."

I had never heard a man pray like that before, and it shook me to my core. Eventually it *would* take the blood of martyrs in Timisoara when the great revolution began.

My dream of reentering the Soviet Union came closer to reality when Pastor Stephanuti gave me the name and number of his friends in Kishinev, capital of the Soviet Republic of Moldavia.

"You need to preach there," he said.

There was nothing I wanted to do more.

CHAPTER TWENTY-SIX

MY GLIMPSE OF MORTALITY

I got word late in 1986 that Pastor Josef Stephanuti had arranged for me to meet with a key person in the Kishinev church. The opportunity to revisit the Soviet Union, after having been deported from there as a young evangelist, was a dream come true.

Fred Gough and a man named Jerry Cadenhead and I flew into Kishinev in Soviet Moldavia in February of 1987. We soon became convinced the authorities were well aware of us and our mission from the beginning.

We were met at the plane by Intourist and assigned a tour guide. As soon as we could politely shake the guy, I wanted to contact the man Stephanuti had told me about. We decided I should make my call from a pay phone to avoid any bugs in the hotel.

I ventured into a raging blizzard to a pay phone in front of the hotel. I needed to know I was talking to a Christian, so when he answered, I said, *"Pace* [PAH-chay; Peace]."

He responded: *"Pace Domnului Isus Kristos* [The peace of the Lord Jesus Christ]."

I immediately said in Romanian, "Good to talk with you, brother. Stephanuti gave me your name and said I should get in touch with you."

With that the phone went dead, and I knew we were being hassled by the secret police. I dialed back immediately and the man said, "I will meet you in front of the hotel in one hour. Wait out by the street."

Fred and Jerry and I waited outside much longer than an hour, and Fred finally said he had to go in and get warm.

Later, he told me the lobby began to fill with what looked plainclothes secret police. None approached the desk clerk or seemed to have anything to do there. A man walked past Fred and whispered in English, "I'm here, but I cannot talk to you now."

Meanwhile, the cold got to me too, so I asked Jerry to continue to wait while I went inside. I sat next to Fred, and without looking at me he said, "Our guy is here. I can't point him out to you, but look around. What do you see?"

"Police," I said.

"They weren't here when I arrived. We need to get out of here."

So in the middle of that blizzard we met up with Jerry and took a walk through the city. Forty-five minutes later we returned to an empty lobby. The woman at the desk said, "Your friend was here. He said he was late but that he would be back at seven."

That's when I knew that the first guy had been secret police. The second might have been, too, but we would have to see who showed up at seven.

When we came down later, Fred didn't recognize either of two elderly men in the lobby. But one kept looking at me.

I walked past him and murmured, *"Pace."*

"Pace Domnului," he said.

I hurried back to Fred. "That's not the guy who said he was here to see us?"

"Nope."

The man approached. "I have nothing to hide. I'll talk in front of anyone." He seemed both nervous and bold. We enjoyed an hour of fellowship, ending in his inviting me to preach in his church.

I did, and though the response was good, the translation was not. I wanted to come back and preach under better circumstances. Native Moldavians are of Romanian heritage, so many speak Romanian, meaning we would need two interpreters.

When we returned to the States, my book *Fire in Your Heart* was released. I took a couple of boxes with me to Singapore '87, a conference for emerging Christian leaders, and that resulted in my networking with other evangelicals all over the world. My ministry began to broaden, and it would never be the same.

I was excited about an opportunity Dave had to go to Kenya and share his faith while playing basketball. I counseled him on how to use the *Four Spiritual Laws* and told him I was praying he would be able to lead someone to Christ. He said, "Dad, I'm only sixteen. That's kind of unlikely."

After the trip he met us in Europe to go into Romania, and we were thrilled to hear he had, indeed, led his first soul to Christ. In fact, he had led twelve!

Titus told me we had been invited to a tiny church in an out-of-the-way town, but I told him it was impossible because I was committed in Bucharest. He said the pastor in Bucharest had released me, "so it's your decision, Sammy."

We stopped and prayed about it and both felt peace that we should go. I had long since learned not to question the leading of the Lord in these matters. If I had passed this up, I would have missed out on a huge blessing.

We drove to the town and found a hundred people jammed in a place no bigger than a typical American bedroom. Others stood outside. I preached, several came to Christ, and I was grateful for the opportunity. But afterward I found out this had been anything but a typical service. An elderly woman ran up to me and began speaking so quickly in Romanian that I needed Titus to translate for me.

She said, "I have not been inside a church for twenty-five years. But last night I dreamt two strangers would be here who I must come and see. When I came in, there you were, the ones from my dream. My son and I gave our hearts to Jesus."

At another small church I asked the people to pray about whom God would have them bring to the services the next night. One of the deacons told me, "I felt led to invite a neighbor who had never been to church. When I went to ask him, he was sitting there dressed and ready to go. He told me he felt like he should get ready to go somewhere, but he didn't know where. But the feeling was so strong, he did it. Then I showed up and brought him to church. He became a Christian tonight."

I had never seen God work in such ways, but you never know what might happen on the front lines. When we were invited to yet another tiny church in Comanesti, I couldn't refuse. Again the building was more like a small room, and four times as many people stood outside. The pastor said it would make more sense to hold the meeting outside, and I agreed.

Titus pulled me aside. "Sammy, it's against the law to preach outside. We could all go to prison. I'm not saying we shouldn't, but we need to know if it's God's will."

So we prayed about it. Again, both of us felt peace.

As soon as we started, people began coming from the high-rise apartment buildings nearby. They filled the courtyard and the street. People climbed trees and sat atop garages. About two thousand gathered for the service, and a couple of hundred prayed to

God's Glory

receive Christ.

We did the same thing the next night, and the pastor told us more people came to Christ in those two nights than in the previous ten years. The church tripled in size, and they were forced to build. Just before the Romanian revolution, that pastor and his four deacons were sentenced to eight years in prison (later reduced to house arrest).

When we got back to Bucharest, we went to the U.S. embassy to retrieve the books we had shipped in through our secret contact. Three of us entered with huge sports bags and left with them weighed down with books. Our bags were checked on the way in but not on the way out.

Our contact person told us, "If you get caught with these, I'll deny ever having contact with you, and I'll not be able to help you."

We kept those books with us everywhere we went. One night we stored them in a church, and our van was broken into. Eventually, a set was sent to Titus, another to Radu, and another to a man in Arad. What a thrill to be able to provide these ministry tools.

During 1987 the Lord let me hear from several people who had come to Him through my ministry throughout the years. I was grateful God had sent them back my way. Coming up on my fortieth birthday, it was wonderful to know that I had had a part in someone coming to Christ.

When I spoke at a church in Oklahoma, the minister of music introduced me, in tears, saying, "Twenty years ago a young man came to the city where I was reared. I gave my heart to Christ through his preaching. I have not seen that man since that day. But he will speak to us now."

A letter to the editor of *Moody Magazine* referred to an article about me and said, "In 1970, I was a seventeen-year-old girl from Monroe, Louisiana, when I met Sammy and Tex on their way to Washington. Their freedom to love and worship God changed my life."

A thirty-year-old from New Orleans wrote to say that both he and his wife were saved as children in different meetings and in different towns before they met, both under my preaching.

I pray that twenty years from now, people from all over the world will have that same testimony. To me it's a glimpse of heaven to learn of the children God the Father has allowed me to help bring to Jesus.

When one of my mentor-encouragers, Mike Gilchrist, asked if I would be willing to minister with him in South Africa in August of 1987, I put it on my schedule immediately. Besides being eager to work alongside Mike, I was curious to see what God was doing in other parts of the world. I saw this as a rare opportunity.

Meanwhile, Tex had a surprise party for me on my fortieth birthday, July 27, 1987. Plenty of friends enjoyed telling me I was over the hill, that I should rest in peace, or that I had one foot in the grave and the other on a banana peel. But, in reality, with all the traveling and working out and jogging I did, I was in unusually good shape for my age. With the Africa trip looming, however, I thought it would be a good idea to get a complete checkup.

I went to the doctor expecting a pat on the back for being in such good shape at my age. He drew some blood, looked me over, asked a few questions, and left the room. When he returned, he looked concerned.

"Sammy," he said, "a couple of things: You've got high cholesterol, well over 250. Further, are you aware of the mole in the middle of your back?"

"No."

"It's large, and of the four signs that a mole is developing into melanoma, you have three."

He was moving too fast "Whoa," I said. "What does that mean?"

"There's no cure and no therapy for melanoma. It cannot be treated with radiation. The only hope is surgery."

"What kind?"

"First, we have to do a biopsy. If it is cancerous, we will remove a large area to be sure we get all the seedlings so it can't spread."

"And if it does?"

"You could be dead in two years."

I told him I was leaving the next day for a speaking engagement in Kansas City, then two weeks later flying to South Africa.

"We can do the biopsy immediately, but if the results indicate the need for removal, you would not be comfortable flying to Africa. We'd perform the operation as soon as possible, and it would require a skin graft."

Of course I needed time to pray about this and discuss it with Tex. "But one thing I know for sure," I told the doctor. "I will go to Africa anyway. I can put up with a little pain for a two-day flight."

"That's a hard trip."

"I know, but if it won't make things worse, I still want to go."

He performed the biopsy and told me he would get the results in five days.

Tex went with me to Kansas City, and we had our afternoons free. Needless to say, we spent every spare minute walking and talking and praying.

"I'm having a rough time with this," she admitted. "I have to think you could handle this better if you risked losing *me.*"

We talked about would happen with our insurance, the kids, the house, even whether she should remarry. It was morbid, but it had to be discussed. For me the biggest problem was not knowing. I believed I could resign myself to it if necessary, and I was determined to change nothing. I had always said I was willing to give my life in service to the Lord, so I would not slow down until I had to. I would continue to preach, and if I was gone in a couple of years, Tex should continue her ministry.

She said she couldn't imagine remarrying. She also felt strongly that if I needed surgery I should not go to Africa. But I remained convinced that unless it hampered my recovery, I would not let discomfort stand in my way.

I was still in shock, but evaluating our life priorities was a good thing. We wanted always to live as if we were going to die soon.

We learned the mole was in a pre-melanoma state, so it was removed with relatively minor surgery. I also had one removed from behind my left ear, just to be safe, and even now I continue to have regular checkups.

Scary and sobering as that episode was, it led to deep reflection and introspection, and I believe our lives, our marriage, and our ministries became better for it.

My mother also kept us on our knees. She accused me of abusing Dave and Renee by taking them to dangerous places. When we visited her, she had my dad's sister and brother, a retired pastor, come to straighten me out.

However, my aunt and uncle were very gracious. They asked about our ministry and seemed pleased. When they left, Mom yelled at me and called Tex horrible names. "Mom, you can scream at me, but I can't allow you to speak to Tex that way."

She told us to leave, and my heart broke.

In South Africa in August of 1987 I was one of three speakers at the well-attended pastors' conference. Mike Gilchrest and a national evangelist were the others.

While we were in Cape Town, I spoke in the afternoons. Not being known or in demand there allowed me time to get alone with God. I went out to a rock overlooking the Indian Ocean every evening to enjoy the sunset and simply listen to God. I had long taught that true prayer was not necessarily talking to God but just enjoying intimacy with Him. On those precious days during those wonderful hours I simply adored the Lord and let Him speak to my spirit in His quiet way. There I was, at the southern tip of Africa, knowing that the same God who had been with me in Eastern Europe was with me there. I meditated on His greatness, and I know now that He was preparing me for a most unusual encounter with Him.

On a Wednesday afternoon I addressed pastors and church leaders of all races who had come from all over South Africa, hungering for a touch from God. I preached on prayer, what it was and what it wasn't.

This was not an unusual service at first—as much teaching as preaching. In fact, Mike had to leave in the middle to help an ailing pastor, and when he returned he was surprised to see what had taken place.

I didn't give any type of altar call. I simply asked the conferees to sing "We Exalt Thee" as we closed. All I can say is that the Spirit of the Lord fell on the place. While they sang, some stood, some knelt, some laid on the floor. Most wept as they sang and prayed. People confessed sin and were restored to God and each other. This went on for at least forty-five minutes, and when one of the hosts announced it was time to go to dinner, no one left. Husbands and wives reconciled, and people all over the room prayed together.

Thirty minutes later the host again tried in vain to dismiss the group, but only much, much later did it finally break up. I felt privileged to have been a part of such a special, holy time.

One of the best experiences in South Africa was meeting national evangelist Malvory Peffer. This precious brother became a member of our staff, heading our efforts in that nation.

I never doubted God was just as much at work in other areas of the world as He was in Europe, but it was great to experience it firsthand. I believe God was getting me ready to send me out to other continents as well. I didn't know my schedule would allow such far-flung efforts, but, of course, He did.

CHAPTER TWENTY-SEVEN

BLACKLISTED

I should have known things in Romania were approaching a breaking point. On our January 1988 trip Tex and I were accompanied by board member Chuck Hollimon and his wife, Nancy, and my new associate evangelist, Brent Saathoff. We stuffed our van with food and supplies for the believers, but when it broke down outside Budapest, we had to leave it and most of the stuff and rent a car.

That worked out for the best because when we got to the Romanian border, we found the guards either heavily taxing or turning away people bringing in supplies.

During our last night in Timisoara, someone broke into the car and stole only the rental documents. It must have been the Securitate because those papers were worth nothing to anyone but us. We needed them to get out of the country.

By that time I was going on very little sleep, and teaching during the day, preaching every evening, and staying up to be sociable with our hosts left me exhausted.

Brent was off preaching with Titus, and Chuck and Nancy and Tex were scheduled to go back to Budapest before dawn. We finished eating well after midnight, but Nelu Dronca and Peter Dugalescu decided it would be best for me to report the stolen papers to the police so we would have something official to help us get out of the country. The problem was that I needed an interpreter, and they were not supposed to be with me. Nelu volunteered to go with me anyway, and we drove to the police station.

Nothing had been resolved by 2 A.M., so I told the police I'd be back. I drove Chuck and Nancy and Tex to Arad, and we rented a hotel room so we could sleep for just forty-five minutes. Before we parted, Tex told me a man had come to her after the service and said he'd had a dream in which he saw me dying in a small room.

I put the three of them on the train to Budapest and drove to Nelu's house, feeling as lonely as I ever had in the ministry. After breakfast we went to the police station again. I was so sleep deprived I felt like a zombie.

After finally getting the documents we needed, I drove to Arad and had lunch with Pastor Titi Bulzan in his home. I was to preach in his church that night. At about two in the afternoon I felt queasy and went to take a nap. When they roused me to go to the meetings, I got up and then collapsed. I had no strength in my hands or fingers, and my legs and feet felt like lead.

They lifted me back onto the bed, but when they came to see if I was able to go, I couldn't move—even to lift my head from the pillow. Titi stayed with me, and while I tried to sleep, he summoned a doctor, who found my pulse dangerously weak. The diagnosis: total exhaustion.

By eleven that night I knew I had to try to get back to the hotel. It was illegal for me to stay in a private home. Titi could be sent to prison, and I could be deported. Now if I could just get out of bed…

"You have to be able to walk into the hotel, Sammy," Titi said. "If they see us helping you, they will take you to a hospital, and eventually they will kill you."

I told him I thought I could make it. He helped me out of bed and left the room when I started toward the bathroom. Titi sensed something wasn't right, rushed back in, and caught me as I passed out in the bathroom. He carried me back to bed like a baby. *Is this it?* I wondered. *Was the guy's dream right? Am I going to die right here?*

Titi decided it was too dangerous for me to try to go back to the hotel. "We'll take our chances here."

I slowly recovered enough to be able to preach the next night and Sunday morning, but when Brent and Titus returned they were shocked by my appearance.

Before we moved on I thanked Titi for saving my life.

From that point on we were followed everywhere we went. At one point Titus counted six Securitate following us. We decided to confuse them by splitting up and meeting back at Titus's place. It worked, but we noticed Securitate agents at every meeting after that—the worst I'd seen in all my years of ministry.

The crowds were also the largest I'd ever seen in Romania, so there was no hiding what we were doing. In Alba Iulia the people were so hungry for the Word of God that they came even to the youth services and what were supposed to be small group discipleship meetings in the afternoons. Later, when we asked new converts to meet with us in the sanctuary after the regular evening meeting, the rest of the crowd began filing back in and filled the place so they could hear what we were telling the new believers. Titus referred to that time as "days of heaven, when people lost all concept of time, and eternity became their focus."

On our way out of the country Brent and I happened to pull up behind a car that also had two Americans in it. The guards must have assumed we were together, and as they had apparently seen a professional photographer in the lead car shooting pictures throughout the country, they confiscated all the film from both vehicles.

After they discovered a videotape of one of my messages and played it, a plainclothes Securitate agent angrily informed me through an interpreter that I would not be allowed back into the country.

I told the girl to ask him why.

"You know why," he spat.

"No, I don't. What have I done?"

The interpreter, clearly terrified, said, "I can't tell him you said that. You'll be in trouble if you talk to him that way."

"Please go ahead and tell him. I want to know what I've done."

When she did, he reddened and narrowed his eyes at me. "You have broken our laws."

"No, I have done nothing illegal. Tell me what crime I've committed." If I was going to be kicked out for preaching Christ, I wanted to hear it from his lips.

"One more minute and you're in very serious trouble. Now get out of here!"

I had been threatened with blacklisting before, and others had been turned away for having been with me. But every time I tried to get back in, I made it. How serious this threat was, I didn't know.

We sent Brent into Romania by train in June to see whether he showed up on the computer as blacklisted, but he got in without a hitch. That made me confident I could do the same.

In July I traveled with Scott Horne, a Georgia acquaintance who had a burden for Romania. All the way there, the song "Great Is Thy Faithfulness" kept coming to mind. I sang it over and over as I gazed out the window during the numerous hours Scott and I spent on the jet.

Sam Friend, ministering in Europe, met us during our stopover in Munich. "Sammy," he said, "what happens if they don't let you in?"

"They issued me a visa," I said. "If I was blacklisted, they wouldn't have done that."

"But what if they don't let you in?"

"Sam, I believe I'm going to get in. I really do."

"But what if they don't?"

I smiled. "I can't imagine it, Sam."

"Look," he said, "let me give you Bryan's phone number. [I use only Bryan's first name here because he was a man near Austria who housed Christians traveling in and out of Eastern Europe. I had stayed with him before.] I'll be there, so call if you have any problems."

In Budapest, Scott and I met Darryl Gardiner, who would be going in with us. We split up on the train, just in case so we were in three separate cars when the train arrived at the Romanian border, just outside Oradea, at 10 P.M., Thursday, July 21, 1988.

Normally this is a one-hour stop, where passports are checked before the train continues into the country. When two hours had passed, it was clear something was wrong.

When the guards finally got to me, one flipped open my passport, pocketed it and said in English, "Mr. Tippit, get your luggage and come with us."

Six soldiers escorted me off and surrounded me until the train slowly began to pull out. I would not see my beloved Romanian brothers and sisters this time, and I wondered whether I would ever see them again.

Scott and Darryl were still on the train, near the back, and I needed to catch their attention so they would know I was not with them. I watched carefully as car after car rolled past. I didn't want the guards to see at whom I was looking. When Scott and Darryl saw me outside, surrounded by guards, their mouths dropped. Looking away, I raised one finger, indicating that they must trust God now. They had depended on me for this trip, but they were on their own with Him now.

As the train slowly disappeared, I was reminded how lonely I felt after putting the Hollimons and Tex aboard in Arad the trip before. This was worse. This was more than exhaustion, more than missing. Besides fatigue and disappointment, there was fear and the frustration of having no information.

Of course I had a good idea why they had taken me off the train, but shouldn't they have told me what would happen next? One guard stayed with me while the others moved fifteen or twenty feet away. I was wearing light summer clothes, but now, past midnight, it was chilly. I walked in place, then I sat on my luggage and felt sorry for myself.

Would they put me in prison? Would I ever see my wife and my kids again?

I knew Titus would meet the train in Oradea and learn I had been detained. He had become my best friend, whom I felt God had provided after the death of Ken Leeburg, who had been such an encourager and a challenger.

I allowed myself to hope I might be put on a later train. The only thing I knew for sure was that my brothers and sisters in Christ would pray for me and try to get word to my loved ones that I had not made it in. I was glad I had Bryan's number in my wallet. Sam Friend had been right after all.

By about 3 A.M. I was chilled to the bone and depressed. Then the Lord brought again to my mind the great old hymn of the faith, and I began singing "Great Is Thy Faithfulness." Then I sang all the verses I could remember to "How Great Thou Art" and "Holy, Holy, Holy." I focused on God and sang great hymns about His character. Frankly, I'm not much of a singer, and some have accused me of trying to torture those guards with my voice before they did whatever they planned to do with me!

I soon I realized I knew enough Romanian to be able to communicate with the guards, so I started making up songs and singing sermons they would understand. I may have been under arrest, but they were a captive audience. By dawn they would know the Gospel.

When I got through singing, I preached to them for about twenty minutes, which exhausted the extent of my Romanian. I said, "Jesus loves you, and He died for you. He wants to forgive your sin and live in your heart." They wouldn't look at me.

Just before dawn I dug a sport coat out of my luggage, but I was still freezing. The guards wore big, heavy coats, and one by one they found places to lean and then crouch and then sit. By 5:30 or so I was the only one awake.

Behind me sat two small buildings—one with people in it, one empty—with a narrow passageway in between. That passageway would be warm, and I could still see the guards in case they woke up and panicked. I tiptoed in there, out of the wind and felt a lot better.

About half an hour later a bus pulled up on its way to Oradea, and several people got on. My mind was racing. None of the guards had stirred. I could grab my luggage and be on that bus and into Oradea before they knew I was gone.

I thought of Titus's brothers, who had risked prison by swimming the Danube to escape to the West. Was I up to that? I knew it would be foolhardy, but I have to admit I was seconds from making a run for that bus. When it pulled away, I still could have walked the ten kilometers or so into Oradea.

I had gone two nights without sleep and had nothing to eat since the flight. When a factory whistle blew, the guards awoke and spun around to see where I had gone. I casually walked out and sat by my luggage again. No one scolded me for having moved because they would have had to admit they had been asleep and didn't know even how long I'd been gone.

I had to look haggard as the morning dragged on. At ten a train from Oradea to Hungary pulled in, and the guards moved me to a holding area with waiting passengers. I didn't want to go to Hungary, but that was better than standing outside all day. I wanted to go to Romania, but I had the feeling that if they didn't put me on that train to the West, I would go to prison.

The passengers were ushered onto the train, but still I stood alone in the holding area. At the last instant, just as the train began to slowly roll, a guard handed me my passport and nodded toward the train.

The train was so full I had to stand all the way to Budapest. There wasn't even room to lean anywhere for a little nap. When I changed trains in Budapest to go to Vienna, one seat was available, and so I was finally able to get off my feet. As we rolled on toward Austria God gave me this promise from His Word: "We are hard-pressed on every side, yet not crushed, we are perplexed, but not in despair, persecuted, but not forsaken, struck down, but not destroyed" (2 Corinthians 4:8-9).

I was also led to this passage:

Do not fret because of evildoers, nor be envious of the workers of iniquity. For they shall soon be cut down like the grass. . . . Trust in the Lord, and do good. Dwell in the land, and feed on His faithfulness. . . . Commit your way to the Lord. . . . The steps of a good man are ordered by the Lord, and He delights in his way. Though he fall, he shall not be utterly cast down, for the Lord upholds him with His hand (Psalm 37:1-5, 23-24).

In Vienna I called Sam Friend and told him all that had happened. I caught a train to where he was staying with Bryan, and they met me at the depot. Finally, I was able to call Tex and get some sleep.

The next day, on a ten-kilometer walk, I let Sam and Bryan get farther and farther ahead as I wept over Titus and Nelu and Stephanuti. I thanked God for the beautiful times we had spent together in ministry and fellowship, and I prayed that one day I might see them again. My love for them and for all the believers in Romania would never cease.

I didn't know where Scott Horne or Darryl Gardiner might be, but I knew they were conducting the ministry I had been denied.

Sammy Tippit could be turned away at the border, but the Spirit of God could not be contained.

CHAPTER TWENTY-EIGHT

THE WORLD AS MY PARISH

Friends and acquaintances smuggled encouraging words out of Romania to me. Titus asked someone simply to tell me, "The glory of God comes only through much suffering."

That fall (1988) I attended the Frankfurt Book Fair for Moody Press and made a strategic contact with Yugoslavian publisher Branko Lovrec. Expanding my ministry through the translation of my books was an exciting proposition. God also allowed me still to have an influence with Romania by speaking at the Romanian Baptist Church in Chicago, where Titus's brother, Lucian, and his family attended.

A new friend, evangelist Steve Wingfield, asked if he could help out in Romania in my absence, and I helped arrange for him to speak in Timisoara the following January (1989). He came back with a message from Nelu Dronca: 'Tell Sammy that I have all the assurance in my heart that one day he will again sit at my table and eat in my house."

My faith was small. I longed for Nelu's prediction to come true, and it broke my heart to have to stay away.

I also received a letter from a minister that told roughly the following story:

> I recently returned from my first trip to Romania. It was thrilling, as I met some wonderful people. One young lady told me she was saved under your ministry and wanted to be baptized. Her parents, with whom she lived, opposed this as they are Orthodox. Her father whipped her thirty-nine times, to the point that she was unconscious. Her doctor said he had never seen such deep wounds.
>
> Her brother is in the secret police and afraid for his job because of his sister becoming a believer.
>
> She left town and was baptized recently. She wanted me to tell you she was disappointed she wasn't able to see you again this summer.

The next month, in a carefully coded phone call from Darryl Gardiner, I learned the Romanian believers desperately needed preachers to come in and fill speaking obligations. More meetings had been lined up than speakers, and Darryl wanted me to suggest some possibilities. I called throughout the U.S. but found no one available or willing. I felt terrible, knowing the Romanians would feel we in the West didn't care.

I had very little chance of getting in, but I had to try. If word got to the Romanians that at least someone tried, it would encourage them. Fred Gough agreed to go with me on hardly any notice, so we flew into Belgrade, Yugoslavia, hoping to get in through a border we had never attempted before.

When we changed our money into Romanian currency, it appeared we would receive our visas. But all of a sudden I sensed a different atmosphere—lots of scurrying about, impromptu meetings, and concerned looks.

Sure enough, my name had turned up on the computers as an undesirable. I was not welcome in their country, but they didn't know why. They interrogated us about drugs and tore apart our vehicle and all our belongings. In the end we were deported, but I knew word would get to our brothers and sisters that we had done our best to get in.

That summer I went to Manila for the Lausanne II International Congress on World Evangelization, where I made friends with leading believers from all over the world. In 1989 alone I preached in Africa, India, Yugoslavia, Ireland, Peru, and Brazil—many times in areas where there were few Christians.

One of the highlights at Manila was meeting a lady who waited at the edge of a crowd after I spoke. When she finally made her way to me, she said, "Are you the Sammy Tippit who was arrested in Chicago years ago."

"I am," I said.

She said, 'Today God has answered my prayer that He would let me meet you again someday just to say thank you. When you were passing out tracts on Rush Street, I was a go-go dancer in one of those clubs. I received one of your tracts and actually went and heard you speak. I ended up giving my heart to Christ, and my husband and I are now on the mission field serving Him."

I was left dumbfounded. I thanked God and prayed I would never get hung up on numbers but always remember that people like her are what evangelism is all about.

My schedule filled with evangelistic crusades and revivals all over the world. I felt humbled by all the opportunities but wondered how our little organization could do it all. My board supported selectively accepting strategic invitations. They worried about my health, given my age, my cancer scare, and my grueling travel schedule.

Despite a schedule full enough to keep me busy the rest of my life, by September of 1989 I felt so burdened for Romania that I could barely concentrate on anything else. I called Josif Tson, head of the Romanian Missionary Society in Wheaton, Illinois, and told him that if I couldn't get in, I wanted to do the next best thing and go next door.

"I've been to Kishinev [in Soviet Moldavia] and I told you about that debacle. If you have any solid contacts there, I'd like to go knowing who I'm dealing with."

Josif liked the idea and knew many Romanians in Kishinev. He helped me arrange some meetings during the next opening on my schedule, May of 1990. I secretly hoped that Titus could somehow get to Kishinev.

While all that was being planned in late 1989, I fulfilled commitments in Nigeria in November and Peru in December. It was while I was in Nigeria and deathly ill that I got word from Tex that the Berlin Wall was coming down. My life and ministry would never be the same.

A month later, Tex, Dave, Renee, and I were visiting my mom in Louisiana when we saw a news broadcast about Christians being killed in Timisoara and a revolution in the making. I started receiving calls from the media, asking for comments on what was what was going on. I think that was when Mom realized for the first time that I had done the right thing with my life. I sensed God was changing her heart.

After seeing the impact of the fall of Ceausescu, I knew I needed to be in Romania. When word came that Titus wanted me to come immediately, I couldn't get there soon enough. My suitcase never arrived, so I had only one set of clothes in the dead of winter, but the way the people of God received me warmed my heart. Being invited to the pulpit at the Second Baptist Church of Oradea, even though the service was about to close, remains one of the highlights of my life.

I began the last decade of the second millennium preaching to people just freed from a godless dictatorship. Imagine the looks on the faces of the people who had just seen a miracle.

These people knew I had been blacklisted and also that I had tried to return, but they had not heard the details of my arrest and deportation. Before the revolution it would have been impossible for anyone to tell the story in public without risk.

When Titus translated my account, he and I and the nearly three thousand in the pews were in tears. I concluded: "I can now say publicly that no dictator, no Ceausescu, no Communist, no atheist, not anyone could keep me out if God wanted me here!" The beaming smiles and heartfelt *ahmeens* were glorious.

For the first time ever I was allowed to stay with Titus in his home. Though it was small and they really didn't have room for a guest, he said, "You must stay. We have waited for this day."

We talked until the wee hours and the next day went through Oradea and saw an amazing sight. Everywhere Romanian flags flew, the Communist hammer and sickle had been cut from its center. To me the hole in the flag represented the vacuum in the hearts of the people. Something someday would replace Communism in the country. What would fill the hole in the people's hearts? I knew well the answer to that. The time was now to take advantage of the window of opportunity.

That night at Second Baptist, I spoke on the hole in the flag. Later, Dr. Nick Gheorghita told me, "No evangelist knows Eastern Europe as you do. You must go, not just to Romania, but to the other countries here, and you must call the people to God. He has uniquely qualified you for this."

During the next few days I returned to many of the places in Romania where I had preached in the past. Every church was packed, and with more non-Christians than I had seen before. In Alba Iulia, the last place I preached before being blacklisted, dozens told me they had become Christians at those meetings.

It was so good to see Nelu Dronca of Timisoara and, indeed, to eat with him in his home, as he had predicted I would. "You suffered with our people, and now it's time to rejoice with them."

Pastor Peter Dugalescu met me in the great Timisoara plaza where the revolution had taken place and where he had preached to 200,000 people.

How thrilling to stand where tens of thousands of people had knelt with him and recited the Lord's Prayer, where he had preached the Gospel to them and taught them a song about the return of Christ that became the theme song of the revolution. I would have given anything to have been there when that great mass began to shout in their own language "God exists!"

"Exista Dumnezeu! Exista Dumnezeu! Exista Dumnezeu!"

As Peter told me the story, people in the plaza began to gather around us, soon numbering in the hundreds. I was so full of the joy of the Lord, I said, "Peter, can I preach?"

He said, "Brother Sammy, this is the new Romania."

As soon as I began, they shouted, *"Exista Dumnezeu! Exista Dumnezeu!"* And these were not church people. They had lived under atheistic Communism their whole lives. A cloud of fear had hung over that country for so long that never in my wildest imagination would I have dreamed I could speak in a public square and hear the masses cry out, "God exists!"

New Romania

I spoke of the miraculous, mighty hand of God that could not be held down by any human, any ideology, any regime. And the people shouted, *"Exista Dumnezeu!"*

Titus came to the next God's Love in Action board meeting where I recommended bringing him on full-time as director in Eastern Europe. The board enthusiastically agreed but remained committed not to going public about our need for increased funds.

The month Titus began, our income increased enough to cover both new men, and we've had sufficient income ever since.

One of the best things that happened as a result of the revolution was that the pastor in Comanesti, whose church had tripled after our meetings, was allowed to pastor once again. He had come to the United States, and we had helped him build a larger facility. The Ceausescu regime came to bulldoze it down, the congregation tried to interfere, and the pastor and his four elders were imprisoned and the church leveled. Now he had been released, and they were building again.

Before I left Romania, Titus agreed to come to Kishinev with me and I would also speak in Romania during that time. He immediately went to work arranging sites and cities.

I ministered in Indonesia, Peru, and Brazil before getting back to Romania in May. When I arrived to preach in a stadium following a soccer game in Baia Mare, Titus asked how it felt to walk into history. "This is the first stadium crusade in the history of Romania."

Titus told me of one of the early pastors of the Second Baptist Church of Oradea, who called the people to pray that one day God would allow His people to stand in the great stadiums of the nation and proclaim the Gospel. He also led them to pray the Gospel would be preached through the media.

"Sammy," Titus said, "today is the beginning of the answer to that prayer. For the first time in the history of this nation, the Gospel will be proclaimed outdoors in a great stadium."

That night as I faced ten thousand people for the first time in my ministry, I felt so at home that God gave me a sense that this was what He had created me to do. My public speaking, the ability to minister cross-culturally, and having been willing to go to the hard places all had led to this point.

When I gave the invitation that first night and hundreds and hundreds and hundreds streamed forward, I fell to my face and wept. This was a day I had dreamt of and longed for. In three days four thousand people prayed to receive Christ. About half of those responded on the last night, and it was the largest response I'd seen up to that point.

I was interviewed by a journalist so fascinated by the crusade that he ran a lengthy feature on me in a sports magazine, of all things. He told me he had never been allowed to know about God so he asked if I could get him a Bible so he could understand some of the terminology. We provided all the journalists with Bibles, and the next night we were covered by newspapers, radio and TV stations, and other magazines—a further answer to the prayers of the church in Oradea from years before.

From there we went to Kishinev for the second time (the first time being my cloak-and-dagger experience in the blizzard). Titus, Bill Northfield, my son Dave, and I told church leaders of the historic crusade we had just held. They asked us if we would return to Kishinev in the fall for a citywide crusade. Although I had a full international schedule between May and September, I could hardly wait to get back to preach in both the Soviet Union and Romania in large outdoor crusades.

Whereas I will always be willing to go anywhere and talk to just one person about Christ, it was incredible to see how God opened doors and ripped down the Iron Curtain.

CHAPTER TWENTY-NINE

HARVEST TIME

It didn't seem that long ago that I was a baby Christian mustering the courage to share my faith in the bars around Baton Rouge. Now God had granted me the unfathomable privilege of preaching His Gospel on every inhabited continent, addressing indigenous pastors and leaders, calling the world to prayer and revival through my books, and spending my life the only way I have wanted to since I came to faith in Him.

After the fiasco my ministry friends and I had once endured in Kishinev, I told pastors there that I did not want to hold a big crusade in Moldova without an official invitation from the government. When church leaders sought this for me, officials told them they would first have to check me out.

Surely they would discover I had once been blacklisted from Romania, but worse, years before I had been arrested, detained, and deported from Leningrad. All I could do was what I have done ever since I learned that obedience must be the hallmark of my ministry: I left it in God's hands.

I'll never forget the day the letter came, officially inviting me. All systems were go.

Our fall 1990 trip to the Soviet Union and Romania was unlike anything I had ever experienced. We started in the Soviet city of Belcy in Moldavia, where the city council had originally rejected the idea of an outdoor public crusade. Organizers appealed to the Supreme Council of Moldavia in Kishinev, which overruled the city council.

From the moment the meeting started, things went wrong. I was in the middle of my message when a bottle of carbonated water exploded on the stage and startled me. Then, when I began quoting John 3:16—the essence of the Gospel—the sound system went out. Not one person left as the great crowd patiently waited fifteen minutes until I could finish the verse and keep preaching. Satan may be the prince of the power of the air, but his scheme failed that night.

What happened next was reported a few months later in *Moody Magazine:*

179

Evangelist Sammy Tippit is used to all kinds of responses. From the bars in his native Baton Rouge, Louisiana, in the '60s to the streets of Chicago in the '70s, and in almost every imaginable venue since, he has seen between one person and several thousand come to Christ.

He has ministered at U.S. political conventions and the Communist Youth World Festival. He has been arrested for his bold witness in countries as diverse as the United States, the Soviet Union, and Romania.

He has preached on every inhabited continent, sometimes to huge crowds, sometimes in churches so small and remote that no other evangelist has ever visited. His team consists of a wife, a two-person office staff in San Antonio, a Romanian evangelist and interpreter, and a half-dozen personal evangelists who pay their own way on trips abroad.

His message is simple, clear, old-fashioned, and direct. Jesus is coming again. Be ready. Repent. Get saved.

And now he stands on a makeshift platform at a soccer stadium, preaching the first public Gospel message in the modern history of this Soviet republic. Opposition, particularly from the Orthodox Church, has been intense.

"The evangelicals are not Christians," church leaders say in local newspapers. "They do not revere the Holy Mother."

Yet 12,000 have gathered. The majority of those in the stands are unbelievers; the evangelicals stand at the edges of the crowd. Tippit pauses for the staccato interpretation into Russian after every phrase. While he senses the leading of the Spirit and is confident he is preaching God's own message, he can't help but wonder how the people will respond.

He pleads with them to turn from sin, to come to Jesus, to be assured of heaven. As is his custom, he asks them to show their decision. "If you're willing to make that choice tonight, raise your hand right where you stand."

With arms outstretched, he scans the crowd. How bizarre that they have never heard this message, never worshiped in public. They must wonder about the consequences if they respond—from their friends, from the authorities, from the church. No one raises a hand. "Oh, God," Tippit prays silently, "save souls!"

Nearly a minute passes. Though still no one has raised a hand, Tippit feels led to ask decision-makers to come forward, to take a step of confession before men that they are choosing heaven over hell, life over death, Jesus over self.

From deep in the crowd he sees movement. A peasant woman of perhaps 60 marches down the stadium steps and onto the soccer field, a bouquet of flowers held aloft; she looks like some spiritual statue of liberty. She strides to the end of the platform where she solemnly presents the gift to the evangelist. She crosses herself in the Orthodox fashion and sinks to her knees, crying out to God.

Immediately, from all over the arena, individuals, couples, dozens, hundreds pour from the stands toward the platform. After several minutes, 2,000 stand there smiling, faces wet with tears, praying aloud. At least half are past middle age.

"I want to be there," Tippit says, "when that brave woman is rewarded in heaven."

Following the event in Belcy, the ministry Every Home for Christ helped us mail Christian literature to the people of Kishinev in advance of the crusade in that city. Of 120,000 flyers that offered a free Bible correspondence course, 60,000 had already come back, so many that the Kishinev post office informed us they would not deliver them; we would have to

come and get the responses that stuffed huge mail sacks. Clearly, God had already begun a mighty work in that city.

The morning after the stadium crusade began, I received word that Mayor Nicolae Kostin wanted to see me immediately. I wasn't sure I wanted to see him. The last time I was summoned to face Soviet authorities I had been banished from the country.

After we exchanged pleasantries, Mayor Kostin flashed a huge smile, threw his arms around me, and said, "We are so happy you have come to Kishinev. For many years we have persecuted the Christians, treated them as the dirt on the floor, the scum of the earth. We were wrong. The very morality needed to make society function correctly is the morality of the Christians. Prior to the Communists, our forefathers were people of deep faith. Would you help return our people to the faith of their forefathers?"

Swallowing a big lump in my throat, I said, "Mayor Kostin, that is exactly why we have come! We love the Moldavian people and want them to know Christ."

At a subsequent meeting with the mayor's staff, we discussed what *perestroika* and *glasnost* might mean for cooperation between the United States and Moldavia. They invited us back to their city and expressed interest in visiting the United States.

From there we went to the Romanian city of Iasi *(Yahsh)*, where Orthodox opposition held attendance down for the first few days. The last day, however, the crowd was immense, and later I learned why. We had been videotaped in Kishinev, but the program wasn't aired until two hours before the last meeting in Iasi. When people heard we were coming, they showed up. It was an amazing turnaround.

In Galati we revisited where Titus had expressed his willingness to be martyred for the sake of his countrymen. Then we went to Arad, where we saw our largest crowds ever, around twenty-two thousand the final night.

Before the revolution, I preached in packed Romanian churches, but I never dreamed I would preach in stadiums that could not contain all who wanted to hear the Gospel. Not only had political boundaries been redrawn, but God was also intervening in the affairs of human history.

In Ukraine, the day our Odessa crusade was to begin, we were informed that we had lost permission to use the gigantic stadium. When we pleaded for reconsideration, we were directed to a military authority, who covertly showed us a cross he carried in his pocket.

He felt bad about what officials above him had done, so he gave us permission to use a smaller stadium. The Soviet military was assigned to direct people to the new location, and afterward they offered to feed the choir and the staff. Imagine that! Even better, the crowd that would have looked sparse in the original stadium jam-packed the new venue-

Every day it rained, right up to the time of the meeting. The rain stopped during the meeting and resumed when we finished. One night it appeared to be raining everywhere but at the stadium.

We also uniquely solved an interpreting problem. Our key contact, Vasile Binzar, knew Russian and Romanian but not English. Titus knew English and Romanian but not Russian. So we used Titus as a human language adapter. As I preached in English, Titus stood directly behind Vasile and whispered a Romanian translation into his ear. Vasile translated that into Russian!

In city after city in Ukraine and Romania, thousands came to Christ. I was overwhelmed, worrying how many were sincere, would persevere, and how they would be followed up. It was great to be able to provide follow-up material, and someone reminded me that ninety percent of the counselors at these meetings had come to Christ under my ministry.

I realized that the real work of follow-up was done by the Holy Spirit.

As we left, I wept as I expressed my thanks to the Lord that thirty thousand people had publicly prayed to receive Christ in Ukraine and Romania in just three weeks—many in cities in Ukraine where no one from the West had ever traveled before.

I told the Lord I knew it had nothing to do with me and that everything had been accomplished in His divine plan and time. But I thanked Him for allowing me to see His mighty deeds play out in my lifetime.

Mass evangelism is merely one-on-one personal evangelism on a grand scale. Imagine my thrill, after having been privileged to be used of God in that way, to get a call from my own mother.

"Sammy, I need help," she said, her voice shaky. "I've been a proud woman and bitter woman, and I'm tired of it. I need God."

"Mom, God loves you, and I do, too. We can pray right now. Jesus will take control of your life and forgive you. He will remove all the guilt and set you free from the bitterness."

After we prayed together, she thanked me, and I thanked the Lord. It had been more than 25 years since I had come to Christ. God's faithfulness was key to what happened in Mom and in our ministry. What a privilege to enjoy the spiritual harvest season! Decades of fervent, faithful prayer and Bible study, often led by humble pastors in hard places, resulted in these great outpourings of God's Spirit.

Months later we got reports of how the Soviet and Romanian churches had grown. In Belcy alone, some fifteen hundred at one church said they had received Christ at our crusade.

In Kishinev the churches held special Sunday services for new believers only. There were so many. The government also granted permission to build sixty-eight new churches throughout Moldavia!

In one Ukrainian city, a pastor reported receiving five thousand new people into his church following our crusade.

My goal is to spend my life for God, and He has blessed me beyond measure.

When the Soviet Union began to unravel, I immediately wired Kishinev's Mayor Kostin that I was willing to come and stand with him and his people, even before tanks and guns. Although he did not take me up on that offer, it sealed a bond between us that was never broken. (Mayor Kostin passed a few years later.)

In the fall of 1991 I enjoyed the rare privilege of hosting him in San Antonio, and I set up several meetings for him with senators and congressmen in Washington. Titus came to me one day and said, "We must continue to push eastward to those who've never heard the Gospel. We can't stop with Moldavia or Ukraine. We must go to the furthermost part of Siberia."

"Is that possible?" I said.

The former Soviet Union was one of the darkest places in the world, and Siberia the darkest of the dark. Titus convinced me we could do it, and he and Vasile quickly arranged meetings in three cities in the Krasnoyarsk region, which seemed the end of the world. Located within the Arctic Circle, Norilsk was built by slave labor under Stalin. Millions, many of them Christians, died in Siberian slave labor camps.

There were only a handful of believers in Norilsk, so we had to send a team to prepare the meetings. We arranged with the Emanuel Bible Institute in Oradea, Romania, to send twenty of its students (from Romania, Moldavia, and Ukraine) to Siberia during the summer.

They were the first Christians ever to go door-to-door to share the Gospel in Norilsk. They shared their faith, preached on the streets, and invited people to the upcoming meetings. Their determination and sweet sense of joy deeply touched me, and I would later realize why.

Tex, Clifton Jansky (a musician from San Antonio), and I stayed in the home of a Norilsk lady who, like most everyone else in town, was an atheist. She greeted us the first morning with, "Your meeting today will be a failure. No one will come to the stadium in the rain."

I looked her in the eye and said, "No, madam. This meeting will not be a failure. It will be a success."

"How can you say that?"

"Because our success isn't measured by how many people come to our meetings. It's measured by obedience to God. I will be at the stadium even if no one else is there. I'll be there because God told me to come here and preach the Gospel. And if I'm the only person, then the meeting will be successful because I will have done what God told me to do."

I gathered the team, and we asked God to stop the rain. An hour before the meeting, the clouds blew away, the sun appeared, and the largest crowd in the history of that stadium showed up.

Clifton

When I was arrested in Leningrad years before, I feared the Communists were sending me to Siberia for preaching the Gospel. Now God had sent me to Siberia to preach the Gospel to the Communists!

At the close of my message, as I always do, I invited people to join me at the front of the platform and pray with me if they wanted to repent of their sins and trust Christ to save them. When almost everyone in the stadium began moving, I couldn't believe it. Surely they had not understood.

"Stop!" I cried out. "Please, stop coming! I'm asking you to make a commitment to Christ that will cost you everything! He calls you to holiness and to declare with your mouth that God raised Him from the dead. You must be willing to give Him your entire life and future. Be sure you count the cost before you come."

And still they came, at least ninety-five percent of the crowd. I finally had to instruct them to just stop where they were and I would lead them in prayer that way.

After the service a journalist said, "Many believe we're under a curse because the streets we walk on, the apartments we sleep in, and the offices we work in were built by slave labor. Are we under a curse?"

"No," I said, "I don't believe this city is under a curse. I believe it's under a blessing."

The lady was shocked. "How can you say that?" she said.

"Many of those slaves were Christians, in prison because of their faith. It's not impossible to imagine that when they laid the pavement and built the apartments and office buildings, they prayed that those who walked and slept and worked here would one day hear the message of God's love for them."

A few months later I read in a Christian magazine that several of the Moldavian and Ukrainian students who did the preparation work for our meetings were grandchildren of Siberian prisoners. Their forefathers *had* built those cities. I believe God holds dear to His heart the blood of the martyrs. He answered their prayers by allowing their grandchildren to return to the city to proclaim the name of Jesus.

Some of the students remained in Norilsk for two years to disciple those who came to Christ, and they started churches with the new believers. Several of those felt called to the ministry and went to Emanuel Bible College in Oradea.

When I returned to Oradea to preach in the new church facility of the Second Baptist Church (which had changed its name to Emanuel Baptist Church), Dr. Paul Negrut pointed out a student.

"Sammy, he lived in a Siberian village and followed all the people going into the stadium. He was one of those who came forward."

Paul told me the young man returned to his village and told everyone what had happened to him. The older people wept and one said, "Many years ago the Communists killed all the Christians in this village. But the last one they killed lifted his hands toward heaven and asked God to raise up a new generation that would one day bring the message of Christ back to this village. You're the answer to his prayers."

Imagine how that young man must have felt to hear that.

Oh, God, help me to be willing to go anywhere any time under any circumstances to tell men and women of your love.

Not every effort resulted in such spiritual highs. My next stop would be a house of horrors.

CHAPTER THIRTY

HARD PLACES

I had been back to South Africa several times since the great experience I'd enjoyed there in 1987. Eager to reach other areas of the continent, I was excited to meet Peter Kasarivu from Uganda when he visited San Antonio. A young leader who had come to faith after the murderous Idi Amin had been overthrown, Peter had a burden to reach his country for Christ.

I conducted evangelistic meetings and a pastors' conference in Uganda in 1994, and my heart was knitted with many of those dear leaders. While preaching in an open field to several thousand, I asked how many had a relative or close friend who had died from AIDS. I was taken aback when ninety percent of the audience lifted a hand.

I was gripped with a renewed sense of urgency. Heaven and hell were at stake, and God would expose me to even more—and even worse—tragedy.

Not long after I ministered in Uganda, I read that 500,000 people had been slaughtered in one month next door in Rwanda, simply because of their ethnic background.

Peter Kasarivu contacted me and said Rwandan pastors who heard me in Uganda "desperately want you to come and share Christ with their people. Their fellow Tutsis were slaughtered."

Virtually no outsiders were venturing in to Rwanda, but a few months later Gary Maroney and Billy Honc, an associate pastor at my home church, and I boarded a plane bound for there. A fellow passenger heard where we were going and stared at me, eyes wild. "You could be killed!"

We brought money to help rebuild fifty homes and clothe 250 families, and Peter met us at the airport with a group of pastors (Leo, Joseph, and Norman) who took us to breakfast and briefed us. "You must understand how deep the hurt runs in the hearts of the people and how difficult your task will be," Peter said gravely.

New friend Pastor Leo spoke up. "The nation is still in shock. The press says half a million people have been killed, but everyone here believes it was more than a million."

I was aghast. "Why would anyone do such a thing?"

"The political leadership [the Hutus] was afraid of the minority Tutsis," he said. "Government radio told the people constantly that the Tutsis were half animals—and dangerous."

Joseph added, "The order was given. 'Kill all Tutsis.'"

Norman said, "Hutu husbands killed their Tutsi wives, and Hutu wives killed Tutsi husbands. If the children looked like the Tutsi father, sometimes mothers slaughtered their own children. Neighbors murdered neighbors. It was mass insanity."

"How could people buy into something so obviously evil?" I asked.

Joseph's look gave me chills. "The entire nation came under the possession of Satan's demons. The church was at the center of the genocide. Many priests and even evangelical pastors participated. They gathered the Tutsis of the community to the church and told them it was a safe haven. Then they locked them inside and had the militia come and throw grenades into the building. Tutsis who tried to escape were shot point-blank. And if the militia ran out of ammunition, they used machetes."

"Oh, God," I cried, my head in my hands.

Norman said, "The government doesn't trust any minister of the church. But even worse, the people don't trust each other. When you preach Sunday, there may be two women present. The husband of one may have been killed by the husband of the other. Can you imagine the bitterness?"

We had heard all we could stand for one morning. How could anyone who claimed faith in Christ engage in such heinous barbarism?

The pastors took us to a room so we could nap before our journey to Butare. But as the three of us lay there, all we could do was weep and moan as though one of our own had been murdered. Though we hadn't slept all night on the plane, rest was impossible.

In Butare we would conduct a pastors' conference each day, I would speak at the national university each night, and I would also preach a community evangelistic campaign outdoors. Christian students had organized these first evangelistic outreaches since the genocide.

Before we went to the university, we had lunch with government leaders, and the mayor confided to me that just a few months earlier he had been a professor at the university.

"When the order was given to kill all Tutsis," he said, "I was frightened for my wife and our seven children. Our neighbors, some of our best friends, said we must hide and offered to take five of the children while we hid elsewhere with the other two. They said the Hutus would never suspect them. We thanked them for their love and concern, believing it was the only way to keep all the children safe." Tears welled up in his eyes. "Once our friends took our five into their home, they called the militia, who came and slaughtered them."

I was speechless.

"I'm not bitter," he said. "I miss my children so very much, but God has given me the grace to forgive."

I wanted to go to bed and wake up to discover this was just one bad dream. But I was to speak to a thousand university students that night. How could I speak about hope, peace, and love when everything they had ever known had been shattered by revenge, hatred, and discrimination?

Moments like these determine how real and deep-rooted one's faith is. Could Jesus really heal the broken heart? Could He give victory over such bitterness? Could the integrity of the church be rebuilt after such a blemish blot on its soul? My message for leaders was the need for revival, and for the general populace my message was simply the Gospel.

Many students came to Christ during several days of meetings. Later the student leadership told me, "Our professors are antagonistic toward Christianity and angry about the church's participation in the killings. Would you share the Gospel with them as you did with us?"

I agreed to meet with them, and close to fifty professors attended, plus the university chancellor. I spoke of God's ability to heal a broken heart and even a broken nation. I told how Christ could bring peace to every person.

Afterward I answered the professors' questions to the best of my ability. Finally the chancellor stood. "Mr. Tippit, one question continues to plague us. Where was the church during the genocide? And where is the church today? Mr. Tippit, where is the church?"

Sadly, we all knew exactly where the church had been. It had played an evil role. I never again wanted to be asked such a question. I could not defend the church in Rwanda that day. But I would dedicate the rest of my life to going to the difficult and dangerous places with the message of God's love. Whatever it cost, I would bring His message to those who desperately needed Him.

At breakfast the final morning Gary asked Norman, "Why have I seen only one dog here?"

Norman looked sheepish. "So many bodies littered the roads that the dogs picked them apart, so we had to kill most of the dogs. And all those big black birds you see used to not be in the country. Thousands came to feast on the bodies."

I was finished eating for the day.

One of the pastors said, "What happened here was demonic. One couple in our church had their arms severed and were locked in a room with starving dogs. They died slow, horrible deaths."

We drove back to Kigali, where I was to lead a nationwide pastors' conference and preach an evangelistic meeting. But I was so emotionally raw that I couldn't talk for fear of weeping. It was just too much. How would I ever be able to preach?

But the pastors pressed, "You must see the result of the massacres firsthand."

The next morning they took us to a community outside Kigali where a bullet-torn church sat in a beautiful, serene setting. In the sanctuary I froze, gasping, "Oh, God!"

There the picked-clean bones and clothes of five thousand slaughtered people were strewn across the pews, on the floor, and around the pulpit. We could not move without crushing a bone or catching a foot on clothing.

Genocide

My emotions ran wild, imagining the moment these innocent men, women, and children realized this place of refuge had become a death chamber.

Norman said, "The new government leaders you will speak to Sunday night have seen this same sight in many churches. It's a miracle they have agreed to the meeting."

When I returned to my hotel room, I cried out, "God, I can't do this. What can I say to the pastors? What can I say to government leaders?" I had never felt so inadequate.

God's grace always amazes me. The Bible says, "His strength is made perfect in our weakness."

Pastors and Christian leaders from throughout the nation came to the conference—both Hutus and Tutsis. At first you could have cut the tension with a knife, but as I opened the Word of God and called for repentance, restitution, and reconciliation, hearts melted with the healing of Christ.

When I invited Christian leaders to repent, many fell to their knees weeping. They went to one another, asking forgiveness. It reminded me of the meetings in South Africa years earlier, a time of revival. God manifested among us.

At the close of the meeting the leaders broke out in the national dance, a beautiful sight, even for a Baptist evangelist! It was as though they had emerged from cocoons, and their joy was indescribable.

Healing had begun with the spiritual leaders and would flow to the general population.

I stood in the open fields the final weekend to proclaim the Gospel. Thousands gathered and many gave their hearts to Christ. The deepest needs in Rwanda were of the heart, and Jesus met those needs.

One man in the crowd would become important to our ministry in the region and eventually a key political leader in another war-torn country.

After the evangelistic meeting, we were rushed to a historic meeting with government and Christian leaders. Members of Parliament, the president's cabinet ministers, city officials, and leading pastors all gathered under one roof at the nicest hotel in the city. It was the first time such groups had sat together since the genocide. I was nervous about what to say and how they would respond.

Pastor Leo opened the service and took everyone by surprise. "Before we do anything else, we want to admit that Christian leaders participated in the genocide. That's an awful blemish on the name of Christ and on the church, and we want to ask our government leaders to forgive us."

A deathly silence fell upon the room. A presidential cabinet minister next to me at the head table said, "I never thought I would hear those words from a Christian leader."

When it came time for me to speak, I told them my story of traveling as a teenager and speaking about

Leaders

the need for peace in the world while having no peace in my heart. I explained how I came to know Christ and the great transformation in my life. I spoke of the need for repentance, faith, and reconciliation. A holy hush fell over the room. As one we prayed to the God of both the Hutus and the Tutsis, the blacks and the whites, the men and the women.

After the meeting the vice mayor of the city told me, "I came here very disturbed in my heart. I had no peace and saw our situation as hopeless. But tonight I gave my heart to Christ, and I have experienced that peace. Thank you for this message to me and to our nation. This is our only hope."

Before we left, many Rwandan pastors met with me and asked if I would return to bring this message to the masses. I promised we would.

I arrived back in San Antonio mentally, emotionally, and physically exhausted. I tried to explain to Tex what had happened, but I couldn't bring myself to tell her everything. That weekend our Sunday school teacher, Mike Scalf, surprised me by asking that I report on trip."

I trembled before the fifty or so in the class. I began, "Rwanda was very—" but I broke down crying and couldn't stop. Mike gathered the men around me, and they prayed for me for the entire Sunday school hour as I wept.

Mike didn't know it, but he was about to become part of the story.

CHAPTER THIRTY-ONE

TREACHEROUS PLACES

I promised Tex long ago that our lives would never be boring. God has taken us to some of the most difficult places in the world, and we've seen Him meet every financial need.

The countries we travel to enjoy few, if any, resources. Our ministry pretty much pays for everything, and the budget grew from sixty thousand dollars in 1986, the year we left the church at Bothell, to more than a million dollars by the end of the century. I keep our overhead low, our staff small, and our salaries (set by the board) extremely modest, and we have maintained our policy of informing supporters of our ministry but never asking for money. We believe that if God puts it on our hearts to minister somewhere, He will provide what we need. And He always has.

My son Dave and his wife Kelly preceded us to Rwanda to prepare for our return trip there, and when Tex and I arrived, we found the country had begun to heal since our last visit, but war in neighboring Burundi weighed heavily on the minds of the leaders in Rwanda. Soldiers drilled in the stadium each day, preparing for battle, so we were allowed in only at the last minute for our meetings.

We were fortunate that the vice mayor of Kigali, who had become a Christian at our meetings two years before, helped Dave navigate a lot of red tape. Mass meetings like ours were usually forbidden in countries on the brink of war.

Thousands came to Christ, and Joseph Karasanyi informed me that the pastors in Burundi had invited me to come and share the message of Christ with their people. "They heard you were not afraid to travel here during tumultuous times. Will you go?"

I assured him I would after a brief ministry trip to Great Britain. Joseph met with Burundi leaders to plan a large-scale evangelistic meeting, and God knitted my heart and Tex's with those of Joseph and his wife, Rose. True servants of Christ, they plunged headfirst into His plans, even in dangerous places.

Joseph told me there were no flights into the country, but that a Rwandan charter company might be willing to fly me in. I took a deep breath. This was going to be a tough one, but God has always provided just the right person at the right time. He led Mike Scalf, our Sunday school teacher and businessman with a knack for team building, to come and work with us. We decided he would go ahead of me into Burundi, as Dave had done in Rwanda the year before.

Joseph found us a flight, but at a price of six thousand dollars. I always want to honor the trust of those who sacrificially support our ministry, and I knew they'd understand that people were dying in Burundi. I felt compelled by the love of God to go.

And He provided as He always does. The Missions Committee at Wayside Chapel, an Evangelical Free church in San Antonio, offered to help.

Mike met Joseph in Rwanda a week later, and the two of them flew into Burundi. Meanwhile, Tex and I arrived in London where the next day I was to meet another team member, Martin Ntende, who would go with us to film the meetings.

We were awakened that night by a call from Mike Scalf's wife, Norma. Voice quivering, she said, "Sammy, I just talked to Mike in Burundi. He's running a fever and having hallucinations, and I'm scared to death for him. But that's not all. His mother's been taken to the hospital, and they don't think that she's going to live more than a couple of days. Plus, he told me someone threatened Joseph, demanding thousands of dollars from you."

I said, "Norma, if he's that sick, it's urgent we get him out immediately. I don't want to scare you, but he may have malaria."

Tex prayed while I called Mike. He sounded awful. "There's no way out of here, Sam," he said. "The charter plane dropped us off and left. The airport was desolate, the terminal building full of bullet holes. There wasn't a single person around. No planes either. The glass had been shot out of the doors. It's strange here. Hardly any cars on the streets, very little food in the hotel, and the hotel is almost empty. I'm the only one on my floor."

"Tell me about this threat to Joseph," I said.

"Three men stepped out of the dark outside his hotel and told him they knew he was working with an American who must have a lot of money. They wanted three thousand dollars right then. Joseph told them he didn't have any money, that he had prepaid all the expenses. They told him they'd return when you arrived. They want money, or the life of everyone who attends the crusade will be in danger."

"Mike, get Joseph to stay where you're staying. Then we need to work on getting you out of there. Is it safe for Tex and me to come in?"

"Sammy, that's your call."

I told Tex I needed to walk and pray. I felt guilty and stupid. How could I have put everyone in such danger? Why did I send my friend and colleague into such a situation?

But God gave me peace. The same God who had delivered me when I was arrested had it all under control. The God who protected us at the Romanian border could protect my team in a war zone.

I went back to the room and told Tex, "Sweetheart, I love you and you're the most precious person in the world to me. I couldn't stand it if we went into Burundi and—"

"Sammy," she said, her eyes filling, "you're not the only one who's been praying. I believe God wants me to go with you. I'm with you all the way."

We held each other. "You've been through so much with me," I told her, weeping. "I can trust God with my life, but it's so much harder to trust Him with yours."

She turned my face toward hers. "Remember what the people cried out in the Romanian Revolution."

How could I forget? Lives on the line, they shouted, *"Dumnezeu este cu noi!"* [God is with us!]

I went to work getting Mike out of Burundi and to a doctor, but not before he called his mother for the very last time. Norma held the phone to his mother's ear as they spoke.

She died twenty-four hours before Mike arrived back in the United States. Our pastor, David Walker, met him at the airport in Houston and broke the news to him.

Tex and Martin Ntende and I flew from London to Kigali, Rwanda, and then took the charter to Bujumbura. When the plane touched down at the deserted airport, Joseph emerged to greet us with flowers and a speech. Over a hundred Christians were lined up to welcome us. When we all left the airport, not another soul was in sight.

The three of us and Joseph and Rose stayed on the same floor and were not to leave the hotel except for the meetings. The stadium was just across the street, and over two hundred armed soldiers would be there, but we weren't allowed to walk over. A car and security guards would pick us up.

It was like being under house arrest, but I was also excited about the opening of the meetings the next evening. I sensed God was saying, "It's time. Thousands of people are waiting to hear from Me."

When it came time to go, six bodyguards with hand-held radios escorted us to the middle car of three. Imagine having to caravan across a street the size of a driveway.

At the jammed stadium the bodyguards escorted us through the cheering throngs. We weren't used to being treated like royalty. We felt more at home when people persecuted us. Tex said, "I don't like this."

"I don't either, sweetheart, but they're trying to express their appreciation."

The atmosphere was supercharged and it was clear the people had been starving for a message of hope. I began, "I've come to Burundi with good news! God loves you! God loves your family! God loves Bujumbura! God loves Burundi!"

The crowd roared. I preached the Gospel of God's love, of our need for repentance from sin and putting our faith in Christ. It was obvious God was deeply at work in the hearts of the people.

"If you want to have a personal relationship with Christ," I concluded, "then I want to pray with you. I'm going to ask you to join me at the front of the platform."

Normally people come and stand at the front, but when these people came (close to two thousand each day), they fell on their faces and wept openly. I had never before seen such brokenness and repentance.

The top story on the evening news that night showed the stadium filled with Hutus and Tutsis worshiping together. That shocked the nation, because six miles down the road, Hutus and Tutsis were killing each other.

Following the news, Joseph received a call from the presidential cabinet minister in charge of the peace negotiations. He asked to meet with me at his home on the following Saturday morning.

When we arrived, members of South Africa's Parliament were leaving. One reached out to me and said, "Thank you for what you're doing for this country. You're accomplishing more than you'll ever know."

The minister of peace and reconciliation, Mr. Ambrose Niyonsaba, welcomed me with open arms and told me he'd been out of the country trying to negotiate peace with the leaders of the two factions. "It's too dangerous to attempt that here, so we were in Tanzania. When I returned, I wanted to see what the news media had to say about the negotiations. But the main report was what you're doing in the stadium. I couldn't believe my eyes. Thousands of Hutus and Tutsis were meeting together peacefully and worshiping God. What we've tried to do for years, you've accomplished in one week. It's absolutely incredible, people prostrate on the ground and praying with each other and for one another.

"I implore you, bring this message of peace with God to every person in Burundi. It's our only hope."

God had again accomplished far more than I could have imagined. More than eight thousand people had prayed to receive Christ, finding peace with God and with one another.

Before we left Bujumbura, a delegation of pastors from the Democratic Republic of the Congo invited me to come to their nation in the summer of 2000. We found the situation even worse there.

Mai-Mai rebels had slaughtered people in a nearby village a few months earlier and now threatened to stone and beat anyone going to our meetings. They also threatened to bomb the stadium.

That affected attendance the first day, but when no bomb went off, the crowds began to build, and an average of thirteen thousand came daily. About thirty-five hundred people placed their faith in Christ.

The governor phoned and told me, "Thanks for bringing this message of peace to our country. Many are afraid to come here. Thank you for not being afraid."

CHAPTER THIRTY-TWO

RUNNING AS A CHAMPION

I'd be perfectly happy simply to be a secret agent for God, going wherever He leads me. He's given me a special burden to proclaim His name among those who have never heard the Gospel. That's why it has surprised and humbled me to be used to preach to hundreds of thousands of people in some of the largest cities of the world.

Seeing God move mightily in Rwanda and Burundi, Joseph Karasanyi was hungry to reach all of Africa. One of his top priorities was Ethiopia, which had also long fascinated me because it had been under Communist domination for nineteen years. Following the collapse of Communism, Ethiopian evangelicals were divided, seemingly unable to cooperate for the sake of their country.

Joseph called one of his pastor contacts there and said he had an American evangelist friend he felt God could use in the country. His contact was stunned almost speechless and finally told Joseph, "I'm amazed. We didn't expect God to answer so quickly." He said a group of pastors had recently decided to get on their knees for an all-night conversation with God. They became burdened to ask God to send a mighty revival to their land. One prayed, "Oh, God, please send an evangelist who can explain clearly Your salvation to the people."

Joseph told him and then me, "This is going to be the largest harvest of souls in the history of Ethiopia."

To be honest, I was skeptical. God had used Joseph to get us in to dangerous and nearly impossible places. But the greatest harvest in Ethiopia's history? Wasn't he being a bit unrealistic?

Joseph made several trips there to prepare for the event. Each time he would call Mike Scalf and me and say, "God is going to do something special here. Trust the Lord, He is going to work."

He told us a mighty Ethiopian prayer force had been unleashed, focused on our meetings.

But at the same time, war broke out between Ethiopia and neighboring Eritrea. As the days drew closer, the government threatened to cancel our meetings, afraid of large gatherings during wartime. Perhaps mercifully, I was unaware of this, giving me one fewer thing to stress over. My throat had been giving me major problems, and my voice was beginning to fail.

Believers in Addis Ababa, the capital city, continued to pray. They believed God had orchestrated my coming, and they would not give up.

Tex and I flew to Ethiopia, blissfully unaware of the 90 percent chance the meetings would be canceled. I boarded the plane believing God would heal my throat and move mightily.

Normally I sleep on overnight flights, but my favorite movie was showing—*Chariots of Fire*. It's the story of Eric Liddell, a Scottish Olympian who would become a missionary to China.

In one great scene, Liddell's sister Jenny expresses her concern that Eric's love for running will surpass his missionary calling. He tells her, "I believe God made me for a purpose, but He also made me fast. And when I run I feel His pleasure."

I wept as I watched, knowing God had created me to speak to the masses with the message of His Gospel. I sensed the Holy Spirit saying to my heart, "Run as a champion."

Joseph and the pastors and church leaders who met Tex and me at the airport were ecstatic. Excitement about the meetings filled the air. That's when we learned that the government had planned to cancel the campaign because of the war, but the day before, a peace accord was signed with Eritrea. Joseph gave me a knowing look. "Expect great things, Sammy."

I was astonished at the crowd at Ethiopia's national stadium. Normally, the first day has the smallest crowd, but every seat was filled and more sat on the ground. What would happen during the coming days? The atmosphere was electric, Burundi times ten.

In one area of the stands approximately two hundred men sat, and after forty-five minutes they left, replaced by another two hundred. That happened four times.

I asked one about it and one of the pastors explained, "They are the praying men. A prayer room under the stadium holds two hundred men who pray for forty-five minutes and then trade places with another two hundred. Eight hundred men pray throughout the service." I knew that was why God was working in such a marvelous way.

When I invited people to come to Christ, God's awesome presence filled the stadium. It was as if they had been waiting for a moment like this for more than a quarter of a century. Thousands flooded from their seats and came forward to receive Christ. The rest roared and applauded.

I returned to my hotel room so overcome with emotion I could hardly speak. Even more people jammed the stadium the next day, and more than seventy-five thousand people attended the third day. It was the largest crowd I had ever preached to, up to that time.

I had awakened filled with anticipation and leaned over to kiss my wife. "Hi, sweetie," I croaked. My voice was gone!

God, You told me to run as a champion! What is going on?

"Son," He seemed to gently say, "this is how a champion runs in My kingdom—not by human ability or great oratory is the world won, but by My Spirit. Run with the wind—the wind of My Spirit. Trust in Me and Me alone."

I had no choice. I could quit, or I could trust God. That evening when I arrived at the stadium, I was barraged with questions about my voice. I eked out, "I don't know."

When the choir finished, I stepped to the microphone, cleared my throat, and could barely be heard. But I was loud enough for the interpreter to hear. He translated, and God worked. Thousands came to Christ.

I went back to the hotel with a clearer understanding. God had raised me up to proclaim His Word. And God would get all the glory. I was learning to run as a champion.

More than 300,000 attended the four-day crusade, and more than 9,000 had prayed to receive Christ.

That Sunday morning, when I spoke at the largest evangelical church in Addis Ababa, thousands stood listening outside. Four thousand converts from the crusade had shown up. They matched the new believers with cell group leaders who would disciple them.

Ethiopia

I was scheduled to preach in the world's largest stadium two months later, and I felt inadequate. In the heart of Rio de Janeiro, Brazil's great soccer stadium, Maracana, holds over 150,000 people.

I had loved Brazil since the late 1980s, when Wade Akins, a missionary there and longtime friend, had invited me. Wade is one of the greatest missionaries I've ever met and one of my personal heroes. The largest crowd I preached to during that first trip was only thirty people. Now I was to preach in Maracana.

As much as an evangelist might consider this an honor, I had long before explained to the organizers that I was simply a man God had chosen to use, but I didn't have a huge organization like many others. It would take an incredible organization to do what they had in mind.

This was a task only God could accomplish. He would have to raise the funds, the organization, and everything else necessary for such a large crusade. Our small staff in San Antonio was nowhere near able to lead such an effort in one of the largest cities in the world.

Yet, I had a sense of peace. I left it with the Brazilian pastors.

God began to work in marvelous ways. The first evangelical governor of Rio de Janeiro was elected within the next few months and threw his support behind the campaign. Other evangelical denominations came on board. One by one, God provided the resources.

But I still had severe throat problems. By May I lost my voice, and with one week until the meetings, my spirits were low. We had a team of 75 people, the Tennessee Baptist Convention had a team of more than 300, and International Crusades had 150, all in churches throughout Rio preaching, witnessing, and sharing Christ in anticipation of the crusade.

Tex and I spent the week on a lonely beach in southern Brazil, updated daily on our teams in Rio. I used the time just to talk to God.

One night I faced a crisis of inadequacy. I cried, "Oh, God, I can't do this. I don't have the human resources. I don't even have a voice."

I sent an urgent e-mail to our intercessors, pleading for prayer. A longtime friend replied with an e-mail that, though simply written, blanketed me with serenity. He knew our ministry well enough to remind me of all God had done with us in the past and urged me to go forward by looking back. God would be faithful.

After a couple of more hours talking to God on that lonely beach, that still, small voice said, "Run with the wind. Run as a champion."

I was caught off guard at the airport in Rio when Tex and I were met not only by Christian leaders but also by a convoy of police vehicles behind and in front of us, rushing us to our hotel. One of the leading sociologists in the nation had been assigned by the governor to ride with Tex and me and brief us on the problems facing the city.

Tex and I had lunch with son Dave and his wife, Kelly, and our daughter, Renee. I was reminded how faithful God had been and how He had brought us through so much. What a precious time with our children, now grown and living for Him.

For so long I had felt like God's secret agent—and I relished that role. Now I was to stand before the governor, the vice governor, the mayor of Rio, and the international press as I proclaimed the name of Christ to people in world's largest stadium.

God coated my voice with strength, and when I gave the invitation, it appeared half those in attendance responded. It sounded like roars of thunder as thousands prayed aloud with me in that great stadium.

Would God now open doors in the other great cities of the world? How could He use me if I didn't have a voice?

Part Four — The Autumn of Life

CHAPTER THIRTY-THREE

'BE STILL AND KNOW...'

Around this time I was challenged to go to Iran, a country so hostile to the Gospel that even sharing Christ with one individual meant a death sentence. Evangelicals had dubbed it "the nation of martyrs." Yet I was invited to join a few others there to do nothing but pray for the nation.

Imagine a mass evangelist making such a trip knowing I could not mention the name of Christ to anyone! And neither was I to tell anyone I was going. Still I went, and God gave me such a burden for the people that I merely walked the streets and prayed God would open doors there someday.

God gave me a burden for the entire Middle East, one of the most difficult regions of the world to reach with the Gospel.

When I returned to the United States, I was invited to speak in a church in California made up mostly of born again Iranians. Several people from other religious backgrounds came to know Christ that day, confirmation that God was going to work mightily in that land of martyrs.

Meanwhile, Joseph Karasanyi thought we should go to the Middle East for a major evangelistic campaign, focusing on Egypt and the United Arab Emirates.

Despite that God had put that area on my heart, I confess that at first I thought, *No way we'll be able to minister there.* But I was to eat my words. Joseph, a man of huge faith, persisted, convinced God would open doors.

Finally I asked Mike Scalf to go with him to meet with city leaders to check it out. They discovered a network of eight hundred churches interested in a major evangelistic thrust.

The Middle East wasn't even on my radar when I first began traveling into Eastern Europe. Soon friends in India invited me there for major crusades. Here I was at the dawn of the new millennium, in my early fifties, and it appeared my greatest ministry opportunities still lay ahead of me.

I don't deny that I had long dreamt of preaching the Gospel to massive crowds. But I had always been careful not to get out ahead of God and His plans. I didn't develop a big organization, just enough of a staff to allow me to follow His leading.

I have always had an insatiable desire to know and walk with God. And while He's given me a big vision, He's also opened more doors than I could have ever hoped for. A simple motto God has burned into my life is: "Before He works through us, He always works in us." How often I've been taught that lesson!

My voice problems continued until I finally sought help from a surgeon who videoed my vocal cords and found them severely bruised and swollen. A speech therapist, medication, and exercises helped, but I still struggled.

Needless to say, to a preacher the voice is vital. I did everything my speech therapist instructed, but one day she said, "Something doesn't sound right," and videoed my vocal cords again.

She was alarmed to discover polyps and immediately called the specialist again. Though he was in surgery, she had him paged, which told me this was much more serious than I imagined. He wanted to see me that week.

I awoke early the day of my appointment, and a verse of Scripture burned in my heart: "Be still, and know that I am God; I will be exalted among the nations, I will be exalted in the earth" (Psalm 46:10, NIV).

Be still? As is true for most preachers, silence has never been my spiritual gift. God had given me an ability to communicate, but He's also often reminded me that He doesn't need my oratorical skills. What He desires is my availability to Him.

The specialist looked grim. He gave me a choice between surgery to remove the growths or complete silence for two weeks, along with medication that might make them disappear.

God had already impressed upon me to "Be still...," so I said, "I don't want surgery unless it's absolutely necessary."

The following Monday I was to speak in Sacramento to mission leaders from all over the world. The specialist prescribed two weeks of absolute silence beginning the day after that.

When I returned to my car, Tex called for an update, and tears streamed down my face. I didn't understand why this was happening, but I had peace.

At home, Tex and I discussed the ramifications of two weeks of silence and even the prospect of losing my voice. In a strange way, I was excited about the two weeks of silence. So was Tex!

I knew that if I stayed in San Antonio, I would be tempted to talk. So after I spoke in Sacramento, we flew to Phoenix for a week for some quality time with God and to enjoy the Grand Canyon. Then we would return to San Antonio to celebrate Thanksgiving with our family—who would understand and honor my silence.

The two weeks proved to be some of the greatest of my life. When Tex would tell people why I wasn't talking, some assumed I couldn't hear either and would speak louder or even try to communicate with me in sign language. Even funnier, some made up their own sign language.

Most of all, the two weeks became a unique time with God. I was consumed with reading my Bible. If God was trying to tell me something, I wanted to make sure I heard everything. My responsibility was to be still. He would be exalted in all the earth.

The beauty of the Grand Canyon declares the glory of God. Tex and I spent hours every day seeking Him, and in my quietness, I met with Him and He with me. I'll never be the same person.

Tex and I had much for which to be thankful: children who loved the Lord, friends on every continent, an unbreakable commitment to each other, and a lifetime adventure with Christ.

But I also sensed we'd only just begun. I knew there were no guarantees, but I envisioned another thirty years of ministry and couldn't wait to get back to it.

When I returned to the specialist, the growths had disappeared and I wept yet again. God is amazingly good.

I had campaigns scheduled in Eastern Europe, Asia, Africa, and South America. In my own country few people had heard of Sammy Tippit, and that was all right with me. The kingdom of God is about making Christ known.

George Whitefield, the great evangelist of the 1700s, once said, "Let the name of George Whitefield rot in hell, but let the name of Jesus Christ be glorified forever."

Someone once said, "If God can keep a man hidden, then He will be able to use him."

Keep me hidden, Lord.

CHAPTER THIRTY-FOUR

LIGHT IN THE DARKNESS

It's difficult to remain hidden when God has called you to be light in a very dark world. Our difficulties in Eastern Europe during the days of Communism seemed minor compared to the mortal threats we faced in war zones in Africa and from Islamic terrorists in the new millennium.

Joseph Karasanyi kept telling me we would see huge crowds in Cairo because of the sheer size of the city. I was skeptical. Egypt was predominantly Muslim, and I wasn't sure how many contacts Joseph had. I finally sent Mike Scalf to meet him in Cairo and look into the possibilities.

Mike discovered that Joseph only had one acquaintance there, Pastor Bakki from the Assembly of God (AOG) church. But his faith alone made up for any shortfall in contacts.

Providentially, the AOG was having a leadership conference in Port Said, and Mike and Joseph were able to meet with 15 key leaders. They told Mike only one Cairo church could organize such a meeting, the Kasr el-Dobara Evangelical Church.

Mike and Joseph met with their skeptical leaders, who had created a network of six hundred like-minded churches throughout the country. They had been involved in Billy Graham and Luis Palau crusades and had been praying for another such opportunity, but who was Sammy Tippit?

As Mike tried to explain who I was, a young pastor excused himself and returned with a copy of my book, *The Prayer Factor*. The atmosphere turned from suspicion to excitement. Plans for a large event in Egypt were birthed.

When Mike returned to San Antonio, we assembled a team that assisted me in a conference on spiritual awakening for pastors and leaders throughout the Middle East.

The Egyptian Christians used technology rather than a stadium as a platform for the Gospel. It gave me a vision for the future of our ministry, especially in countries closed to the idea of mass meetings or where it was dangerous for people to meet publicly.

They would film the services each evening at the Kasr el Dobara Church, then immediately copy videos and deliver them throughout the nation to the other 600 churches—by foot, bicycles, cars, and airplanes.

I was nervous the day before the first meeting. I had seen God's Word melt the hardest Communists but wondered how it would go over in the Islamic world. Our team took an evening sailboat ride down the Nile River the night before we began.

That evening is etched into my memory. All was quiet on the Nile, and as we sailed past the multitude of homes and apartments, God's love flooded my soul. My heart cried out, "Send revival to Egypt, oh, Lord!"

I slept very little that night as I tried to discern God's message for the people. I paced the room wondering about this new type of audience. What should I preach to people steeped in their own religion? Would they respond?

Frankly, the message God seemed to place on my heart sounded preposterous. *Preach in an Islamic country what I preached to secular American youth?*

The answer kept coming back a resounding *Yes.*

As I participated in the worship preliminaries that first evening, I still had to wonder whether I had understood the Lord correctly. But as some of the locals shared their personal stories of how they had come to faith in Christ, I was stunned to realize they weren't about Islam. These testimonies could have come from any church in the West. Human nature was the same wherever you go. Men and women talked of their search for purpose and meaning in life—how they'd been involved with drugs or gone through a divorce. Some told of suicide attempts.

I preached on the fear of rejection, told my own story, and proclaimed Jesus as the only One who can provide the acceptance for which our hearts long. When I invited people to place their faith in Jesus, I was astounded at the massive response.

As I was leaving, one of the pastors ran to me, waving. "Brother Sammy, this is exactly the message our people need to hear."

Tex and I both had tears rolling as we prayed before we went to bed. Deep in the heart of every human are the same needs. That truth provided a framework from which I would minister throughout the Islamic world.

Concurrent with our meetings, the church also hosted a pastors' conference for Christian leaders from eight nations throughout the Middle East. One of the leaders told me, "We are experiencing something unusual from God. The sense of His presence is wonderful."

The Kasr el Dobara Church pastor told me of a village of about 20,000 in upper Egypt that was predominantly Orthodox. Because of good relations with the Orthodox, the Evangelicals used the Coptic Orthodox Church's video center antenna, which covered the whole village. Volunteers went door to door, asking people to adjust their TVs so the entire village could live stream our meetings. They also went to coffee bars to adjust the televisions. And they even put posters on governmental buildings—something unheard of. The entire village listened every evening!

Even when things went wrong, God's hand could be seen. As I preached one evening, the video went out in an overflow area where eight students had been laughing and mocking the meetings. When the video went out, they entered the church to find out what was happening.

They stayed and listened and when I asked those who wanted to accept Jesus to stand, all eight stood. The leader of the counselors worried they might make fun of the appeal. But when he sent counselors to each of them, they found all of them under a deep sense of conviction from the Holy Spirit.

The final evening, the atmosphere was so electric I kept bouncing on my toes and my hands tingled. The auditorium filled and overflow rooms were packed. Many more people stood outside.

I fought tears as I looked into the faces of the people and preached. When I gave the invitation, throughout the sanctuary people stood and wept.

As we were leaving the church, a counselor grabbed my coat. His eyes sparkled. "You need to hear this lady's story."

Happy tears ran down her face. "I dreamt last night that I should go to a Christian church. But when I awoke, I didn't know where to go. As I walked down the street this evening, I saw many people outside the church and asked what was happening. Someone helped me to go inside.

"Your message was for me. I believed in Jesus."

What happened at the Kasr el Dobara church extended far beyond the meetings. The pastors' conference helped us establish relationships with several churches from other Islamic countries.

Christian leaders from throughout Egypt traveled to Cairo on the final Saturday for a national conference on spiritual awakening. Most had seen a harvest during the evening evangelistic meetings.

My ministry had been birthed in the revival in Monroe, Louisiana, and the outpouring of God's Spirit in Romania had shown me that there's no place too difficult for God. Now He was knitting my heart with followers of Jesus in the Islamic world.

At the close of that meeting, I extended an invitation for leaders to pray for revival in Egypt. Mike Scalf told me that the administrator of the church said, "Come quickly. You must see this." Mike came to the sanctuary to find hundreds of leaders on their knees, broken before God.

God's Presence

I thought I'd never fall asleep that night. We had entered a new moment in our ministry. Several pastors from other Middle Eastern countries asked us to come to their nations. Two pastors, Emmanuel Bandi and John Chiek Boom from Sudan, told me, "It is very dangerous in our country, but please come. We will try to get a big stadium."

I said, "Is that possible?"

They didn't need to answer. I saw it in their eyes.

CHAPTER THIRTY-FIVE

PERIL

Joseph Karasanyi was thrilled about Sudan. He believed no country was too difficult for God. I agreed but also understood the persecution and danger we might face.

Sudanese leaders believed we would be given permission to conduct a large event in a major stadium in Khartoum. I thought that would be impossible without a miracle. Osama bin Laden had once lived there and in the early 1990s had formed an alliance with the National Islamic Front of South Sudan. Even after he was kicked out of the country, the people held him in high esteem, and the government continued to persecute Christians.

But as I prayed through this during my daily quiet times, I felt a definite urge from the Lord that I should go to Khartoum. That was all I needed. In June 2001, I asked Mike Scalf to travel with Joseph into Khartoum to begin preparations.

Mike immediately called me in the States. "Sammy, you need to know that Christians invited German evangelist Reinhard Bonnke to lead an Easter celebration at the central Green Square. But the police refused to allow the meetings, and Bonnke and his team left the country."

Mike paused. "The believers gathered at All Saints Cathedral to pray, but the government sent in troops and, uh..."

"Mike, are you okay?"

He struggled to speak. "Yeah, but Sammy, what I saw..."

I waited.

"I saw the blood of Christians splattered on the walls of that church. The troops threw grenades and shot and wounded ten believers, three seriously. A hundred were detained. Fifty-three men were flogged with fifteen lashes and sent to prison for twenty days. Several women and children were also flogged."

Persecution

Mike paused to compose himself. "Church leaders collected shrapnel embedded in the platform and pews and filled a large barrel three quarters full."

I could barely speak. "What are our friends saying? Do we need stop our preparations?"

"They want to move forward, Sammy, but they will understand if you decide not to come."

I sucked in a huge breath. "Mike, tell them as long as they feel we should come, I'm coming. God spoke to my heart to go to Sudan, and I haven't heard anything different."

By the end of July 2001, the Sudanese government had granted the organizers permission to hold the meetings in one of its largest stadiums. That alone sounded like a miracle, but I said, "We must have permission in writing."

"Sammy," I was told, "that will take time. Nothing happens quickly around here."

"I understand. But, we can't commit without absolute assurance they won't do to us what they did to Bonnke."

Before I left to minister in Brazil during the first 10 days of September, I got word the Sudanese government had said it would grant written permission. We could pick up the document September 11.

"Perfect timing," I said. "I get back to the U.S. that day. I'll call you as soon as I'm in the country."

Meanwhile, the Egyptians would go and train the counselors. They'd done the best job of following up new believers of anyone we'd worked with.

Tex and I enjoyed a sweet time of ministry in Brazil, but my heart was heavy the whole while. I couldn't get the Sudanese Christians off my mind.

When we arrived at the Rio airport September 10 for our late flight home, security seemed tighter than usual. Our bags were searched, and airline personnel seemed to ask more questions than normal. I didn't care. I just wanted to get home to the fax from Joseph with the written permission. I hardly slept, wondering if they would really grant it.

It always feels good to land in America, though we still had to fly from Dallas to San Antonio. After going through customs at DFW that morning, Tex and I went to the Admiral's Club to await that last leg home. She found a desk to do some writing, and I sat in front of a television to catch up on the news.

I couldn't believe what I saw happening to the World Trade Center towers in New York. I yelled down the hall, "Tex, come here! Hurry!"

"What? What's wrong?"

"Our country is being attacked!" I said, pointing to the television.

Just then an announcement came over the P.A. "The airport is being closed. Please leave immediately. I repeat. The Dallas/Fort Worth airport is being closed. You must leave immediately."

"What do we do?" Tex said. "How will we get home?"

"Check car rental agencies."

All the agencies Tex called had already rented their last cars.

"See if we can rent a van," I said.

She found a van within a few minutes, but due to my lack of sleep on the plane, we didn't get far before I needed a cup of coffee. The lady at the cash register in a gas station just south of Dallas had panic written all over her face. "Is this the end of the world?"

"No, ma'am," I said. "This isn't the end, but we need to be prepared, and only Jesus can make us ready."

Fear descended on the country like a fog.

I worried about what had happened to the Egyptians. Had they made it out of Khartoum before the attack in New York? With air traffic at a standstill all over the world, what about Joseph? Had he made it in?

Should I cancel? And even if I decided to continue, what about the team that planned to travel with me? The biggest question was what the pastors and leaders in Sudan were thinking. I believed God had told me to go to Khartoum. Could I have been wrong? Did the current circumstance change the mission?

Fortunately, our annual board of directors meeting was only a couple of weeks away. They've always provided sound advice.

Mike learned that our Egyptian friends had successfully trained counselors and made it out of Sudan before the terrorist attacks. As for Joseph, he had been on a flight into Khartoum from Nairobi when the pilot said they were returning to Nairobi.

After spending time in prayer, I still wasn't sure what I would do, but at least I knew I needed to release the team from its commitment to go. I didn't want anyone to feel guilty if I did go and they chose not to.

Alerts from the U.S. State Department advised Americans to immediately leave Sudan. It appeared the U.S. might attack there after launching offensives in Afghanistan.

I contacted John and Emmanuel, the Sudanese pastors I'd met in Egypt. I had one question: Should I still come?

They didn't hesitate. "Yes, Sammy, you must. If we cancel now, they will think we are fearful and have no support from abroad. They will do everything possible to destroy the church. Please, don't cancel."

"I need to hear clearly from the Lord on this again, because I don't want my presence to put your lives in danger."

"We are willing to die. But we will pray that God will show you what to do."

I got away to my special place of prayer, a spot under a clump of trees where on my morning walks I got alone with God. "Oh, Lord," I said, kneeling in the grass, tears rolling, "I don't want to die. Yet if that is what You want, I'm willing. But I don't want to go to Khartoum by myself. Would You send someone with me?"

I was exhausted and needed to talk to Tex. She's walked with me through so much, I knew she'd have some insight.

She saw the stress on my face as soon as I walked in the door and hugged me. "Are you okay?"

I stared at the floor. "I don't know what to do. I'm willing to go, but I'm afraid to go by myself."

"I'll go with you."

I lifted her chin so we were eye to eye, and I smiled. "I can run faster without you. If I have to get out of Dodge, I'll need to do it quickly."

Just then the doorbell rang and our son Dave greeted me. "I need to talk to you," he said as he came in. "I guess you've cancelled your trip to Sudan."

"No. I was just telling your mom I believe God wants me to go."

"Interesting."

"Why?"

"We had an all-night prayer meeting with the young people in my discipleship group, and I felt God wanted me to go to Sudan."

Chills ran up my spine. It seemed like an answer to prayer, but could I put my son in harm's way? "Have you discussed this with Kelly?"

He nodded. "She only wants God's will."

I urged him to pray more with her and be absolutely certain they were both at peace this was of God.

They spent the next few days praying while I travelled to a meeting in Georgia. There, Greg Williams, a local pastor, told me he felt God leading him to go with me. By the time I returned to San Antonio, Dave and Kelly had decided that it was God's will for him to go.

I asked three Brazilian friends—who had traveled with me to other countries to video and photograph our work—if they would pray about going. Daniel, Josias, and Selio came back with a yes within twenty-four hours.

Not only would I not have to go alone, but God put together the team. One last piece of the puzzle was that our board of directors needed to feel peace about the situation.

We had scheduled our annual board meeting in Tennessee. Everyone would be there except Joe Ragont, so I called and asked if he had any counsel.

"Sam, I would say only this: Don't make any decisions based on fear. Base your decision on God's leading. If He leads, you must go. If not, you have to cancel."

I knew deep in my heart that God wanted me to go. I also knew if He was in it, He would give the entire board the same peace.

They peppered me with questions, then asked me to leave the room. I spent a long hour praying and pacing. When I returned, one of them said, "We believe God wants you to go to Sudan. We don't know whether He wants you to come back. If you are willing to go, understanding that you might die there, you have our blessing." They also tried to put my mind at ease about Tex, promising they would take care of her the rest of her life, should something happen to me.

CHAPTER THIRTY-SIX

IN THE LION'S DEN

When word came, in writing, that the Sudanese government had granted us permission to hold evangelistic meetings in the Khartoum stadium, I sensed God had great things in store.

Before we left the States, Dr. Michael Wirth, a close friend and faithful prayer partner, asked to meet. He told me God had spoken to him from the book of Esther about her role in saving the Jewish people from destruction. He said, "Sammy, I believe you will have an opportunity to speak to the leaders of Sudan about the plight of Christians."

Frankly, I often take with a grain of salt the many specific messages people claim to have about wherever I'm going. I thank them and am polite, but so often their "revelations" exhibit an ignorance or at least naiveté about the region or country in question. But I knew Mike, and he wasn't the type to make those kinds of statements flippantly. He's one of the foremost orthopedic surgeons in America, a deep thinker, and a man of prayer. Plus, he had not been overly specific, the way many are when passing along such "words of knowledge" just for attention.

Mike had simply felt led to say he believed I would have opportunity to talk to Sudanese leaders about the plight of the Christians there. I couldn't pass that off. I wanted to be alert and ready for any such opportunity.

Our Brazilian cameramen met Dave, our new pastor friend Greg from Georgia, and me in Kenya before we continued to Sudan. Joseph and a contingent of Sudanese pastors met us in Khartoum. The gleam in Joseph's eyes matched the thrill flooding my heart.

The Christians drove us to our hotel with their own security team ahead and behind us. Two security guys searched my room before I settled in, and the pastors told me to be careful at meals and not to engage in conversations with anyone I didn't know.

The next day ministry board member Dave Engbrecht, pastor of the Nappanee (Indiana) Missionary Church, called my room just before we left for the meetings and recorded an interview with me.

He posted it on our website, and people around the world gathered to pray.

Before I left the room, I prayed. "Oh, God, draw people to Jesus."

Dave Tippit, Greg, and the pastors had gathered in the lobby, and a convoy of vehicles took us to the stadium.

A large group of young people formed a barrier between the platform and the crowd, which I estimated at between 25,000 and 30,000 people.

God filled my heart with love for the Sudanese people, and it was amazing to see the attentiveness on their faces as I started my message. It seemed no one even moved, remarkable for such a large crowd.

When I came to the close of the message, I was stunned as a large cloud of dust rose throughout the stadium from approximately 5,000 people responding to the invitation and joining me at the front of the platform.

I was so overwhelmed that I once again had trouble falling asleep that night. Fortunately, I had nothing planned for the next morning.

However, a loud bang woke me early, and I jumped out of bed. "Who is it?"

"Joseph! And the leaders from the Council of Churches are with me!"

I opened the door to panic-stricken faces. Joseph put a hand on my shoulder, and rasped, "Al Qaeda and the Muslim Brotherhood have threatened to bomb the stadium this afternoon, promising a bloodbath. Soldiers have surrounded the stadium and told us we can't return."

I staggered as the room spun. "What do we do?"

Pastor Apollo Alfred, head of the Council of Churches, said, "Meet with all the leaders of the churches and challenge us to bring the Gospel to all the people of Khartoum. Revive us and we will go back to our churches and spread the revival."

I took a deep breath. "Okay, let's do it."

"But," Apollo said, "you and everyone on your team must understand: We have secured a hall that will hold 500 people—every

Christian leader in Khartoum. The terrorists could kill all of us with one bomb. No one should come unless he is willing to die."

"I'll tell our team."

"One more thing," he said. "I'm trying to set up a meeting with the Vice President of the nation. He's responsible for interacting with the churches. Are you willing to meet with him?"

My meeting with Dr. Wirth and his word from Esther raced through my mind. "Yes, I would like that."

My team—son Dave, Greg (the Georgia pastor), and the Brazilian cameramen (Daniel, Josias, and Selio)—came to my room, where Joseph told them about the threat to the stadium and the suggested alternative.

After an intense time of prayer, I told the guys what Pastor Apollo Alfred had told me and made clear that anyone willing to go to the meetings must also be willing to die.

They gaped at me, silent. "No one needs to feel guilty if you don't sense God's leading," I said.

Daniel said, "Pastor Sammy, what has God told you?"

I pressed my lips together. "I believe He wants me to go."

Daniel said, "Josias and Selio and I discussed this before we came. We believe God wants us to go wherever you go. So, we will be there."

Greg quickly agreed. "I'm ready to die for my Savior."

"Dave?" I said.

"I don't know," he said, tension in his face. "I spoke last night with some people who've been working here for quite some time, and they're very concerned." He sighed. "One had a dream that we would be killed. I need more time to pray."

I put a hand on his shoulder. "That's okay. Stay here and pray during the first meeting. God will show you His will in His time." I had peace about Dave's ability to discern and follow God's lead.

When it came time to leave, Dave was still praying. Security guards surrounded the rest of us in the lobby and escorted us to the cars.

The hall was packed, the tension crackling. Pastor Apollo introduced me, and I spoke about our victory in Christ. "They may be able to stop us from preaching," I began, "but they can't stop us from following Jesus! We are more than conquerors through Christ!" The crowd roared. "They may be

Revived

able to keep us from the stadium, but they can't stop the prayers of God's people." The leaders cheered, joy making them smile in the midst of suffering. When we closed with a time of corporate prayer, they cried to God with a fervency I've seldom seen.

When we returned to the hotel, Dave was eager to hear all about it. "Dad, as I prayed God gave me peace that He wants me to be a part of the meetings. If I'm killed, I'm ready."

I hugged him and told him I loved him.

Alone in my room, I knelt, emotion flooding my heart as I remembered God's promise so many years before that He would use Dave for His glory. I worried for his safety, of course, but I also felt blessed to have such a man of God as a son.

The next morning both Pastor Greg and Dave spoke before I preached. The pastors and leaders fell to their knees and wept, and their love for Jesus so inspired those of us who had come to serve them.

As the meetings drew to a close, you would have thought our team had been ministering together for years. It seemed God made the time with the leaders a tapestry upon which He wove a beautiful message of revival. The leaders shouted with joy, focusing not on their suffering, but on the One who had suffered for them.

Saturday evening, November 3, 2001, our team and a small contingent of Sudanese pastors were welcomed to the residence of Macar Kacuol, Vice President of the Republic of Sudan. I knew God had ordained this and prepared me through Dr. Wirth, but that didn't make me any less queasy.

Mr. Kacuol had a small group of advisors with him, and after everyone had been introduced, the Sudanese pastors got right to the point. "Why couldn't the government protect us when we were assembling peacefully to worship?"

The Vice President hung his head and struggled to respond, but I didn't feel he gave an adequate answer.

The time had come for me to speak up. My heart pounded, but a small voice deep within me said, "Don't be afraid."

"Mr. Vice President," I said, "before I came to Sudan a friend reminded me of how God raised up Esther to save His people from harm. My friend felt I might have an opportunity to speak to leaders of the nation on behalf of Christians. Sir, if you want God's blessing, you must protect the Christians."

The Vice President fixed his eyes on me and didn't move.

"I urge you to use your position to give Christians the freedom to worship."

I shared the Gospel with him and his aides, and they listened politely. Then we prayed for them.

When we departed Sudan, Pastor Apollo gave me a big hug. "Please ask people around the world to pray for Christians in Sudan. We are suffering, but we believe God is going to do great things here."

CHAPTER THIRTY-SEVEN

THE CLOSED COUNTRIES

The prayer walk in Iran gave me a vision for revival in the Persian world.

The crusade in Egypt showed me how useful technology could be in Islamic nations.

And our time in Sudan exposed me to Christians in the midst of suffering.

God had thrust me into ministry in the most difficult areas of the world, and that would come with a heavy price.

An Armenian Iranian pastor in Los Angeles encouraged me to develop a Farsi language website, translate my books into Farsi, and conduct conferences for Iranian Christian leaders. My book, *The Prayer Factor,* was translated and distributed throughout Iran, and I soon got reports of God using it powerfully there.

When I conducted a *Prayer and Revival* conference for Christian leaders and pastors from Iran, I met many whose family members and colleagues had been killed for their faith in Jesus. One person identified and brought together about thirty-five Afghan Christian leaders for a meeting with 350 Iranians where I spoke and taught on the subject of prayer.

Apparently nothing such as that had ever been done with Afghan Christians. A spirit of revival gripped them from the opening moment. One said he didn't even know there were other Afghan believers. A young lady fell on the floor weeping when she met other Afghan Christians.

A missionary recalled going to the stadium in Kabul "where thousands came to watch an execution. As they shouted Islamic slogans I asked God to let me see the day when Afghans would worship Jesus. He let me see it today."

After the conference I was invited to speak at the annual gathering of the Christian agencies working in Afghanistan. I made arrangements to fly directly to their conference from a ministry trip Tex and I were on in Brazil. Due to previous commitments, she flew directly back to the United States.

The conference organizer emailed that a lady would pick me up and drive me about an hour and a half to the conference. I called him right away.

"We need to make other arrangements for transportation," I said. "I'm sure the lady you have scheduled to pick me up is a wonderful Christian, but my wife won't be with me, and I don't think it should be only the two of us traveling to the conference."

Silence.

"Are you still there?"

"Yes, I'm here," he said somberly. "I'm not sure what to say."

"I'm not saying there's anything wrong with the lady..."

"No, no, that's not it. I think God is trying to tell us something. Two of us have been organizing this conference for years because of our deep burden for Afghanistan. Now, I'm doing it myself because my colleague has just separated from his wife. He's been involved with another woman. I think God is using you to speak to us even before you arrive."

My Iran prayer-walking friend Peter met me at the conference center, concern written on his face. "There's a split among the agencies about how vocal they should be in sharing Christ inside Afghanistan," he told me. "Some believe they should witness only by deeds, whereas others believe that there must be verbalization. We need to pray for unity."

I sensed so much tension in the first session that afterward I mingled with participants and learned more was at work than disagreeing over methods. Fear and discouragement seemed to rule.

A number of conferees lived in Pakistan but worked among the Afghans. Terrorists threw grenades into the Protestant church near the American Embassy in Islamabad and killed five, two of them Americans.

Just a few weeks before the conference, terrorists had also struck at the heart of Christian agencies in Pakistan. They attacked a school that housed the children of missionaries, and security guards and employees were killed.

My heart broke as I listened to their stories. And as I ministered daily on prayer and personal revival, I could tell by the moisture in their eyes and the softening of their faces that God was working. I didn't understand how deeply until the last session.

I spoke about absolute surrender to God and invited them to make the front of the auditorium an altar. People flooded forward, weeping, some even wailing. They embraced one another and prayed together.

I sat and watched God transform hearts filled with fear into hearts full of faith.

Peter came to me and asked if I would pray with one sobbing woman. I knelt beside her. "What's on your heart?" I said.

She tried to regain her composure. "God has called me to martyrdom," she managed.

My eyes widened. "Martyrdom? I don't understand."

She wiped the tears from her face. "My husband and I were told we would be killed if we returned to Pakistan. Now God is telling me we must go back to minister to these people."

A tear rolled down my cheek. Shame on us Americans who get teased about our faith or feel persecuted because saying "Merry Christmas" is considered intolerant. "Oh, God," I prayed, "give my sister and her husband wisdom. Lead them by your Spirit. Keep them safe."

As people returned to their seats, the organizer opened the floor for anyone who had something to share. One after another stood with stories similar to the one I'd just heard. One couple said, "We had decided that this would be our last conference. We had seen too much terror and suffering. But, God has changed our hearts. We must continue to serve the people."

When we finished, the conference host (I'll call him Curt) pleaded for some time with me. "I need your counsel." We arranged to meet later for a meal, because right then I was emotionally washed out and needed time alone.

I found some nearby woods where I could pray and be refreshed. For some reason I always seemed at home praying in a wooded area.

When Curt and I met later, he came right to the point. "My wife thinks I love Afghanistan more than I love her."

"Why?"

He held up his hand. "You see my wedding ring?"

I nodded.

"Do you know what the other ring is?"

I shook my head.

"It signifies my commitment to Afghanistan. But my wife's jealous. She doesn't want anything to do with Afghanistan. What should I do?"

Having experienced a revival in my own marriage in Germany years earlier, I said, "You need to take off that ring, go home, and love your wife the way Christ loves the church. You can always rebuild your ministry if you have kept your commitment to your wife. But, if you violate your commitment to your wife, you will also lose your ministry. You need to leave here committed to let your wife know how much you love her."

After the conference, Peter, Dave Tippit, two Afghan Christians, and I joined a couple of others and made a prayer walk in Afghanistan similar to what we had done in Iran.

When we arrived in Kabul we prayed at the stadium where the Taliban hung or shot those considered sinful under Islamic law.

In Herat, not far from the Iranian border, the women wore burkas and covered their faces. At the ancient mosque in the heart of the city, stern looking men watched us. I thought I'd try to engage them.

As I passed them, I said, "The architecture is beautiful." Their countenance immediately changed. A bearded man explained in English the carvings on the mosque and led us to where the stone carvers worked. I asked if it was possible to purchase one of the stones.

"Oh, no," the bearded man said. "These are property of the government." As we were about to leave, an elderly man handed me a stone bearing the inscription "Thank You."

A young man introduced himself as the administrator of the mosque and invited us to have tea.

As we followed him to his office, one of the Afghan Christians whispered, "Sammy, if you have a gift you could give this man, that would be very good."

What could I give him? I patted my pockets and finally noticed the special pen I always carried. It had been given to me by the Christian Writers Guild after I had spoken at its annual conference, and I cherished it, the only pen that had ever had any special meaning to me.

Over tea, the young administrator touched me deeply when he said, "I have never known peace." He said there had been fighting and killing in his country since he had been born.

When he finished, I was expected to respond. "You and I have something in common," I said. "You grew up without peace in your land. I grew up without peace in my heart. I have something for you. This pen was given to me as a Christian writer. I want to use it to write how I found peace in my life, and then I want you to have it."

I wrote in their guest book of how Jesus had come into my life and given me peace. "I hope you'll read this and that every time you use this pen you'll to remember what I wrote about the true source of peace."

The young man accepted it with a smile.

The two Afghan believers with us were developing a Christian radio program for the country. I would provide teaching for the many new believers we were anticipating, and they would translate my messages into Dari.

A month later I was invited to lead a pastors' conference in Pakistan. Gulf War fighting in Baghdad had just ended with Islamic clerics in Pakistan vowing to kill Americans. The stories of my friends at the conference, willing to go back despite such threats on their lives, were fresh on my mind and embedded deep in my soul. We asked the Christian leaders whether it was wise to come, and they urged us to move forward.

Once there, I met with a Christian who would translate my materials into Pashto. I was thrilled with that but both Tex and I were sobered by the atmosphere the first night I preached in Faisalabad.

Armed guards met us at the grounds, and I was ushered to the platform and surrounded by men wielding shotguns and automatic rifles. Armed soldiers lined the rooftop of a nearby building.

I passionately preached who Jesus is and what He could do in the lives of the people. At the close of my message, when I called for people to join me at the front of the platform to pray, the armed soldiers rushed to form a wall between the people and me.

Did they think I needed protection from new converts? I was frustrated, worried no one would respond. But chills ran up my spine as hundreds came anyway, tears streaming down their faces.

"Oh, God, forgive my lack of faith."

I concluded our meetings in Karachi, where Christians asked if they could broadcast my messages on cable television.

"Is that possible?"

They told me that not only was it possible, but if I had other recorded messages, they could translate them and produce a regularly scheduled broadcast.

I had seen the potential of television when I walked in Iran. And I had seen how God used technology in Egypt. Here was an opportunity to proclaim the Gospel throughout Pakistan. Yet I would need to be very careful not to further endanger the Christian workers there.

We had dinner in the home of a man who had worked for a Christian welfare organization. During the meal he grabbed his wife's hand and said solemnly, "Every day is a gift of God's grace. A few months ago I was delayed and couldn't go into work on time." His lips trembled. "I arrived to find terrorists had stormed our office, tied up my colleagues and shot all seven of them to death. We need you to pray for us."

I was learning to pray as I had never prayed before. I had never felt so inadequate to fulfill God's call on my life.

CHAPTER THIRTY- EIGHT

A HEAVY HEART—THE HIGH COST OF MINISTRY

God opened doors for us to partner with friends for television broadcasts into Iran, Pakistan, and India and a radio broadcast into Afghanistan. That enabled us to bring the good news of God's love to millions in the heart of Islam.

Joseph Karasanyi also continued to press me about preaching in war zones of Africa. Kisangani, located in the Democratic Republic of Congo, had been devastated by war, and Joseph felt the people were desperate for a message of hope.

It seemed we had something going on every inhabited continent. On the trip to Kisangani I stopped for a major outreach meeting in Nairobi, Kenya.

I took a team of pastors, evangelists, and laypeople to minister in churches, and I planned to preach a large combined meeting the final weekend in the center of the city.

Though God had done more than I could have ever imagined, I still occasionally struggled with insecurity. Few people realized how much I needed encouragement. Developing friendships had become nearly impossible due to my heavy travel schedule.

God had been gracious to provide encouragers in the past. In Germany, Tex and I had developed great friendships. Ken Leeburg and I became running partners and dreamed of doing what I am doing today. We also dreamed of running the original Greek marathon together. But then Ken was tragically killed.

At First Baptist Church of Bothell, Washington, General Errol Van Eaton was part of my men's discipleship group and stayed in contact after I left to travel as an evangelist. But he was killed in a helicopter rescue mission off the coast of Haiti. Both Ken and Errol knew my strengths and weaknesses and encouraged me to become all that God desired. I missed them.

God provided new encouragers for Tex and me in Billy and Kristi Hobbs in San Antonio. Billy had been a professional football player before becoming a Christian, and he had served on the staff of our

227

home church for several years before being called to full time evangelism. I invited him to travel with me.

When we were in town, he and Kristi met with Tex and me every Wednesday night before church services for a meal. We spent time praying and dreaming, just as I had done with Ken and Errol. God met that need for friendship.

Billy and Kristi traveled to India with us. He shared his testimony at the evangelistic meetings and preached alongside me in pastors' conferences.

When Billy and Kristi went with us to Kenya, the experience changed their lives. Billy fell in love with the kids who lived on the streets and ate at the garbage dump. In fact, he and Kristi decided to try to adopt some of them.

"Sammy, some people in America are African-Americans. I think I'm an American-African. This feels so much like home."

I laughed. "Hobbs, only you could be that."

Before I left Kenya to fly to Kisangani, he promised to pray for us until we arrived home safely. I told him not to worry and said Tex and I would plan on Wednesday night dinner with him and Kristi as soon as we got back.

There were no commercial flights into war zones, so we hired a private company to fly the Brazilian cameramen and us into Kisangani.

As we descended, the pilot announced that it didn't appear we could land. He said he could see thousands of people at the airport but it had been bombed out. "They have no communication, and there shouldn't be anyone there." He said he would circle the airfield to see if he could learn any more."

Tex squeezed my arm, Daniel's eyes widened, and Selio said, "*Vamos orar* (Let's pray)!"

I knew Billy and Kristi were praying and hoped they were getting others to as well. When the pilot came back on, he said, "I don't see any fighting. We're going to land."

I couldn't believe my eyes when we got off the plane. A band played. Choirs sang. Joseph rushed to the plane with local pastors.

"This city has had nothing but devastation for so long," he said, "and these people heard you were bringing good news. So, thousands have come to meet you, and a parade through the city is planned for you and Tex."

They placed Tex and me in an SUV with an open top. I stood and waved to the multitudes who lined the streets. Tex, one of the humblest people I know, was embarrassed. She quietly said, "Remember, this is about Jesus."

Buildings had been bombed, windows shattered, filling stations closed. Young men on the streets sold gasoline in jars. Yet we saw smiles on the faces of thousands that day.

Kisangani

The parade took us to the Governor's office, where he and a delegation of political leaders welcomed us, and I prayed for them.

The stadium and grounds were packed, and the governor, military officials, and United Nations peace-keeping forces attended. Thousands responded to the message and gave their lives to Christ.

Harvest

We returned exhausted but overflowing with joy. Wednesday evening Billy and Kristi updated us about their plans to adopt some of Nairobi's street children. Our time together, laughing, dreaming, and praying, recharged my spirit.

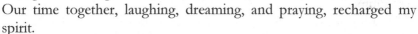

I told them I wanted them to go to Pakistan with us in September for a pastors' conference and evangelistic meeting.

Billy's eyes sparkled. "We're in."

Tex and I were soon off to Cambodia, and for some reason I had never felt so exhausted when we returned. I laid on the couch in our living room and couldn't get up. I simply didn't have the strength. Except for the bathroom break, I lay there for more than 30 hours.

Tex was worried, because for the first time ever she was scheduled to travel to another country without me. She was to speak in Canada and was leaving in a couple of days. Meanwhile, I had foolishly accepted an invitation to speak in Haiti because I didn't want to hang around the house by myself.

Tex contacted Billy and Kristi, and they immediately came over. Billy pointed at me. "You're not going to Haiti."

"I can't cancel on them now."

"Then I'm going with you. No argument. Listen, I pray for you every morning. I'm not going to let you hurt yourself. Understand?"

I knew Billy was right. And if something happened to me, he could finish the conference.

It all worked out, and Tex and I both enjoyed good meetings. I knew I needed to slow down, but God was blessing in such a mighty way that I didn't want to. That stretch on the couch should have been a major red flag, and no doubt the Holy Spirit was trying to speak to me, but I was clearly not listening.

I was caught in a web of the work of God while losing sight of God Himself.

At the close of July 2004, we launched an outreach in Sao Paulo, Brazil, one of the world's largest cities. I was intimidated by the prospect of preaching at Portuguese Stadium, one of their professional football venues. And this would be the most ambitious effort we had ever been involved in. We partnered with the Brazilian Baptist Convention, longtime friend Wayne Jenkins brought a team of about two hundred pastors and workers, and our ministry also brought one hundred pastors, evangelists, and leaders. This massive team preached in local churches during the week and then everyone came together for the evangelistic crusade the final weekend in the stadium.

One morning while we were checking things out at the stadium I noticed the local professional soccer team gathered around someone. Our Brazilian camera crew was filming whatever was going on, and my translator, Pastor Tercio was there too.

I headed that way to see what was going on, only to find Billy sharing his testimony with the team while Pastor Tercio translated. I couldn't have been happier as Billy forcefully told of having played professional football in America, "but my life was a mess. Fame couldn't give me peace. Money couldn't give me peace. Only Jesus gave me what I needed."

Billy Hobbs

He asked the players to pray with him when a man showed up who looked like he might be the coach. *Lord, take control,* I prayed. *Protect Billy.*

"How many of you want to follow Jesus and allow Him to take control of your life?"

Ninety percent of the players lifted their hands while the coach folded his arms. *Uh-oh.*

Billy prayed with the guys, then the coach approached him. I hoped we wouldn't have problems, but I knew everything was all right when I saw Billy's big smile. He waved me over and introduced me to the coach. "He says the rest of the team will be here this afternoon and wants to know if I can tell them about Jesus. Can I get a ride back over here?"

I laughed and slapped him on the shoulder. "Billy, Billy, Billy. You bet we can get you back here."

The team made him an honorary member and gave him a jersey they had all signed. Billy gave it to the youngest person in our group, a teenage boy who had hoped to buy a Brazilian soccer jersey before returning to the States.

We returned to the States after having seen thousands come to Christ in Brazil. Still running on adrenaline, I took Tex with me on a quick trip to Michigan for a board meeting with Life Action Ministries. While on a break, I got a call from my office—and they knew not to call unless it was urgent. I excused myself.

Chris Dillashaw, a young man on our staff, blurted, "Sammy, have you heard about Billy Hobbs?"

"No, what's going on?"

"Billy was just killed."

"No! No!"

My knees buckled and a couple of the other board members helped me to a conference room where I could only weep. Finally I was able to tell them what was wrong.

They had already sent for Tex, and when she saw me, her mouth fell open. She pulled me into her arms as I told her about the call. "We need to call Kristi," I said.

"I know, but you and I need to talk and pray first."

I knew she was right. I was in no condition to talk to a grieving widow until I could get my own emotions under control.

When we finally did connect, Kristi explained that Billy was hit by a car while on his motor scooter. He had died instantly. She added, "Sammy, I know Billy would want you to be one of the speakers at his funeral."

I didn't know if I could get through that, but I told her Tex and I would be on the next flight home. "Just know that we love you and are praying for you."

I stared out the window as the plane took off. This had to be a bad dream. Several minutes later Tex's sweet voice awakened me. "A penny for your thoughts."

I covered my face with my hands. "Do you think I'm a jinx?"

"What are you talking about?"

"Every time I make a close friend he gets killed."

"You know where those thoughts are coming from. You need to reject them right now."

"I know, but this hurts so much. It's like strike three and I'm out." Tex took my hand in hers. "I even feel guilty thinking about myself at a time like this."

Kristi asked our pastor, David Walker, Billy's former football coach, Gene Stallings, and me to speak at the funeral. And she asked if David and I would also speak at a second service in Amarillo, where Billy was a hometown legend. I told her I would do whatever she asked to honor Billy's memory.

I dreaded the funeral, but the service was packed with friends and old football teammates. After Pastor Walker and Coach Stallings and I spoke, the church played a video of Billy himself preaching just two weeks earlier. In it he called for people to come to Christ. It was just what Billy would have wanted.

We hosted a lunch for out of town friends, and Gary Maroney, who had traveled with me more than anyone else, asked if I would say a few words.

I followed him toward where most of the people were, but before I got there, pain shot through my stomach and bent me over.

"Sammy," Gary said, "are you okay?"

"Something's wrong." I grabbed my stomach and cried out as everything went blurry.

People began to gather, so Gary barked, "Everyone back up!"

Tex knelt next to me.

Gary yelled, "Call 911!"

I groaned and everything went black. The next thing I knew, medics were putting me in an ambulance and Tex was holding my hand.

They took me to the Emergency Room at Methodist Hospital. I was spent—and embarrassed. I had lost control of my bodily functions.

They kept me for several hours, diagnosed it as a vasovagal attack, and released me. I had never felt so depleted. Back home I called Kristi and apologized profusely because I simply didn't have the strength to go to Amarillo.

She was gracious, but guilt rolled over my soul like a tsunami. It took a few days before I could even get to my special place of prayer under the trees. I sat on a large rock, weeping over Billy and my other two friends in heaven. I noticed a blade of grass, bent and broken under three dewdrops. *I feel like that.*

Three friends—all great blessings to me, but the weight of losing them had broken me.

CHAPTER THIRTY-NINE

DARK CLOUDS

I had looked forward to going to Pakistan, but it would be tough without Billy and Kristi. Again, my son Dave stepped up. "I know you're struggling," he said, and went with me. What a relief! Dave proved especially helpful in our conferences for leaders, as well as evangelistic events. I loved watching him minister.

We spent most of our time in Karachi, but Tex fell ill the day before we were to drive a couple of hours to Hyderabad for our last events. We decided Dave should stay with her in Karachi.

I found the hotel in Hyderabad creepy. The halls were dark, some guestroom doors stood open. I heard someone praying and saw a bearded man swaying. My room had no lock, only a latch. *God, I'm trusting You.*

Many came to Christ that evening, but I didn't sleep much that night. Noises in the dim lit hall kept me on edge. I was very glad to get back to Dave and Tex, who had recovered. But I was exhausted.

On our flight home I felt ill and continued to get worse. We got through customs at DFW and headed toward the gate for the last leg to San Antonio, but I told Dave and Tex, "I don't know if I can make it."

Just in sight of the gate, I grabbed Dave's arm. "You go ahead and get back to that sweet wife of yours. Your mom will stay with me."

After Dave boarded, my knees buckled and I dropped to the floor, clenching my stomach. I felt stares all around and couldn't believe this was happening again. I was rushed to the Baylor Medical Center where doctors assumed I had picked up some kind of bacteria and kept me a few days.

Tex was always patient and kind. I asked her, "Why is this happening?"

"All I know is that we need to pray."

"I'll be okay if I can just get home."

She squeezed my hand. "We'll be there soon enough."

I took a couple of months off, trying to overcome the toll the storms of life had taken on me. Yet, my troubles seemed minor compared to those of so many friends around the world. A tsunami struck India on December 26, 2004, not far from where I was scheduled to speak at a pastors' conference. One of my dearest friends miraculously missed being swept into the ocean.

In a strange way my sufferings enabled me to minister to many hurting leaders in India. I also preached an evangelistic meeting and many responded. That helped heal my broken heart.

Tex and I flew from India to Hawaii, where our daughter Renee was to marry Paul Barker. She wanted a small destination wedding with only family present, and we secured a beautiful spot on the beach. However, it rained daily.

"Dad, could you ask God to give us sunshine for the wedding?"

I'd seen God hold off rain in stadiums around the world, but for a wedding? "Sure, sweetheart, but I don't know…"

I found myself asking God, "Is there any way…?"

His Spirit spoke gently to my heart, "Don't you remember? I've worked miracles at weddings."

The morning of the ceremony there wasn't a cloud in the sky, and it was the most beautiful wedding I've ever seen. Being both the officiating pastor and the father of the bride proved challenging, but what a fulfilling day! *Thank you, Lord, for answering Renee's prayer, and for not forgetting me.*

I felt I was on the mend, but storm clouds formed quickly. Our Pakistani translator, Babar Shamsoon, asked if we could provide a bodyguard, believing his life was in danger. It seemed he was under some sort of spiritual attack.

- One of his co-workers had a heart attack.
- Someone stole Babar's computer, containing most of the recordings for our broadcast.
- He worried about trying to record the message one more time in Peshawar. He believed it was too dangerous and wanted to know if someone could find a safe place in another city to record the messages.

I told Peter, my prayer-walking friend, to let Babar know we would provide funds for him to hire a bodyguard and would see if we could set up a safehouse for him in Karachi.

Chris Dillashaw, in charge of the media for our ministry, had traveled with Dave Tippit and knew how to navigate dangerous situations. He said he could work with Babar on the recordings.

I immediately called a friend in Karachi and arranged a safehouse, knowing the project—and Babar's safety—was in good hands.

During the next few weeks I spoke in the U.S. and in Holland and felt my heart was slowly being refreshed.

Speaking at an evangelistic meeting in Louisiana gave me the opportunity to visit Wayne and Martha Jenkins. He and I had known each other since high school, and he had become the Director of Evangelism for the Louisiana Baptist Convention. Tex and I were enjoying lunch with them April 6 when my cell phone rang.

It was Peter, telling me Babar had been kidnapped. "They are demanding $60,000."

"What about the bodyguard we hired?"

"They're holding both of them."

Nothing prepared me for that moment. That afternoon I found a wooded area to seek God. The heaviness had returned to my heart with a vengeance.

At the service that night, I asked the people to pray for Babar and his bodyguard and for wisdom for me."

When my cell phone rang the next morning and I saw it was Peter, I dreaded answering. My fears were well founded.

"They found Babar's body," he said. "Tortured and mutilated."

"Oh, no!" Time seemed to stop. "And the bodyguard?"

"Murdered also."

The world was spinning. I thought that I had made it through the valley of Billy's death, but now a cloak of heaviness overwhelmed me.

Was I responsible for Babar's death? I knew better, but the thought plagued me. Could we have done more to protect him?

I told Peter to find out what it would cost to take care of Babar's and the bodyguard's widows, and we immediately partnered with another ministry to meet their needs.

Naveed Malik, who had translated for me during my evangelistic meetings, told me, "You must not return to Pakistan for a few years. The terrorists have the computer with your messages, and they will kill you."

For the first time in my life, I actually considered quitting the ministry. The pain was unbearable. I hung my head as I spoke with people. I would break down in the middle of preaching.

I prayed constantly, trying to regain my spiritual and emotional balance. I had seen God on the mountaintops. Now, I needed to know Him deeply in the valleys.

James Robison, who led me to Christ, asked to interview me on his television broadcast in May. I told Tex, "This will be good. I need to return to my roots and be reminded of all the good things God has done."

She gave me a peck on the cheek. "You go, and I'll pray. When you get home, the skies will look much better."

Reconnecting and reminiscing with James was more than I hoped it would be. He couldn't have known how much I needed it.

Tex was waiting at the airport, and I was glad to be able to tell her I thought I saw the light of hope in the valley.

A couple of days later I was excited to preach at the ordination service for Chris Dillashaw at my home church. I knew he would eventually leave us for a pastorate, but I was happy for him.

I got a call from my sister just as Tex and I left for the church. She told me a pastor had come to her with a letter from a man in Portugal. "It says he has evidence he's our brother, and he wants to talk to you."

I rolled my eyes. "You've got to be kidding! Is this some kind of a hoax? If he's looking for money, he didn't do his homework."

"I don't think that's what he wants. The letter seemed sincere."

I chuckled. "Most people find their long-lost brother in Houston or Dallas. Ours is in Portugal?"

How much can happen to one person in less than a year? If it hadn't been happening to me, I wouldn't have believed it.

After the service that day, I told my pastor, "David, I think I need counseling."

He tilted his head. "About?"

"Can I tell you at breakfast in a couple of days?"

Meanwhile I Skyped the man in Portugal, compelled to find out if this was a scam or if I really had a brother I'd never known. All I knew was that life had become so strange that I needed answers. I had to wonder whether God was up to something in my life.

I quickly realized the man wasn't after money. He was a retired, wealthy Englishman living in a resort area. He had built and sold a company, then searched for his true father. He knew more about my father than I did.

Dad's history was a little sketchy to me. He grew up in a remote area in the forests of southwest Louisiana. He became seriously ill when I was ten, and after that we rarely visited any of his family. His parents had died before I was born, so though I was named after my grandfather, I knew nothing about him. My mom's parents died when I was just a child, so I didn't know them either.

At the time of my Skype call to the Englishman, my dad had been gone thirty-seven years. Mom had died nearly ten years before.

"I've done DNA testing, and I am from Native American background, just like you."

"Sorry, but you're mistaken," I said. "I'm not Native American. I have light skin and hazel eyes."

"You don't know?"

"Know what?"

"That your cousin and aunt are members of the Nansemond Indian tribe. Your grandmother was Eliza Bass, a direct descendant of John Basse of the Nansemond."

"I know nothing about the Nansemond Indian tribe."

"Check it out. You'll see."

"Believe me, I will."

I must have set Google on fire, comparing my searches with a genealogy book that my cousin had written about our family, but which I had never read. To my amazement, most of what the Englishman said was true.

The great irony in what I discovered was that if I really was a descendant of the Nansemond, it would mean that I was not at all who I thought I was. My whole life I had assumed I was just a white kid from Baton Rouge, ignorantly reared to hate black people merely because of the color of their skin. God had completely delivered me of that racist bigotry, and I had come to love everyone in His name and for His sake, regardless of ethnicity.

But my forefathers were part of what came to be known as the Louisiana Redbones, who migrated to southwest Louisiana around the time of the Louisiana Purchase. The Redbones were a mixed-race people, a combination of Black, Native American, and English. In fact, one of my ancestors had been legally designated "colored," which meant he would have not been welcome in some churches I attended when I was younger.

The truth was, if I were Redbone, I was not just a European white, but also sub-Saharan African and Native American. It was not uncommon for white-appearing Redbone to produce dark-skinned children.

Not knowing for sure just added to all the mental anguish I was suffering just then.

When I met for breakfast with my pastor, David Walker, he could tell immediately I was troubled and asked what was going on.

I could barely get the words out. It was as if the past nine months burst from me in a sea of tears. "I don't know."

"Tell me, Sammy."

"I don't know who I am!"

"What are you talking about?"

He knew a lot of what weighed on me, but I told him everything again, beginning with Billy's death, my physical collapses, and about this man who claimed to be my brother. "I don't know what's going on, David. I don't even know my own ethnicity."

A godly man and a longtime, dear friend, David pointed a finger in my face. "Sammy, you do too know who you are! You are a child of the King! You're a new creation in Christ. You are a servant of Jesus. Whatever you find out about your family, that's who you are—in the deepest part of your being."

His words planted a seed of healing in my aching heart. Even his tone was exactly what I needed, jolting me back to reality. No matter what happened. No matter how I felt. No matter what I learned about my family. A child of God was who I was. And nothing could alter that.

I soon discovered that my cousin was well-respected among Louisiana genealogists. She had written much on the history of the Louisiana Redbones.

When I called her about the man from Portugal, she said, "Oh, Sammy, I'm so sorry. He asked me how to get in touch with you, but I wouldn't tell him. I don't believe he's your brother. Most of the information he has about our family came from me."

I peppered her with questions, suddenly passionate to learn more of my heritage.

The man in Portugal remained adamant that he was my brother, and as he didn't seem to have any ulterior motives, he was very convincing. I wanted only to know the truth. We agreed to submit to a DNA sibling test to determine the facts once and for all. And then we waited for the results.

Meanwhile, Tex and I traveled to a secret location in the Middle East to minister to Iranian Christian leaders. Pastor Hormoz Shariat, an Iranian who had come to Christ and begun a television broadcast, asked me to produce a program with him. That fulfilled the dream God had instilled in me when we prayer-walked through Iran.

The believers at the secret conference were very sweet. Though they had greatly suffered, they expressed deep joy in the midst of their pain.

Between sessions I hurried to an Internet cafe to see if my DNA report had come. Though it didn't arrive while we were overseas, God continued to grant me peace.

When we returned, the results came through. The Englishman in Portugal was not my brother.

It was as if a thousand pounds had been lifted off me. But the whole experience had changed me. I became obsessed to learn about my family background. In the process, some incredibly wonderful discoveries lifted me out of the slough of despondency.

My DNA test revealed that I was, indeed, Redbone. That was quite a shock, as you can imagine, yet I found it somehow defined me. I had identified with the disenfranchised my whole ministry. I always felt an immediate kinship to minorities and the oppressed, especially the rejected.

I always thought that was because of the rejection I had felt from my mother and others in my family when I came to Christ and entered the ministry. That immediate bond I felt with anyone of any race, especially when I went to the hard, remote places, now made sense! I was one of them!

Also, I had always believed I had no Christian heritage, that I was the first in my lineage to come to faith in Jesus. But during my genealogical search, I learned that my fourth great grandmother and her husband had donated the land for the first Baptist church west of the Mississippi River—the Calvary Baptist Church of Bayou Chicot.

My third great grandfather and grandmother, John and Delaney Bass, had helped start some of the first Baptist churches in Louisiana.

Most thrilling of all, I learned my grandfather, Sam Tippit, was passionate about the Lord and continually brought his family by horse and wagon to brush arbor revival meetings. My grandmother, Eliza Bass, was known as a woman of prayer. Are you ready for this (I wasn't!): She had a place under the trees where she regularly met with the Lord.

I read a poem about an experience one of my aunts had as a young girl. While in the barn, she heard her mother, my grandmother, talking to someone about personal things and thought she shouldn't. She peered out to find my grandmother under a clump of trees, talking to Jesus.

I told Tex, "I can't explain it, but I just need to see where my grandmother prayed."

Two of my cousins in Louisiana met Tex and me and showed us the spot. It proved to be just a simple piece of ground surrounded by trees! The older of the cousins said he had once known an old preacher who said our grandmother was so passionate that when she prayed in church, the doors rattled.

So prayer was part of my spiritual DNA! When I became a Christian, I met with friends to pray. When I became pastor in Germany, God led me to teach the people to pray. When I went to Romania, I found a praying church.

My pastor was right: I knew who I was. I still do.

It was no accident that I have gone to the most dangerous parts of the world. When I was a new Christian, God gave me a word while at Louisiana College. A young preacher read, "Then the word of the Lord came to me, saying: 'Before I formed you in the womb I knew you; before you were born I sanctified you; I ordained you a prophet to the nations'" (Jeremiah 1:4).

Back home on my knees in my own special prayer spot, I came to realize that ironically God had used my mother to instill in me a pioneer spirit. Had I been reared in a warm Christian family, I probably would have become pastor of a nice, respectable church in Louisiana.

But that's not what God created me to do. He had charged me with taking the Gospel to the dark and dangerous places. If Mom had not been so hard on me, I probably would not have developed a pioneer spirit.

For the first time in my life, I was able to thank God even for the bitter rejection I had felt from Mom when I was a young Christian. Who but God would think to use a bitter woman, negative to the things of Christ, to help shape me for my calling? The ways of God are greatly higher than our ways, His thoughts so much greater.

God began the healing process with David Walker's admonition, and it culminated in October when I spoke in a small town in Romania. Scornicesti was the birthplace of Nicolae Ceausescu, the deposed and assassinated Romanian dictator. The town had become a despised place following the revolution. However, some Romanian Christian youth set out to love the people and serve the town. They dug a well to provide clean water for the community, and they shared Christ with the residents.

They invited me to conduct evangelistic meetings in the center of town, then held a final service on Sunday at a small church they had recently built. Because of the historic nature of the church, being in Ceausescu's hometown, they invited David Funderburk, former U.S. Ambassador to Romania under Ronald Reagan, and me to speak at its dedication.

That thrilling event seemed to serve as the final bandage God applied to the pain I had accumulated during the past few years. Complete joy in my calling had returned.

CHAPTER FORTY

CANCER

Not only did I grow in my prayer life during the next few months, but I also grew physically. I gained a lot of weight. I didn't pay much attention to it because God had restored my vision for the ministry, and things were going so well with it. I was busy, conducting evangelistic meetings and leading conferences on revival around the world. The ministry among the Iranians had exploded, not because of anything we were doing, but because God was working in a special way among them.

Hundreds of thousands of Iranians watched my television broadcast. I heard about one house church in which an entire group of drug addicts came to Christ. I had become their pastor. It was too dangerous for them to go to a Christian church. Therefore, they met secretly in one of their homes every Tuesday evening to listen to my teachings via satellite television. They then prayed and sang and worshipped Jesus.

I went for an annual physical checkup with my primary care physician in March 2007.

When the doctor walked into the room, I saw anxiety on his face. "We received your blood work, and most of it looks good." He paused. "But, there's something that concerns me. Your PSA has risen dramatically." He cleared his throat. "It could be a sign of prostate cancer."

My mouth dropped. "You've got to be kidding. Could it be a mistake? Could they have gotten my blood sample mixed up with someone else?"

"I doubt it. But we can retake it."

"I'd like to do that."

I wanted to know as soon as possible because I knew how dangerous prostate cancer could be. The second blood test showed my PSA had gone even higher.

My doctor ordered a biopsy next.

On my way to that procedure, I stopped by my place of prayer and met with God. After two blood tests, I knew the biopsy was just a formality and that I had cancer. But something odd happened. I was systematically reading through the Bible each day, and that day's passage was Hebrews chapter twelve, which includes this phrase in the first verse: "…let us run with endurance the race that is set before us…"

Despite years of experience viewing Scripture as whole and reading it in context, I couldn't deny that one word leapt off the page and into my heart.

Run.

Run?

I couldn't shake it. This ancient letter to the Hebrew Christians compared the believer's life to a long distance race, yet the word seemed to scream at me. You don't have to be a scholar and certainly not a theologian to see this as the metaphor it is. So why was it so impacting me?

Run. I sensed I was to take it literally. My pulse raced, my breath came short. I paced under the trees.

Run? Run. I knew it would not let me go and could only shake my head as I left to pick up Tex. Whatever it meant, right now I had to deal with a biopsy.

We endured an edgy week waiting for the results, and I spent a lot of time at my special place. I knew what the diagnosis would be and researched treatment options. Meanwhile, the word *run* continued to invade my mind.

Both Tex and I held out a sliver of hope for better news, but deep down we both knew. And the doctor confirmed it. We agreed on robotic surgery, and since I had never been operated on before, I asked the doctor how best to prepare for it.

He said two things would help. "First, you need to lose some weight, because we'll be cutting through your stomach. And second, you need to build endurance. That'll help with your recovery."

I couldn't help smiling, though I had just learned indisputably that I had cancer and needed surgery. Why? Because I also knew plainly how to lose weight and build endurance: *run!*

God had been so good to me throughout my life, instilling dreams in me He's fulfilled every time—except one. My late friend Ken Leeburg and I had dreamed of running the Greek Marathon—the route of the original run of legend. That dream had died with Ken, but now was the time to resurrect it, despite my age. I needed a goal, something that would carry me through the surgery and the recovery—something to look forward to down the road. I needed to run the Greek Marathon. And while training for it, I would be doing what I needed to prepare for surgery.

Tex and I met with Dave and Renee to give them the news and assure them we had complete peace. If I survived, I would continue to live for Christ. If I died, I wanted my death to glorify God. I determined to embrace whatever He had in mind for me, given this situation.

Surgery was scheduled for June 27, 2007, exactly one month before my sixtieth birthday. I had a full schedule before then:

- Another conference with Iranian Christian leaders in May at a secret location in the Middle East.
- Recording several broadcasts for Iran television.
- A conference in Canada the middle of June.
- And I needed to start running.

I shared openly about my cancer diagnosis and asked people to pray for me. Sweet, encouraging responses came from everywhere.

One Iranian lady emailed a friend: "Sammy is speaking about cancer in his body and how God told him that if he dies or lives the Lord will be glorified. I felt a revelation that I am far from God. Now, revival is happening in my heart. I don't know how to describe it. I just want to fall at Jesus' feet and repent."

Imagine how that made me feel. God was going to use the cancer in ways unknown to me. Strangely, I was actually excited about what was coming and what God was going to do.

God had told me one thing: to run. I started while in the Middle East, but it was difficult because I was so out of shape and I didn't accomplish much. Then, it became impossible while in Canada. I developed plantar fasciitis, a foot condition so painful I could barely walk, let alone run.

I found a private place in Canada to pour out my heart to God. "Lord, if you want me to run, You need to heal my feet."

The only response I sensed was *Run!*

I shouldn't have been surprised. That had been God's way with me for more than forty years. He called me to impossible situations, which drove me to a life of prayer.

But either I was mistaken and God *didn't* want me to run, or He wanted me to run later. Because He pretty much put me on the shelf until well after my surgery.

No doubt rest was one thing I *really* needed, because, I would have to wait until after the surgery even to consider running. I pumped weights and lost a few pounds, but I did not build endurance.

Shortly after we returned from Canada, Tex took me to the hospital for the operation. I was encouraged when the receptionist told us that people regularly traveled from around the country to watch our surgeon perform robotic surgery.

The last thing I remember before going under was holding Tex's hand and the surgeon's hand and saying, "Let's pray." Who knows what I prayed?

I was released a couple of days later with instructions to walk as much as possible inside, but no regular exercise for six weeks. If all went well I could resume my travel schedule in three months.

Generous people kindly sent me books and DVDs to fill all that down time, but generous as that was, I knew I would have no time for reading or watching. I wanted to invest every waking hour of my recovery seeking God. I wanted only my Bible and my worship music.

The first night home I suffered some unexpected bleeding and fell into a fearful, uneasy sleep. Soon I found myself dreaming so vividly that I sensed it was something I would never forget. Usually I don't remember my dreams, but this one would stay with me the rest of my life.

Two Native American men, one young and one older, sat on a hill quietly looking over a harvest field. A thundering voice from heaven said, "Wounded deer!" and the words began to echo and wouldn't stop. Again and again and again the words rang out. "Wounded deer. Wounded deer. Wounded deer."

I awoke, my heart racing, and still I heard the voice! "Wounded deer. Wounded deer." I lay back and shut my eyes, trying to go back to sleep, but I continued to hear the voice.

I switched on a lamp and opened my Bible, but I couldn't concentrate with the voice in my head repeating, "Wounded deer."

I struggled out of bed, carrying my catheter bag and limping toward the living room. I had to look like death warmed over. The echo continued so I stopped in the hallway and gazed up. "God, what is this?"

The Lord immediately brought to mind Psalm 42:1, 2: "As the deer pants for the water brooks, so my soul pants for You, O God. My soul thirsts for God, for the living God..." (NASB).

Tears poured down my cheeks. "Yes. That's who I am, a wounded deer, and my soul longs for You. I need You. I can't live without You. I need the waters that flow from Your throne!"

Indescribable joy flooded my soul. I'd never experienced the presence of God like that—more real than any other time in my life. All the sorrow and pain of the past three years were swept away by a tidal wave of peace that came rushing over my soul.

While I still had to heal physically, God had healed my ravaged heart. Those minutes in His blissful presence turned to hours, then days, and weeks. I spent most of the next three months reading the Bible and worshipping Jesus.

Thirsty

I also began trying to prepare myself for running. I went to a rehab center for therapy and stretching and even slept wearing a boot. My plantar fasciitis was almost completely gone by the time the doctor gave me permission to run.

Knowing my personality, I realized I could become so gung ho to progress so quickly that I could hurt myself. So I searched the Internet for a coach.

The resume of a trainer in California intrigued me. Kevin Morning held a couple of world records in Masters Track and Field (for men 30 to over 100). His site said his great love was Jesus and that he served on the worship team at his church.

When I introduced myself, told him my situation, and asked if he would help, I included a link to our ministry. His response thrilled me. He wrote, "I'll do what I can if you'll help me become a man of prayer."

That email just further confirmed that I was doing what God wanted. As Kevin advised me on line, I slowly started walking, then jogging. I went to a local high school to see how far I could go. I was able to walk and jog two and a half miles.

I thought it would be best if I ran a half marathon before attempting a full one. I found one in Baton Rouge, my physical and spiritual birthplace. The only problem, and it was a big one, was that it was scheduled for December 1, less than three months away. I would have to do a lot better than walk/jog two and a half miles. And soon.

My first ministry trip was to Canada. Still feeling full of the presence of God, I flew to Seattle, rented a car, and stopped for the night at a hotel just inside the Canadian border. The conference center would be a three-hour drive the next day. Or it should have been.

As I drove the next morning I felt so connected to all of God's creation that when I saw a sign for "Waterfalls," I smiled and couldn't resist taking the exit. At the end of the road lay a walking trail, so I hiked through the forest to a beautiful waterfall.

I spent the next hour alone, singing and worshipping Jesus. I prayed. I cried. I laughed. And I thanked God for His love.

I drove another hour and stopped in a small town located on a river. I sat by the river for lunch and spent another hour silently pouring my heart out to God.

Worried my hosts might be wondering what had become of me, I drove on. I was almost to the center when I came upon a beautiful lake, stopped again, and sat on a rock overlooking the water, reading my Bible.

It struck me that God was bringing me to a new level of ministry, but first bringing me to a new level of prayer. He had used all I had endured the last three years to deepen my intimacy with Him.

At the conference, I had a few hours between the morning and evening sessions, so I went for my walk and jog. I was getting stronger each day.

When I returned to the States, I continued working out based on Kevin's helpful routines, to which I added waiting upon the Lord. I trained at a local high school track and also a park near my home that was full of deer. It always reminded of who I was—a wounded deer. I grew to cherish Isaiah 40:31: "… those who wait upon the Lord shall renew their strength; they shall mount up with wings like eagles, they shall run and not be weary, they shall walk and not faint."

Every day for the next twelve weeks I would pray and then run. My speed, endurance, and strength rapidly improved, and I increased my distance to ten miles. When Tex and I returned to my hometown for the Baton Rouge Beach Half Marathon, I was ready to run 13.1 miles.

December 1 broke sunny and crisp, perfect for the race. Tex grabbed my hand to stop my fidgeting. "It's going to be okay. You'll do all right."

We got off by ourselves to pray before I lined up with thousands of other runners. In my excitement I started too fast and after a mile forced myself to slow to my training pace. At the five-mile mark I came upon Tex, cheering me on, and I thanked God for such a wonderful wife.

I felt good throughout the race and still felt strong at ten miles. I began hurting about a mile later, and prayed God would sustain me and see me through to the end.

Tex was waiting at the finish line with a trophy that she had secretly bought for me. We hugged.

"I did it!" I said as we embraced. "God gave me the strength."

Tex patted my chest. "Yes, He did. They have refreshments over there. I think you need some."

Louisiana has to be the only place in the world where they serve jambalaya at the end of a marathon. We found a place to sit, and the food was great. As Tex was calling Renee to let her know how I did, the presentation of awards began over the P.A. system.

When the announcer got to the results for the 60-64 age category, he called out the third-place finisher. "And in second place, from San Antonio, Texas, Sammy Tippit!" My mouth flew open and I stared at Tex. My skin tingled.

"Hold on, Renee," she said as I went to receive my medal.

When we got back to our hotel, I slowly put down the medal and Tex's sweet trophy, then burst into tears.

"Sweetheart, what's wrong?"

I pulled her to me. "It's true."

"What's true?"

I looked into her eyes. "God's Word. He said if I waited upon Him, He would renew my strength. He did it—not just spiritually, but physically also."

Tex gently wiped the tears from my eyes.

CHAPTER FORTY-ONE

RUNNING WITH ENDURANCE

Running not only renewed my health, but it also showed me the path to continuous personal revival. The book of Hebrews speaks of an endurance race. I found many verses in the Bible that compare running to the Christian life. I recommend such a search.

As I trained, I asked God to teach me how to finish well the race of life. And the more I trained, the more I learned about the disciplines I needed.

It soon became a challenge to maintain my travel schedule and train for the Greek Marathon eleven months away. One day out of the blue I received an email from Kirsta Leeburg, Ken's eldest daughter.

"I hear you're planning to fulfill the dream you and my dad had. If so, I want to run in Dad's place." What a blessing that would be!

Kirsta had a greater challenge than I. She had a young family and a demanding job as a lawyer in the District Attorney's office. Yet, she was like her late dad—persistent and determined.

We were able to train together only a few times because of my travel schedule. My calendar was packed with ministry opportunities, which—despite my dream—had to remain my top priority. Running was to be an addition to the ministry, not a hindrance.

Early in the new year I led a team to Angola for a nationwide evangelistic outreach. I preached each afternoon at the national bullring in the capital city, Luanda. Tex and I stayed in a compound near the center of the city, and I must have looked comical getting my miles in by running countless small circles inside the area.

Not only did we see a great harvest of souls in the meetings, but other team members also saw many come to Christ as well. Wayne Jenkins flew to preach in a remote province where a cult in the area said they had "received a word" that God would send a prophet from America to teach them about Him. The entire group showed up at his meetings in their cult garb.

Wayne told them, "I'm not a prophet and not the son of a prophet." But when he preached the Gospel the entire cult came to know Jesus.

When we returned from Africa, I faced a new battle. An Iranian friend told me that one of the leading universities in Iran had placed on their home page my testimony of how I came to Jesus. I found that so unbelievable that I asked another Iranian to check it out.

She wrote me, "It's true! They took it from your international website and changed nothing. They even included your invitation and prayer for people who want to follow Jesus."

I was amazed, but I feared for the safety of the person who posted it, and I worried too about repercussions for our ministry.

Soon my worst fears were realized. Someone hacked into our international websites and deleted them. And when we checked our backups, we discovered they had deleted those first! Our international sites were empty, and we had to recreate them from scratch.

Despite that devastating cyber-attack, I didn't lose heart. Regardless the battle, I would do what God had called me to do—proclaiming the Gospel in the difficult places.

In August Dave Tippit, Tex, and I ministered in South Sudan, which had broken away from Sudan. The people were hurting, so I hope we were an encouragement to many of the friends I'd made when in Khartoum. It was such a joy to see them. .

Mani Erfan, an Iranian American friend, joined me and when he shared how he had come to faith in Christ out of a Muslim background, the crowds—who themselves had been persecuted by an Islamic government—cheered and danced.

To continue training for the Greek Marathon, I ran before dawn every morning and carried a flashlight so I could avoid creatures or potholes. With only two and a half months to go before Greece, I was running long distances and couldn't afford an injury.

Back in San Antonio, I turned up the heat on my training. I knew the pace I'd have to run, and by mid-September, I was on target. I was to meet Kirsta Leeburg on a Saturday morning for a long run. As I tied my shoe, pain shot through my back and I crumpled to the floor, screaming. When Tex tried to help me up, it hurt even worse.

"What should I do?"

"Help get me to the bed."

Even with her help, I was in agony.

Tex called our chiropractor who agreed to come in on his day off if we could get to his office. Somehow Tex was slowly able to help me into the car.

"I can't believe this," I wailed. "There's no way I'll be able to run in six weeks."

Tex urged me not to give up yet.

Our chiropractor discovered that my pelvis had shifted because one of my legs was shorter than the other. Apparently I was born that way, and the longer I ran, the more my pelvis shifted.

"Does this mean my running days are over?"

The doctor smiled and shook his head. "I'll do an adjustment and try a simple fix—a heel lift."

I was running again in two weeks, but those had been critical weeks to miss.

Though this whole marathon effort was a dream come true, I didn't feel right about traveling to Greece only to run. A Greek friend arranged a conference so I could teach and minister to pastors there before the big event.

Kirsta and her husband Wade joined Tex and me a couple of days before the race, and we drove the course from Marathon to Athens to get a feel for it. The first eight miles looked fairly flat, but then, oh, the hills! We would climb and descend, climb and descend. But around mile eleven we would start climbing again and continue for *another* eleven miles before finally descending to the original Olympic stadium. It appeared to me that nearly half the 26.2 miles was uphill!

You probably know that the marathon originated in 490 BC when the Greeks defeated the Persians in the Battle of Marathon and sent Pheidippides to Athens to announce the victory. Legend says he ran the entire way—26 miles—declared the news, and dropped dead.

I could see why!

I told Tex, "If I can reach the top of this mountain, I can coast the last four miles. I just need to make it to the top."

Her eyes sparkled. "You'll do it."

The night before the race, Kirsta, Wade, Tex, and I enjoyed dinner with several other American runners. We went around the large table introducing ourselves and telling what had drawn us to the Greek Marathon. Most of the others had run multiple marathons, and now this was their pilgrimage to the "mother of all marathons."

Kirsta and I were the only newbies. Everyone seemed deeply moved when she told her dad's story and said she was running in his place.

I told them how my cancer diagnosis had revived Ken's and my dream. I concluded, "I also want to qualify for Boston."

I saw several trying to keep from laughing. Imagine this old man entering such a grueling race for his first marathon! One told me, "I know a nice flat course in the States that might help you qualify for Boston."

Tex wasn't feeling well and seemed to get worse before bedtime. I got up early to check on her and found she was running a fever. I held her as she cried. "We've been through this together, Sammy! I want to be there for you. I want to watch you cross the finish line."

"Your health is more important. I'm not leaving you unless I know you'll be all right."

"I don't want to keep you from running."

"I know, Sweetheart," I whispered. "I love you. I'm going to find a doctor before we decide."

The hotel had a physician in our room within an hour. He gave Tex some medicine and told me she was in no danger and I should feel free to go. I told Tex the decision was hers, and she insisted I run.

"Don't worry about me, Tex. By God's grace, I'll finish this journey today."

I grabbed my gear and headed to find Kirsta and Wade. When she and I got on the bus to the starting line, we were the only two speaking English. As I stared out the window, emotion overwhelmed me. It had been thirty years since this dream had been birthed in Ken and me. It seemed a lifetime ago.

Once we arrived, Kirsta met a group of American military personnel who planned to run at her pace. She lined up with them, and I found a place a little closer to the front. *God, I commit the next 26 miles to You. Please be with Tex.*

Thousands of runners shouted along with the countdown to the gun, and finally the race was on.

The farthest I had run during training was twenty miles, due to my two-week hiatus. I had been on track to get to around twenty-three miles before that. Could I make the entire distance today?

I quickly settled into my pace and felt great at the five- kilometer (3.1 miles) marker. My breathing was good and my legs fresh. I felt strong and reached ten kilometers ahead of my goal. By the halfway mark I was right on target, though we had already started the hills. I wasn't breathing heavily and my confidence grew. *I'm going to make it. I'll qualify for Boston.*

Just beginning the long, single climb, I reminded myself I had trained for this. Ken's chants from thirty years before echoed in my mind: "Up the hill, over the hill, through the hill, conquer the hill! Come on, Sam! You can do it!"

A Greek friend named Johnathan was filming me at around mile eighteen, and by now I was going to finish for sure. *This will be great!*

When I finally made it to the top of the incline, I was elated. My time was perfect. I would qualify for Boston.

Only four miles to go—and all downhill. I'll cruise from here.

Once I started down, everything changed. First my knees began to ache. Slowing to a walk could jeopardize my chances for Boston, but soon I couldn't help it. I decided just to walk till I gathered myself, but when I tried to run again, my feet were on fire. My calves knotted. I had zero energy left.

Father, help me make it to the next refreshment table. Once there I drank and ate.

I tried to run again, but failed. I walked, then jogged, pain coursing through my hips and down my legs. But my feet remained the worst. Every step they burned hotter and hotter. But the finish line was just a kilometer away. I couldn't collapse now! I had to make it!

But suddenly that last kilometer loomed longer than the entire rest of the race. My body fell apart, and I couldn't move.

Just a few yards from where I stopped was a corner, around which I would be able to see the stadium. I knew if I could just come within sight of it, I'd find a way to finish.

But I simply couldn't move, couldn't lift either foot from the pavement. Crying, I prayed, *Oh, God. I'm so close. Help me!* I put both hands under my hamstrings and lifted one leg, then switched to the other. Could I do this all the way to the end, and how long would it take?

Manually forcing one foot in front of the other, I was finally able to round that corner and see the stadium in the distance. But more than that, thousands of Greek citizens lined both sides of the street and cheered, "Bravo! Bravo! Bravo!"

I'll never understand how that affected me. All I know is that suddenly I could run. I rolled into a trot and then ran without pain!

As I came across the finish line, Johnathan pointed the camera at me and said, "How does it feel to finish the original Greek Marathon?"

I didn't even have the energy to smile. "This is the hardest thing I've ever done in my life," I rasped. "And I think I'm going to faint."

That's the last thing I remember until I roused on a cot in a tent, hovered over by doctors and nurses with Johnathan by my side.

A nurse kept trying to get a needle into a vein, sticking me here and there, and it hurt! A doctor came in and took over, but when he was about to shove the syringe into my arm, I said, "Sir, please don't do that. I'm a Christian, and I'd rather go to heaven than be stuck with that needle again."

Unable to get fluids in me intravenously, they gave me a drink and a banana. More than an hour later, Johnathan found Kirsta and Wade and brought them the tent.

Another hour passed. I whispered I wanted Johnathan to call and check on Tex, but when he reached her and found she was doing much better, naturally she asked about me. Not sure what to tell her, he just said, "Sammy has finished, and he's resting now."

Half an hour later, they were still unable to get a needle into me. The doctor called for an ambulance and I was whisked away to a hospital. I found out later that another runner about my age had collapsed and died, so they weren't about to take any chances with me.

At the hospital, they were finally able to rehydrate me and get me back to normal. As Johnathan and I waited for me to be released, we saw two very distraught young men who turned out to be refugees from Afghanistan. They were excited when they found out I was an American, hoping I could help them.

We shared Christ with them and were thrilled to be able to tell them that Johnathan ran a center for refugees and would be able to help. It was just like the Lord to present that opportunity at the end of such a grueling day.

Finally back at the hotel, I found Tex healthy and we fell into each other's arms. "I did it, Sweetheart," I said, weeping.

"I'm so thankful."

We went out for a late dinner with Wade and Kirsta, and she and I traded the stories of our respective races. "Well, Kirsta," I said, "any advice for me for the future?"

"Yes," she said with a smile. "Next time, don't wait thirty years to follow your dream."

CHAPTER FORTY-TWO

HILLS

I had finished the race, but poorly. I wanted to understand why, because I didn't want to do the same in the race of life. I wanted to finish well.

I had run the marathon the way too many my age approach the final season of life: I thought all I needed was to reach the top of the hill so I could coast the rest of the way. Hard lesson learned.

A couple of months later, Paul Negrut invited me to speak at the Emanuel Baptist Church in Oradea, the first church I had preached in when I had traveled to Romania thirty years earlier. Paul had been a young psychologist then, and my first translator in the country. Now he was Dr. Paul Negrut, Rector at Emanuel University, and he asked me to speak there too.

It deeply moved me to realize that many of the current students had not been born when the country was under the grip of Communism. I could teach them openly in an accredited university instead of their having to climb a mountain to listen to me in secret.

But what could I say to this generation with their smart phones and iPads? Could they grasp the great truths of prayer and revival borne of the kind of suffering their parents and grandparents knew so well?

I chose to speak from Hebrews chapter twelve, from which I had learned so much: *Run with endurance the race set before you.*

I rarely use notes when I speak, which enables me to gauge the response of the audience. The students were on the edge of their seats, eyes wide, clearly hungry for the Word of God. I realized why He had told me to run. The Lord had burned a message into me that not only prepared me to finish well the race of life, but which also served as a relevant message for a new generation of believers.

I was invited to lead a men's conference in Greece for Iranians who had fled their country. The message brought the same response. One man who had just been released from the infamous Evin Prison told me of lying in his cell all night, listening to the screams of his fellow inmates. He grabbed my shoulder. "Your message was exactly what I needed. I must never give up!"

Another told me in tears, "I have been revived. I want to run with endurance. I must go back and minister to refugees fleeing their countries."

I had heard of runners becoming addicted to marathons, but believe me, that was not going to be my problem. In fact, any time I was asked when I would run the next one, I always smiled and said, "Never." And I meant it.

But all that training had allowed me to drop all my excess weight, and despite that I was officially a senior citizen, I was in the best shape of my adult life. I needed an outlet for my energy and my need to achieve, and I certainly didn't want to squander the results of all the work I'd put in.

My friend and virtual trainer, Kevin Morning, had represented the U. S. in the *Masters Track and Field World Championships*. I learned that there were local *Senior Games* in San Antonio and that their annual track meet was just a few weeks away. I became intrigued with the possibility that I could compete in the 400-meter race, something I had done in high school. I learned that a friend of mine, Tom, had run the fastest time in the San Antonio Senior Games among people my age. He would be back to defend his title.

The 400 is literally less than one-one thousandth the distance of the marathon (42,168 meters). So it should be a lot easier, right? Let's just say all the torture of the marathon is condensed into a little over a minute for men of my vintage.

The 400-meter dash is simply a long-distance sprint, in fact bordering on the longest distance just about anyone could maintain his speed. Many believe it's the most difficult race of any distance. One of the legendary adages about the 400 is: *The best thing to do in the final 100 meters is pray.* Well, I had plenty of experience in that discipline! Maybe my prayer life would give me an edge.

I quickly adjusted my workout routines to emphasize sprinting rather than distance running. The 400 is one lap around a flat track, so pushing yourself to build your power and hone those fast twitch muscles is crucial.

I didn't really have enough time between deciding to do this and the day of the games, but I worked hard and was eager to see how I stacked up against the competition.

The day of the race I immediately sought out my friend Tom, gave him a fist bump, and asked a lot of questions. He was open and encouraging, despite that we would be in the same race.

The *Senior Games* were more nerve racking than the marathon, because in the long distance run so many were competing that no one really noticed how fast (or slow) you ran. In this meet, especially in the shorter distances, only eight people ran at a time, and everyone's eyes were on them.

As I took my place for the 400, I found myself bouncing, not because I was cold but because I was a bundle of nerves. I kept my eyes on Tom. *Just hang with him,* I told myself.

When the gun sounded, I couldn't believe what happened. Everyone passed me on the first curve! Tom was *way* ahead. I struggled to pick up my pace and finally passed one runner.

I finished second to last.

Tom won, and his time was even better than the previous year. I congratulated him and asked, "How did you do it?"

He told me he'd been training with a guy among the top in the world for his age and introduced me to Julio. I told him how impressed I was with what he'd done for Tom, and he asked if I'd like to train with them.

"Man, I'd love that."

A few days later I met up with Tom and Julio. We stretched, walked a fast mile, then jogged another mile. It was easy and fun. "Thanks for the workout, Julio," I said, reaching to shake his hand.

He let out a belly laugh. "That wasn't the workout, Sammy. That was the warm-up."

I felt my face flush.

Julio pointed up a hill. "We're going to the top." He paused and smiled. "I know guys like you. You're gonna to want to race. But this isn't a race. Stay with me." He raised an eyebrow. "Understand?"

"No problem."

When we reached the top, I discovered it wasn't the top. The trail curved and we kept ascending. *Aah,* I thought, *there's the top.* But it wasn't the top either! I set my jaw and determined to stay with Julio. By the time we really reached the top, I was gasping.

Julio turned, "Hey, man, you okay?"

"I'll be okay."

"Then let's walk down."

"Yeah," I managed, sucking air. "Good idea."

Tom was grinning. Did I look that bad?

I had just caught my breath when we reached the bottom, and Julio asked, "You ready?"

"For what?"

"We're going back up."

I sighed. "Sure."

By the time we reached the top that time, I was bent over, panting.

"Hey, you sure you're okay?" Julio said.

I lifted a hand, trying to speak. "Yeah, just give me a minute."

Once I was able to stand erect, we ambled back down. Now *that* was a workout. Julio smiled. "You ready?"

I couldn't believe it, but I wasn't about to quit. If these guys could do this, so could I. But this time hurt so bad I didn't even try to speak at the top. I just tried to recover.

Just before we started up the hill for the sixth time, my resolve was wavering. If this wasn't the last time, maybe I *would* have to cry uncle. As Julio lit out again, he told me, "I love to run hills because hills make you strong!"

I thought I would die, and I was about ready give up. Julio must have sensed it. "Keep going, Sam," he said. "I'm right here with you. You're gonna make it. Hang in there."

His encouragement made all the difference, and, fortunately, six ascents was finally it for that first day.

Julio and Tom and I ran hills for six months.

Then came the *Texas Senior Games Championship* in Houston. Tom couldn't go, but Tex and I drove the two hundred miles east, eager to see how much I had improved.

I lined up with guys I remembered from the San Antonio meet, but, *uh-oh,* also the best runners from Dallas, Houston, Ft. Worth, and elsewhere in the state. I realized I could have greatly improved in six months and still wind up last. Still, this would be good experience, and I told myself, *Just have fun.*

The gun sounded, and as I rounded the first curve, I felt strong. Not only had no one passed me, but I was passing others. On the backstretch I continued passing runners until, coming into the final curve, only one remained ahead of me. My lungs and legs were burning, but I had trained for this. I bore down on the leader, caught up, and passed him on the final stretch! I couldn't believe it. I won the state championship!

A guy from San Antonio asked how I had improved so much. I laughed. "You need to meet Julio. He loves to run hills because hills make you strong!"

On the way home I called Julio, and he was happier than I was. I told Tex that what I appreciated so much about Julio was that he wasn't like so many trainers who just tell you what to do. He does it with you.

"God is teaching me something through all this, Sweetheart."

"What's that?"

"No one ever climbed a hill as difficult as the one Jesus climbed. Later, He told His disciples to go into the world and preach the Gospel and promised, 'I will be with you always.' Whatever hill He gives me, when I want to give up, He whispers, 'I am with you. You can make it.'"

It wasn't long before my confidence in that promise was put to the test. Pakistani Christian leaders believed the time was right for me to return to the country. That was where our translator, Babar Shamsoon, and his bodyguard had been murdered.

I kept putting off the Pakistanis, needing clear leading from God and full confidence that the meeting sponsors had the correct motives. Having felt responsible for Babar's martyrdom, which had brought me closer to quitting than at any other time in my ministry, I would return to Pakistan only under the protection of the Holy Spirit. While I was willing to die for my faith, if God called me to, I would not put anyone else in that position. It made no sense for me to go if it meant putting beloved brothers and sisters in danger.

After a year and a half of corresponding with several ministries, I contacted Naveed Malik, my first Pakistani translator. He was the one who had told me following Babar's assassination, "You must not return for a few years. The terrorists will kill you."

Now I brought him up to date on the new invitation. He said he wanted to pray about it. After a few months, he emailed me, "I believe God wants you to come. But we must be careful." He told me of a group of small Baptist churches in Karachi that didn't have a lot of resources or numbers of people. "But I trust them," he wrote, suggesting they host the meetings.

I assured Naveed that I trusted him and urged him to discuss it with the Baptists and let me know if they were willing.

They were, and so we scheduled the meetings for early in 2013, giving me nearly a year to obtain a visa. A longtime friend from the state of Washington agreed to travel with me, but by January neither of us had heard a word from the west coast or Houston Pakistani Consulates regarding our visas. I finally contacted Naveed and told him we'd better cancel, because even if our visas came now, there would be no time for publicity or preparation.

He urged to me not cancel but rather postpone the meetings till October and keep pushing for the visas.

Our annual Board of Directors meeting was scheduled for early October, so we decided that if our visas came through, we would leave for Pakistan three days after that.

When I finally received my visa at the last minute, I knew God had to be in it because I had declared in my application that I would be speaking at churches and meeting with pastors and other Christian leaders. Plus, it would have been likely the government was well aware of my TV broadcasts there.

Strangely, my Washington friend's visa was denied, though he wasn't speaking and had no history with Pakistan.

It was too late to get someone else to go with me (it had taken nearly two years to get one visa!), and though traveling alone would be an exception to our standard procedures, I knew God would be with me.

Then, in late September, a week before our board meeting and two weeks before I was scheduled to leave, devastating news came from Pakistan. Two suicide bombers invaded the All Saints Church in Peshawar, killing 127 and wounding more than 250. It was the worst mass murder of Christians by Islamic extremists in the history of Pakistan.

Was I planning my own suicide mission and risking the lives of all my brothers and sisters in the country? The terrorists had my name and my messages Babar had stored in his computer.

I rushed to my private place of prayer and paced, pleading for God's wisdom. I needed information from someone I trusted in Pakistan, and I needed input from my board.

Providentially, that board meeting was already going to be different. As the youngest member of the board was in his fifties and all the rest of us were in our sixties, we decided that each would bring with him a member of the next generation. The idea was to have the younger guys sit in and critique what we were doing and how we were doing it. We were eager to get an idea of how we came across from an entirely new perspective. How could we most effectively reach this new generation?

Meanwhile, I contacted Naveed and asked if he and the leader of the Baptist churches could have a Skype call during the Board meeting to discuss whether we should proceed.

I brought my son Dave, and most of the guys brought their sons or a staff colleague. I don't know what the young guys expected, beyond hoping to bring us senior citizens up to speed in the areas of technology and social media. But I know they weren't expecting what they encountered when we started.

I had arranged a Skype call to Naveed so we could come to some conclusion about whether I should risk going to Pakistan. We invited our wives to join us too, so with the younger guys, the boardroom was packed and the mood somber.

When Naveed appeared on the screen with the Baptist leader next to him in a cramped office, our boardroom fell so silent that I wondered if everyone could hear my heart pounding.

Here were two men mourning the loss of their countrymen and knowing their own lives were on the line. Pastor Naveed reported that Pakistani Christians were confused, fearful, and angry. "Sammy, we are hurting, and no one knows what to do."

"Should we postpone again or cancel altogether?"

Naveed did not answer immediately, and I wondered if there was a delay in the Skype connection. He finally shook his head sadly and said, "I don't know."

That made me shiver. When we'd faced the same danger in Sudan, the Christian leaders were certain we should come.

Naveed continued, "I have two reservations, Brother Sammy. There is so much confusion among believers, I don't know if we can mobilize everyone. But my greatest concern is you. The terrorists have two primary targets—Americans and Christians."

The Baptist leader said, "I believe you should come. You must come. We need your revival message, especially now."

I could tell by the looks on the faces of the younger guys—with the exception of Dave Tippit, of course—that they were shell-shocked.

They may have grown up reading stories of missionaries and Christian martyrs from decades past, but this was now. We may have been a bunch of gray-haired old men, but this was life and death stuff. My board faced the responsibility of sending me somewhere from which I might never return.

Naveed and I agreed that they and we would give ourselves to prayer over this and would reconnect in twenty-four hours to make a final decision.

I didn't know the Baptist leader, but I knew Naveed. For that reason, though I was torn, I trusted him and leaned toward not going.

Before we prayed, we went around the table and shared our feelings. There was no consensus. Some agreed with my confidence in Naveed. Some didn't want to commit until they felt a leading from the Lord.

But when we got to Dave Tippit, something began to change in my heart. My son had been with me both in Pakistan and in Sudan. He didn't say I should go, but he was positive about the trip.

I knew what I needed to do. Barring God changing my mind after a day of prayer, I decided, *I must go.*

The next day, the board came to the consensus that it would trust my judgment. If the Lord was telling me to go, I should go. As I was reminding them to pray for me, I said, "If I *am* to die there, I'm willing. But I really don't want to be beheaded. So if you think of it, pray for that."

Pakistan

When we informed our Pakistani brothers that I was willing to come, Pastor Naveed suggested we move the pastors' conference from the outdoor grounds in the center of Karachi to the Marriott Hotel. He said the hotel maintained tight security, but that it would cost more. He added that the room would accommodate a thousand leaders."

That sounded good to me, "but what about the evangelistic meeting?"

"That is much more difficult and would be very vulnerable to attack."

I told him to plan for the evangelistic meeting at the grounds in the city. "But, we'll keep open the option of cancelling it if necessary. We can make that decision at the pastors' conference."

What I had feared in Sudan, I now faced with Pakistan—going alone. Dave Tippit, Brandon Ford (son of Board Chairman, Joe Ford), and Evan Walker (son of my pastor, David Walker), offered to go—which deeply touched me—but it would be impossible to get visas for them in three days.

Tex and I were subdued at the airport before I left. I promised to call her every night after the meetings and when I awoke each morning. She would report what was going on to the many people she had mobilized to pray.

"No matter what happens," I said, "remember that I love you."

"And you remember that I love you more."

As the plane ascended, a still, small voice whispered to my soul, "And, lo, I will be with you."

CHAPTER FORTY-THREE

FINISHING WELL

Naveed, his family, and the Baptist pastor met me at the Karachi airport, and in a nearby coffee shop they brought me up to speed. They had booked me a room at the Marriott where the pastors' conference would be, and they recommended I not leave the hotel compound until the evangelistic meetings at the end of the week.

It seemed I had a million questions. Would pastors dare come to the conference? What had they done about publicity for the evangelistic meetings? "It's too dangerous for posters, isn't it?"

The Baptist pastor assured me the conference at the hotel would be full. "Christian leaders are hurting and scared, but they feel the Marriott is safe and that the meetings will greatly bless them."

Naveed's son grinned. "And don't worry about publicity for the end of the week. I have 2,000 names on my texting list. We'll get the word out."

We endured an exhaustive security check—similar to what I'd experienced at border crossings—just to get into the Marriott parking area. Another check at the hotel was much more thorough than at many airports. As my luggage slid through x-ray machines, I thought, *This is a fortress, but will the pastors put up with it?*

Once settled in my room, I Skype-called Tex to let her know I had made it. An eerie peace filled my heart, like the calm I once experienced in the middle of a hurricane as a teenager.

Still, I slept soundly, and after breakfast, I followed the signs in the lobby to our conference room. The Baptist pastor had been right. Pastors and leaders were crammed in there, worshipping Jesus! Such a spirit of revival permeated their songs and prayers that I was overwhelmed.

I expressed my love and concern for them and the families of those who had been killed. At the end of my message I issued a call for prayer, asking them to gather in small groups. Clusters of pastors and leaders passionately sought God.

When it came time to close, I was overcome with emotion. "Oh, Father, send a sweeping revival to the Christian leaders of Pakistan."

From all over the room, shouts of "Amen!" and "Praise the Lord!" ascended to heaven.

Representatives from the Parliament's committee for Religious Minorities arrived the second day to reassure the leaders their rights would be protected. A pastor near me whispered, "These men sincerely want to help, but they don't have the authority."

After the political leaders addressed the group, I asked a handful of pastors to join me on the platform to pray for them. The Holy Spirit swept through the room and a deep sense of brokenness and renewed hope saturated the pastors. Fear seemed to flee as joy erupted. Disheartened pastors were encouraged, and the fearful became fearless.

That night I told Tex, "Even if nothing else happens, I know this was the right thing to do. God has truly revived these pastors and leaders. You can see it in their faces. I needed to be here."

"What about the evangelistic meetings tomorrow evening? Have you made a decision about those?"

"We haven't had any problems, so we're going forward. But I'm nervous."

"Why?"

"I have no idea what to expect. Will anyone show up? Will terrorists try to kill us? It's the unknown that bothers me."

"Let me pray for you," Tex said.

Her prayer was so sweet that it gave me the confidence to face whatever came my way. I had posted on Facebook how God was working, so an army of prayer warriors joined us online.

Naveed told me not to come to the grounds during the singing. "It will be safer if you arrive immediately before you preach." I was disappointed because I love to worship with people in different languages.

Traffic was heavy and a brick wall encircled the grounds, motorbikes parked against it. *It would be easy for a terrorist to park a motorcycle and throw a bomb over the wall.* I told myself to stop thinking like that. I tried to focus on my message. It didn't help that the metal detectors looked shoddy.

The atmosphere inside wasn't anything like most of the evangelistic events I've preached. Normally, excitement is in the air. Here the fear was so thick I would have needed a chainsaw to cut through it. Attendance was decent, but not great.

I preached with all my heart and invited people to become followers of Jesus. While I rejoice with every person who comes to saving faith in Christ, I confess the response was similar to the attendance.

At breakfast the next morning, the waiter handed me an English language newspaper—something he hadn't done before. I immediately saw why. The front-page headline read: *Bomb blasts rock the four provincial capitals; 10 killed, over 60 injured; Three suspected terrorists die.*

Suicide bombers had killed people in every capital city of Pakistan except Karachi. Some had tried to get here on a motorcycle but their bombs went off before they arrived at their destination, and authorities couldn't determine their target.

Could it have been the grounds? Had God intervened? I called Tex and asked her urgently to tell her prayer groups to intercede for us.

What would this news do to attendance? When I arrived I found the place full! And I noticed an unusually large number of young adult men.

The services were incredible. Normally I see a lot of movement in a large crowd. But here everyone sat motionless throughout, as they seemed to be soaking up the message. Thousands responded to the invitation, and it appeared that more than 2,000 of them were young men.

As we left the compound, Naveed's son raised his cellphone and smiled. Later Naveed told me that his son had texted his huge list of friends a word-by-word description of my message the night before. Many of them showed up the next night and came to Christ.

We completed the meetings Sunday without incident. Naveed gave me a big hug as I departed Karachi. "Thank you for loving Pakistan."

The trip home was long, but gave me a lot of think time. It struck me how fragile life is. God had been extremely good. I was amazed to have lived so long when many of my friends' lives had been cut short. *Oh, Lord, I want to finish well.*

I now wanted to focus on reaching this new generation. The young men who'd met with our board offered great counsel and would offer more. For me, the handwriting was on the wall. I wouldn't be able to make many more trips like this. My 2017 birthday would be my seventieth.

I returned to Tex, our kids, and grandkids with a fresh appreciation for life. I knew every day was a gift. No matter how many more I had, I wanted every one to count for God's glory.

I spent much of the flight mulling over the future of our ministry. My road hasn't been traditional. Although I've been privileged to preach some massive meetings, God didn't call me to build a large organization. He didn't want me building my empire, but rather to seek His kingdom.

I decided I would not worry about passing "my" ministry on to a successor but rather—for the rest of my life—just continue preaching the Gospel and calling God's people to pray for revival.

I did, however, want to add one more element to the ministry. I wanted to pay forward all I had learned, to impart to this emerging generation of leaders the life and ministry principles God had taught me during the previous fifty years.

My most valuable resource was relationships. In every country and culture my heart had been knitted with likeminded people of faith, people I had come to cherish. They represented the type of leader I longed to pour myself into. I don't care to build a bigger organization. I want to build better people—people who can lead the cause of Christ long after I'm gone. The success of any ministry, regardless how big or small, rests with the hearts of those who lead it.

CHAPTER FORTY-FOUR

THE CORNER OF SMARTPHONE AND iPAD

God had long ago set me a path to mentor young leaders around the world. Now it was time focus on that.

Fabricio Freitas was fourteen years old when he read the Portuguese version of my book, *Fire in Your Heart*. God inspired Fabricio to seek Him for revival. Sixteen years later he was serving as associate pastor of a church in Brasilia when I asked the leaders in Brazil to give me twelve young men and women I could teach the truths of prayer, revival, and evangelism.

Fabricio implemented the truths I taught in more than 200 churches in the Brasilia area. The National Mission Board of the Brazilian Baptist Convention made him National Director of Evangelism. He and I traveled together throughout Brazil, reaching people with the Gospel and seeing churches revived. Fabricio also showed me how to use social media to reach Brazilians, and we planned to live stream the first national conference on prayer, revival, and evangelism.

Pastor Nazir Masih, who had hosted me to preach in Punjab, India, had taken in a young man from a Sikh background as his spiritual son. Jolly had been put out of his home when he became a follower of Jesus, and Pastor Nazir saw potential in him and had him translate for me.

But Jolly did much more than that. This twenty-eight-year-old pastor pumped me with questions about prayer, revival, and evangelism, then translated much of our material into Punjabi.

Lazarus Yeghnazar asked me to partner with him to reach Iranians. We helped him build studios in Holland for 222 Ministries, where he and I have recorded more than 120 television broadcasts to be transmitted into Iran via satellite. Millions are watching the broadcasts.

Lazarus also asked me to help him reach more than 200,000 refugees flooding Turkey and settling in camps just across from Syria. Lazarus told me one of the attendees of the men's conference in

Greece returned to Turkey where he has a camp that feeds and houses 10,000 refugees. A refugee told him, "We fled Syria because our Muslim brothers were torturing and killing us. We came here, and you Christians are feeding and taking care of us."

Lazarus and I knew that merely getting a picture of Christianity in action was not enough. "Their hearts must be converted," he said. "We have started a small church there and want you to preach the Gospel. Will you help us?"

"Absolutely!"

Mike Scalf had developed a burden for refugees around the world and had started a ministry among them. I asked if he would join me in reaching the refugees in Turkey. On our way to meet him there, Tex and I attended a conference with Lazarus and Iranians scattered throughout Europe.

The stories of those attending overwhelmed us. A former Communist who'd spent five years in prison came to Jesus after being released, then was sent back to prison for his faith. He and his wife eventually fled to Afghanistan and had just arrived in Holland when we met them.

A former drug addict who had come to Christ had spent time in prison for sharing the Gospel, as had his wife. He now pastors an Iranian congregation in Holland.

Following the conference with the Iranians, Tex flew home and I met Mike Scalf. We linked up with the Iranian leaders of 222 Ministries in Turkey who had started house churches throughout the country. All of them were younger than my children. It reminded me of the days of the *Jesus Movement*, truly a youth revival.

One of the young leaders told me, "It's hard to believe that we're sitting here with you. We watched you on television in Iran. Many of us have been in prison. Your teaching prepared us for our suffering. You taught us how to pray."

Imagine how that touched me.

Others said, "We are people without a home, but we have hope. Thank you for your love for Iran."

One man in his early twenties who oversaw their technology, asked, "Can you help us develop an app? No one accesses the Internet via computers. But, everyone has a smart phone. An app is much safer."

I assured him I'd like to help and promised to pray about it. I had no idea how that idea would revolutionize our ministry. Later, in a house church, I taught principles of Christian growth in the morning and preached evangelistic meetings in the evening. One man approached me. "I became a follower of Jesus today, but tomorrow I must return to Iran. I don't have a Bible, and there is no church where I live. What can I do?" I told him of our television broadcasts, but when I returned to the States his question still haunted me.

While praying about how we could help develop an app for Iran, my Romanian friend, Dr. Paul Negrut, called to talk to me about the turmoil in Europe, because the refugee crisis had reached critical mass. "No one seems to know what to do, Sammy—but you and I do. We must act now to develop some kind of technology to reach this generation of Romanians, but also the millions of refugees."

I went immediately to my private place of prayer and paced and cried and shouted, "Yes! This generation lives at the corner of Smartphone and iPad, and I must go where they are!"

It struck me that I had relationships in some of the most influential nations of the world. I needed our materials put into a discipleship app and translated into those languages. A friend put me in touch with a software developer, and spent hours discussing how to accomplish this. It had to be highly sophisticated and have extreme security measures built in. If it were to fall into the wrong hands, countless lives would be at stake.

Costs for translation and production of the app were overwhelming. I spent the next year and a half working with the developer as well as with translation teams for Farsi, Russian, Romanian, Punjabi, Portuguese, Chinese, Hindi, and Arabic. Each team had a minimum of seven professional translators.

I couldn't shake the plea of the brother in Turkey. I couldn't give up, regardless the cost. I believed God would provide for this new project, just as he had when our tiny ministry pioneered in countries around the world.

Jolly, my young pastor friend in Punjab, India, had implemented the revival principles I'd taught, and his church had exploded in growth. He asked if I would teach discipleship via Skype to about forty of his church leaders.

That went so well that Jolly suggested we try an evangelistic meeting the same way.

I love technology and the potential is has to multiply my ministry, so I was thrilled to speak via Skype from San Antonio to about 350 inside and outside Jolly's church. I saw them laugh and heard them applaud as if I were right there with them. Jolly heard me in real time as I preached, and I heard him in real time as he translated.

Around a hundred came to faith, and Jolly said, "We must do this again."

We tried our Skype evangelism in a village where there were no churches and wound up planting a church there as another hundred came to faith. In another remote village, three hundred became believers.

When, at yet another one these, 1,000 responded to the Gospel. Jolly said, "Sammy, let's attempt something really big."

At the end of November 2016, the grounds in Giddarbaha, Punjab were packed with 10,000 people, some standing outside. I preached from my study in San Antonio, and more than half the crowd responded and gave their hearts to Christ.

Clearly, we were at the dawn of a new era of evangelism, and it couldn't come at a more perfect time for me. My board of directors urged me to cut down drastically on the international travel that had taken such a toll on me and on Tex. It was becoming clear that it had become too much for Tex, and neither I—nor the board, which has always deeply cared for us both—thought I should be away from her for extended periods.

Until those incredible experiences with the Punjabi people, I didn't know how I would do without traveling the world to preach as I had done or so long. Now I knew God could work the same way through the miracle of technology.

The discipleship app became an even more urgent need. We had to offer its content to the new believers in Punjab. Until the app could be completed, we used social media to help these people grow in Christ. We put the material, including the videos, on Facebook in the Punjabi language. Almost immediately, more than 8,000 Punjabis were watching, listening, and reading materials daily that helped them grow in Christ.

The younger guys at our Board meeting had been right. This generation will respond to the Gospel, regardless the age of the evangelist, if he stays faithful to the unchanging message of God.

I began to pray that at least 100,000 believers would immerse themselves in our discipleship materials in the next year alone— through social media or our app. My prayer is that by the time you read this, we will have all our teaching on prayer, revival, and evangelism translated into nine languages and available around the globe.

At times, it seems that burden God has given me for lost souls is so great that the burden itself has become a burden. I could preach to every people group every waking moment till the day I die, and still millions would not have heard the Gospel.

I know I am only one person and that God has called many others. I pray they will discover the need not only to be called, but also to be broken. I had to learn the hard way that only when God has broken you can He truly use you.

Someone once told me, "You can't expect to win the whole world to Jesus."

But why not? Jesus died for the whole world and commissioned us go into the whole world. I have spent my life taking His message of love and forgiveness to as many as I can, and I don't want to stop. As technology opens the entire globe to us, I feel as though I'm standing at the threshold of world evangelism. There is no nation too difficult, no tribe too obscure, no situation too desperate for the love of Christ.

We can overcome the evil one by the blood of the Lamb and by the word of our testimonies, if we love not our lives "to the death" (Revelation 12:11).

For the rest of my days, I want to give myself to prayer, study, writing, and preaching.

Please pray that:

> I will be Christ-like in character and deed.
> I will be a Christ-like husband, father, and grandfather.
> I will be courageous in calling the church to revival.
> I will depend completely on God.
> I will walk humbly before the Lord and die to self daily.
> And that Jesus Christ will be glorified.

From the privacy of my own home, able to stay with my beloved wife—who continues to bathe our ministry in prayer--I still see the whole world as my parish and get to preach the unsearchable riches of Christ. All I want is for men and women and boys and girls to come to Jesus, have their sins forgiven, and their eternities assured.

At an age when most people are retired or planning to retire, I consider it an unspeakable privilege to be able to stay at the task I was called to so many years ago. I pray God keeps me from coasting through this final stretch of the race. I long to finish and finish well.

ABOUT THE AUTHORS

Sammy Tippit has spent his entire adult life preaching on every continent, in countless churches, universities, and public arenas, seeing thousands come to faith in Christ.

He is founder and president of Sammy Tippit Ministries and is the author of sixteen other books.

He and his wife, Tex, have two grown children and five grandchildren and live in San Antonio, Texas.

For further information, write, phone, or log on to his website:

Sammy Tippit Ministries
PO Box 700368
San Antonio TX 78270
Phone: (210) 492-7501

E-mail: info@sammytippit.org
Website: www.sammytippit.org

Jerry B. Jenkins has written 21 *New York Times* bestsellers, including the *Left Behind* series. His writing has appeared in *Time*, *Reader's Digest*, *The Saturday Evening Post*, and dozens of Christian periodicals.

He has written biographies of Hank Aaron, Walter Payton, Meadowlark Lemon, Nolan Ryan, and many others. He assisted Billy Graham with his memoir *Just As I Am*.

He owns the Jerry Jenkins Writers Guild (www.JerrysGuild.com) and lives with his wife in Colorado. They have three grown sons and eight grandchildren.

Made in the USA
Middletown, DE
28 December 2018